Beginning x64 Assembly Programming

From Novice to AVX Professional

Jo Van Hoey

Apress®

Beginning x64 Assembly Programming: From Novice to AVX Professional

Jo Van Hoey
Hamme, Belgium

ISBN-13 (pbk): 978-1-4842-5075-4   ISBN-13 (electronic): 978-1-4842-5076-1
https://doi.org/10.1007/978-1-4842-5076-1

Managing Director, Apress Media LLC: Welmoed Spahr
Acquisitions Editor: Steve Anglin
Development Editor: Matthew Moodie
Coordinating Editor: Mark Powers

Cover designed by eStudioCalamar

Cover image designed by Freepik (www.freepik.com)

Distributed to the book trade worldwide by Springer Science+Business Media New York, 233 Spring Street, 6th Floor, New York, NY 10013. Phone 1-800-SPRINGER, fax (201) 348-4505, e-mail orders-ny@springer-sbm.com, or visit www.springeronline.com. Apress Media, LLC is a California LLC and the sole member (owner) is Springer Science + Business Media Finance Inc (SSBM Finance Inc). SSBM Finance Inc is a **Delaware** corporation.

For information on translations, please e-mail editorial@apress.com; for reprint, paperback, or audio rights, please email bookpermissions@springernature.com.

Apress titles may be purchased in bulk for academic, corporate, or promotional use. eBook versions and licenses are also available for most titles. For more information, reference our Print and eBook Bulk Sales web page at www.apress.com/bulk-sales.

Any source code or other supplementary material referenced by the author in this book is available to readers on GitHub via the book's product page, located at www.apress.com/9781484250754. For more detailed information, please visit www.apress.com/source-code.

Printed on acid-free paper

Table of Contents

TABLE OF CONTENTS

TABLE OF CONTENTS

About the Author

Jo Van Hoey has 40 years of experience in IT, consisting of diverse functions, multiple IT companies, and various computing platforms. He recently retired from IBM, where he was a mainframe software account manager. He has always been interested in IT security, and knowledge of assembly language is an essential skill in defending IT infrastructure against attacks and malware.

About the Technical Reviewer

Paul Cohen joined Intel Corporation during the very early days of the x86 architecture, starting with the 8086, and retired from Intel after 26 years in sales/marketing/management. He is currently partnered with Douglas Technology Group, focusing on the creation of technology books on behalf of Intel and other corporations. Paul also teaches a class that transforms middle and high school students into real, confident entrepreneurs, in conjunction with the Young Entrepreneurs Academy (YEA), and is a traffic commissioner for the City of Beaverton, Oregon, and on the board of directors of multiple nonprofit organizations.

Introduction

Learning to program in assembly can be frustrating, not in the least because it is an unforgiving language; the computer will "yell" at you on every possible occasion. And if it doesn't, you may just have unknowingly introduced a hidden bug that will bite you later in your program or at execution time. On top of that, the learning curve is steep, the language is cryptic, the official Intel documentation is overwhelming, and the available development tools have their own peculiarities.

In this book, you will learn to program in assembly starting with simple programs and moving all the way up to Advanced Vector Extensions (AVX) programming. By the end of this book, you will be able to write and read assembly code, mix assembly with higher-generation languages, understand what AVX is, and more. The purpose of this book is to show you how to use assembly language instructions. This book is not about programming style or code performance optimization. After you have acquired basic knowledge of assembly, you can continue learning how to optimize your code. This book should not be the first book you read on programming; if you have never programmed before, put this book aside for a while and learn some basics of programming with a higher-level language such as C.

All the code used in this book can be accessed via the Download Source Code link at www.apress.com/9781484250754. The code used in this book is kept as simple as possible, which means no graphical user interfaces or bells and whistles or error checking. Adding all these nice features would deviate our attention from the purpose: to learn assembly language.

The theory is kept to a strict minimum: a little bit on binary numbers, a short presentation of logical operators, and some limited linear algebra. And we stay far away from doing floating-point conversions. If you need to convert binary or hexadecimal numbers, find a web site that does that for you. Don't waste your time doing the calculations manually. Stick to the purpose: learning assembly.

The assembly code is presented in complete programs so that you can test them on your computer, play with them, change them, break them....

We will also show you what tools can be used, how to use them, and the potential problems in those tools. Having the right tools is essential to overcoming the steep learning curve. At times we will point you to books, white papers, and web sites that can be useful or that give more details.

It is not our intention to give you a comprehensive course on all of the assembly instructions. That is impossible in one book (look at the size of the Intel manuals!). We will give you a taste of the main items so that you will have an idea about what is going on. If you work through this book, you will acquire the knowledge to investigate certain domains in more detail on your own. When you have finished this book, you will be able to study the Intel manuals and (try to) make sense of their content.

The majority of the book is dedicated to assembly on Linux, because it is the easiest platform to learn assembly language. At the end, we provide a number of chapters to get you on your way with assembly on Windows. You will see that once you have Linux assembly under your belt, it is much easier to take on Windows assembly.

There are a number of assemblers available for use with Intel processors, such as FASM, MASM, GAS, NASM, and YASM to name a few. We will use NASM as in this book, because it is multiplatform; it is available on Linux, Windows, and macOS. Also, it has a relatively large user base. But don't worry, once you know one assembler, it will be easy to adopt another assembly's "dialect."

We have carefully written and tested the code used in this book. However, if there are any typos in the text or bugs in the programs, we do not take any responsibility. We blame them on our two cats, who love to walk over our keyboard while we are typing.

The ideas and opinions we present in this book are our own and don't necessarily represent IBM's positions, strategies, or opinions.

Before You Start

You should know some basic things before you start reading this book.

- **You should know how to install and manage virtualization software (VMware, VirtualBox, or similar).** If you don't have a clue what that means, download the free Oracle VirtualBox software (`https://www.virtualbox.org`), install it, and learn to use it by installing, for example, Ubuntu Desktop Linux as a guest operating system (OS). Virtualization software allows you to install different guest operating systems on your main machine, and if you mess things up in the guest system, you can delete that guest system and reinstall it. Or if you have taken a snapshot, you can return to a previous version of your guest installation. In other words, there's no harm to your main (host) operating system when experimenting. There are plenty of resources on the Internet explaining VirtualBox and other virtualization software solutions.

- **You should have basic knowledge of the Linux command-line interface (CLI).** We will be using Ubuntu Desktop here, and we will use the CLI all the time, starting in Chapter 1. You can use another Linux distribution if you want, but make sure you can install the tools used in the book (NASM, GCC, GDB, SASM, and so on). The following is the basic knowledge you need: how to install the OS, how to install additional software, how to start a terminal with a command prompt, and how to create, move, copy, and delete directories and files at the CLI. You also need to know how to use the `tar` utility, `grep`, `find`, `ls`, `time`, and so on. You need to know how to start and use a text editor. No advanced Linux knowledge is required; you need only a basic knowledge of these tasks to follow the explanations in this book. If you do not know Linux, play around with it to get used to it. There are plenty of good, short, beginning tutorials available on the Internet (e.g. `https://www.guru99.com/unix-linux-tutorial.html`). You will see that after you learned assembly on a Linux machine, learning assembly on another OS is not that difficult.

- **You should have some basic knowledge of the C programming language**. We will use a couple of C functions to simplify the example assembly code. Also, we will show how to interface with a higher-level language such as C. If you do not know C and want to fully enjoy this book, take a couple of free introductory C courses at, for example, `tutorialspoint.com`. There's no need to do the whole course; just take a look at a few programs in the language. You can always return later to find out more details.

Why Learn Assembly?

Learning assembly has several benefits.

- You'll learn how a CPU and memory works.

- You'll learn how a computer and operating system work together.

- You'll learn how high-level language compilers generate machine language, and that knowledge can help you to write more efficient code.

- You will be better equipped to analyze bugs in your programs.

- It is a lot of fun when you eventually get your program working.

- And the reason I wrote this book: if you want to investigate malware, you have only the machine code, not the source code. With an understanding of assembly language, you will be able to analyze malware and take necessary actions and precautions.

The Intel Manuals

The Intel manuals contain everything you ever wanted to know about programming Intel processors. However, the information is hard to swallow for a beginner. When you are progressing in this book, you will see that the explanations in these Intel manuals will make gradually more sense to you. We will refer often to these massive volumes of information.

You can find the Intel manuals here:

```
https://software.intel.com/en-us/articles/intel-sdm
```

Just don't print them—think about all the trees you would be destroying! Take a short look at the manuals to see how comprehensive, detailed, and formal they are. Learning assembly from these manuals would be very daunting. Of special interest to us will be Volume 2, where you will find detailed explanations about the assembly programming instructions.

You will find a useful source here: `https://www.felixcloutier.com/x86/index.html`. This site provides a list of all the instructions with a summary of how to use them. If the information provided here is not sufficient, you can always go back to the Intel manuals or your friend Google.

CHAPTER 1

Your First Program

Generations of programmers have started their programming careers by learning how to display hello, world on a computer screen. It is a tradition that was started in the seventies by Brian W. Kernighan in the book he wrote with Dennis Ritchie, *The C Programming Language*. Kernighan developed the C programming language at Bell Labs. Since then, the C language has changed a lot but has remained the language that every self-respecting programmer should be familiar with. The majority of "modern" and "fancy" programming languages have their roots in C. C is sometimes called a *portable* assembly language, and as an aspiring assembly programmer, you should get familiar with C. To honor the tradition, we will start with an assembler program to put hello, world on your screen. Listing 1-1 shows the source code for an assembly language version of the hello, world program, which we will analyze in this chapter.

Listing 1-1. hello.asm

```
;hello.asm
section .data
    msg     db      "hello, world",0
section .bss
section .text
    global main
main:
    mov     rax, 1      ; 1 = write
    mov     rdi, 1      ; 1 = to stdout
    mov     rsi, msg    ; string to display in rsi
    mov     rdx, 12     ; length of the string, without 0
    syscall             ; display the string
    mov     rax, 60     ; 60 = exit
    mov     rdi, 0      ; 0 = success exit code
    syscall             ; quit
```

© Jo Van Hoey 2019
J. Van Hoey, *Beginning x64 Assembly Programming*, https://doi.org/10.1007/978-1-4842-5076-1_1

Edit, Assemble, Link, and Run (or Debug)

There are many good text editors on the market, both free and commercial. Look for one that supports syntax highlighting for NASM 64-bit. In most cases, you will have to download some kind of plugin or package to have syntax highlighting.

Note   In this book, we will write code for the Netwide Assembler (NASM). There are other assemblers such as YASM, FASM, GAS, or MASM from Microsoft. And as with everything in the computer world, there are sometimes heavy discussions about which assembler is the best. We will use NASM in this book because it is available on Linux, Windows, and macOS and because there is a large community using NASM. You can find the manual at `www.nasm.us`.

We use gedit with an assembler language syntax file installed. Gedit is a standard editor available in Linux; We use Ubuntu Desktop 18.04.2 LTS. You can find a syntax highlighting file at `https://wiki.gnome.org/action/show/Projects/GtkSourceView/LanguageDefinitions`. Download the file `asm-intel.lang`, copy it to `/usr/share/gtksourceview*.0/language-specs/`, and replace the asterisk (*) with the version installed on your system. When you open gedit, you can choose your programming language, here Assembler (Intel), at the bottom of the gedit window.

On our gedit screen, the `hello.asm` file shown in Listing 1-1 looks like Figure 1-1.

```
 1 ; hello.asm
 2 section .data
 3     msg db        "hello, world",0
 4 section .bss
 5 section .text
 6     global main
 7 main:
 8     mov     rax, 1          ; 1 = write
 9     mov     rdi, 1          ; 1 = to stdout
10     mov     rsi, msg        ; string to display in rsi
11     mov     rdx, 12         ; length of the string, without 0
12     syscall                 ; display the string
13     mov     rax, 60         ; 60 = exit
14     mov     rdi, 0          ; 0 = success exit code
15     syscall                 ; quit
```

Figure 1-1. *hello.asm in gedit*

We think you will agree that syntax highlighting makes the assembler code a little bit easier to read.

When we write assembly programs, we have two windows open on our screen—a window with gedit containing our assembler source code and a window with a command prompt in the project directory—so that we can easily switch between editing and manipulating the project files (assembling and running the program, debugging, and so on). We agree that for more complex and larger projects, this is not feasible; you will need an integrated development environment (IDE). But for now, working with a simple text editor and the command line (in other words, the CLI) will do. This process has the benefit that we can concentrate on the assembler instead of the bells and whistles of an IDE. In later chapters, we will discuss useful tools and utilities, some of them with graphical user interfaces and some of them CLI oriented. But explaining and using IDEs is beyond the scope of this book.

For every exercise in this book, we use a separate `project` directory that will contain all the files needed and generated for the project.

Of course, in addition to a text editor, you have to check that you have a number of other tools installed, such as GCC, GDB, `make`, and NASM. First we need GCC, the default Linux compiler linker.

GCC stands for **G**NU **C**ompiler **C**ollection and is the standard compiler and linker tool on Linux. (GNU stands for **G**NU is **N**ot **U**nix; it is a recursive acronym. Using recursive acronyms for naming things is an insider programmer joke that started in the seventies by LISP programmers. Yes, a lame old joke....)

Type `gcc -v` at the CLI. GCC will respond with a number of messages if it is installed. If it is not installed, install it by typing the following at the CLI:

```
sudo apt install gcc
```

Do the same with `gdb -v` and `make -v`. If you don't understand these instructions, brush up on your Linux knowledge before continuing.

You need to install NASM and `build-essential`, which contains a number of tools we will use. To do so in Ubuntu Desktop 18.04, use this:

```
sudo apt install build-essential nasm
```

Type `nasm -v` at the CLI, and `nasm` will respond with a version number if it is properly installed. If you have these programs installed, you are ready for your first assembly program.

Type the hello, world program shown in Listing 1-1 into your favorite editor and save it with the name hello.asm. As mentioned, use a separate directory for saving the files of this first project. We will explain every line of code later in this chapter; note the following characteristics of assembly source code (the "source code" is the hello.asm file with the program instructions you just typed):

- In your code, you can use tabs, spaces, and new lines to make the code more readable.

- Use one instruction per line.

- The text following a semicolon is a comment, in other words, an explanation for the benefit of humans. Computers happily ignore comments.

With your text editor, create another file containing the lines in Listing 1-2.

Listing 1-2. makefile for hello.asm

```
#makefile for hello.asm
hello: hello.o
        gcc -o hello hello.o -no-pie
hello.o: hello.asm
        nasm -f elf64 -g -F dwarf hello.asm -l hello.lst
```

Figure 1-2 shows what we have in gedit.

```
1 #makefile for hello.asm
2 hello: hello.o
3         gcc -o hello hello.o -no-pie
4 hello.o: hello.asm
5         nasm -f elf64 -g -F dwarf hello.asm -l hello.lst
```

Figure 1-2. *makefile in gedit*

Save this file as makefile in the same directory as hello.asm and quit the editor.

A `makefile` will be used by `make` to automate the building of our program. *Building* a program means checking your source code for errors, adding all necessary services from the operation system, and converting your code into a sequence of machine-readable instructions. In this book, we will use simple `makefiles`. If you want to know more about `makefiles`, here is the manual:

`https://www.gnu.org/software/make/manual/make.html`

Here is a tutorial:

`https://www.tutorialspoint.com/makefile/`

You read the `makefile` from the bottom up to see what it is doing. Here is a simplified explanation: the `make` utility works with a dependency tree. It notes that `hello` depends on `hello.o`. It then sees that `hello.o` depends on `hello.asm` and that `hello.asm` depends on nothing else. `make` compares the last modification dates of `hello.asm` with `hello.o`, and if the date from `hello.asm` is more recent, `make` executes the line after `hello.o`, which is `hello.asm`. Then `make` restarts reading the `makefile` and finds that the modification date of `hello.o` is more recent than the date from `hello`. So, it executes the line after `hello`, which is `hello.o`.

In the bottom line of our `makefile`, NASM is used as the assembler. The `-f` is followed by the output format, in our case `elf64`, which means **E**xecutable and **L**inkable **F**ormat for **64**-bit. The `-g` means that we want to include debug information in a debug format specified after the `-F` option. We use the `dwarf` debug format. The software geeks who invented this format seemed to like *The Hobbit* and *Lord of the Rings* written by J.J.R. Tolkien, so maybe that is why they decided that DWARF would be a nice complement to ELF...just in case you were wondering. Seriously, DWARF stands for **D**ebug **W**ith **A**rbitrary **R**ecord **F**ormat.

STABS is another debug format, which has nothing to do with all the stabbing in Tolkien's novels; the name comes from **S**ymbol **Tab**le **S**trings. We will not use STABS here, so you won't get hurt.

The `-l` tells NASM to generate a `.lst` file. We will use `.lst` files to examine the result of the assembly. NASM will create an object file with an `.o` extension. That object file will next be used by a linker.

Note   Often it will happen that NASM complains with a number of cryptic messages and refuses to give you an object file. Sometimes NASM will complain so often that it will drive you almost insane. In those cases, it is essential to keep calm, have another coffee, and review your code, because you did something wrong. As you program more and more in assembly, you will catch mistakes faster.

When you finally convinced NASM to give you an object file, this object file is then linked with a linker. A linker takes your object code and searches the system for other files that are needed, typically system services or other object files. These files are combined with your generated object code by the linker, and an executable file is produced. Of course, the linker will take every possible occasion to complain to you about missing things and so on. If that is the case, have another coffee and check your source code and makefile.

In our case, we use the linking functionality of GCC (repeated here for reference):

```
hello: hello.o
       gcc -o hello hello.o -no-pie
```

The recent GCC linker and compiler generate *position-independent executables* (PIEs) by default. This is to prevent hackers from investigating how memory is used by a program and eventually interfering with program execution. At this point, we will not build position-independent executables; it would really complicate the analysis of our program (on purpose, for security reasons). So, we add the parameter -no-pie in the makefile.

Finally, you can insert comments in your makefile by preceding them with the pound symbol, #.

```
#makefile for hello.asm
```

We use GCC because of the ease of accessing C standard library functions from within assembler code. To make life easy, we will use C language functions from time to time to simplify the example assembly code. Just so you know, another popular linker on Linux is ld, the GNU linker.

If the previous paragraphs do not make sense to you, do not worry—have a coffee and carry on; it is just background information and not important at this stage. Just remember that makefile is your friend and doing a lot of work for you; the only thing you have to worry about at this time is making no errors.

At the command prompt, go to the directory where you saved your hello.asm file and your makefile. Type make to assemble and build the program and then run the program by typing ./hello at the command prompt. If you see the message hello, world displayed in front of the command prompt, then everything worked out fine. Otherwise, you made some typing or other error, and you need to review your source code or makefile. Refill your cup of coffee and happy debugging!

Figure 1-3 shows an example of the output we have on our screen.

```
jo@UbuntuDesktop:~/Desktop/linux64/gcc/01 hello $
jo@UbuntuDesktop:~/Desktop/linux64/gcc/01 hello $
jo@UbuntuDesktop:~/Desktop/linux64/gcc/01 hello $ make
nasm -f elf64 -g -F dwarf hello.asm -l hello.lst
gcc -o hello hello.o
jo@UbuntuDesktop:~/Desktop/linux64/gcc/01 hello $ ./hello
hello, worldjo@UbuntuDesktop:~/Desktop/linux64/gcc/01 hello $ █
```

Figure 1-3. *hello, world output*

Structure of an Assembly Program

This first program illustrates the basic structure of an assembly program. The following are the main parts of an assembly program:

- section .data

- section .bss

- section .text

section .data

In section .data, initialized data is declared and defined, in the following format:

<variable name>   <type>   <value>

When a variable is included in section .data, memory is allocated for that variable when the source code is assembled and linked to an executable. Variable names are symbolic names, and references to memory locations and a variable can take one or more memory locations. The variable name refers to the start address of the variable in memory.

Variable names start with a letter, followed by letters or numbers or special characters. Table 1-1 lists the possible datatypes.

Table 1-1. *Datatypes*

Type	Length	Name
db	8 bits	Byte
dw	16 bits	Word
dd	32 bits	Double word
dq	64 bits	Quadword

In the example program, section .data contains one variable, msg, which is a symbolic name pointing to the memory address of 'h', which is the first byte of the string "hello, world",0. So, msg points to the letter 'h', msg+1 points to the letter 'e', and so on. This variable is called a *string*, which is a contiguous list of characters. A string is a "list" or "array" of characters in memory. In fact, any contiguous list in memory can be considered a string; the characters can be human readable or not, and the string can be meaningful to humans or not.

It is convenient to have a zero indicating the end of a human-readable string. You can omit the terminating zero at your own peril. The terminating 0 we are referring to is not an ASCII 0; it is a numeric zero, and the memory place at the 0 contains eight 0 bits. If you frowned at the acronym ASCII, do some Googling. Having a grasp of what ASCII means is important in programming. Here is the short explanation: characters for use by humans have a special code in computers. Capital A has code 65, B has code 66, and so on. A line feed or new line has code 10, and NULL has code 0. Thus, we terminate a string with NULL. When you type man ascii at the CLI, Linux will show you an ASCII table.

section .data can also contain constants, which are values that cannot be changed in the program. They are declared in the following format:

```
<constant name>      equ      <value>
```

Here's an example:

```
pi equ 3.1416
```

section .bss

The acronym `bss` stands for **B**lock **S**tarted by **S**ymbol, and its history goes back to the fifties, when it was part of assembly language developed for the IBM 704. In this section go the uninitialized variables. Space for uninitialized variables is declared in this section, in the following format:

`<variable name>        <type>        <number>`

Table 1-2 shows the possible `bss` datatypes.

Table 1-2. *bss Datatypes*

Type	Length	Name
resb	8 bits	Byte
resw	16 bits	Word
resd	32 bits	Double word
resq	64 bits	Quadword

For example, the following declares space for an array of 20 double words:

```
dArray resd 20
```

The variables in `section .bss` do not contain any values; the values will be assigned later at execution time. Memory places are not reserved at compile time but at execution time. In future examples, we will show the use of `section .bss`. When your program starts executing, the program asks for the needed memory from the operating system, allocated to variables in `section .bss` and initialized to zeros. If there is not enough memory available for the `.bss` variables at execution time, the program will crash.

section .txt

`section .txt` is where all the action is. This section contains the program code and starts with the following:

```
        global main
  main:
```

The `main:` part is called a label. When you have a label on a line without anything following it, the word is best followed by a colon; otherwise, the assembler will send you a warning. And you should not ignore warnings! When a label is followed by other instructions, there is no need for a colon, but it is best to make it a habit to end all labels with a colon. Doing so will increase the readability of your code.

In our `hello.asm` code, after the `main:` label, registers such as `rdi`, `rsi`, and `rax` are prepared for outputting a message on the screen. We will see more information about registers in Chapter 2. Here, we will display a string on the screen using a system call. That is, we will ask the operating system to do the work for us.

- The system call code 1 is put into the register `rax`, which means "write."

- To put some value into a register, we use the instruction `mov`. In reality, this instruction does not move anything; it makes a copy from the source to the destination. The format is as follows:

  `mov destination, source`

- The instruction `mov` can be used as follows:

  - `mov` register, immediate value

  - `mov` register, memory

  - `mov` memory, register

  - **illegal**: `mov` memory, memory

- In our code, the output destination for writing is stored into the register `rdi`, and 1 means standard output (in this case, output to your screen).

- The address of the string to be displayed is put into register `rsi`.

- In register `rdx`, we place the message length. Count the characters of `hello, world`. Do not count the quotes of the string or the terminating 0. If you count the terminating 0, the program will try to display a `NULL` byte, which is a bit senseless.

- Then the system call, `syscall`, is executed, and the string, `msg`, will be displayed on the standard output. A `syscall` is a call to functionality provided by the operating system.

- To avoid error messages when the program finishes, a clean program exit is needed. We start with writing 60 into rax, which indicates "exit." The "success" exit code 0 goes into rdi, and then a system call is executed. The program exits without complaining.

System calls are used to ask the operating system to do specific actions. Every operating system has a different list of system call parameters, and the system calls for Linux are different from Windows or macOS. We use the Linux system calls for x64 in this book; you can find more details at http://blog.rchapman.org/posts/Linux_System_Call_Table_for_x86_64/.

Be aware that 32-bit system calls differ from 64-bit system calls. When you read code, always verify if the code is written for 32-bit or 64-bit systems.

Go to the operating system CLI and look for the file hello.lst. This file was generated during assembling, before linking, as specified in the makefile. Open hello.lst in your editor, and you will see your assembly code listing; in the leftmost column, you'll see the relative address of your code, and in the next column, you'll see your code translated into machine language (in hexadecimal). Figure 1-4 shows our hello.lst.

```
 1     1                                  section .data
 2     2 00000000 68656C6C6F2C20776F-       msg db       "hello, world",0
 3     3 00000009 726C6400
 4     4                                  section .bss      |
 5     5                                  section .text
 6     6                                      global main
 7     7                                  main:
 8     8 00000000 B801000000               mov     rax, 1          ; 1 = write
 9     9 00000005 BF01000000               mov     rdi, 1          ; 1 = to stdout
10    10 0000000A 48BE-                    mov     rsi, msg        ; string to display in rsi
11    11 0000000C [0000000000000000]
12    12 00000014 BA0C000000               mov     rdx, 12         ; length of the string, without 0
13    13 00000019 0F05                     syscall                 ; display the string
14    14 0000001B B83C000000               mov     rax, 60         ; 60 = exit
15    15 00000020 BF00000000               mov     rdi, 0          ; 0 = success exit code
16    16 00000025 0F05                     syscall                 ; quit
```

Figure 1-4. *hello.lst*

You have a column with the line numbers and then a column with eight digits. This column represents memory locations. When the assembler built the object file, it didn't know yet what memory locations would be used. So, it started at location 0 for the different sections. The section .bss part has no memory.

We see in the second column the result of the conversion of the assembly instruction into hexadecimal code. For example, mov rax is converted to B8 and mov rdi to BF. These are the hexadecimal representations of the machine instructions. Note also the conversion of the msg string to hexadecimal ASCII characters. Later you'll learn more about hexadecimal notation. The first instruction to be executed starts at address 00000000 and takes five bytes: B8 01 00 00 00. The double zeros are there for padding and memory alignment. Memory alignment is a feature used by assemblers and compilers to optimize code. You can give assemblers and compilers different flags to obtain the smallest possible size of the executable, the fastest code, or a combination. In later chapters, we will discuss optimization, with the purpose of increasing execution speed.

The next instruction starts at address 00000005, and so on. The memory addresses have eight digits (that is, 8 bytes); each byte has 8 bits. So, the addresses have 64 bits; indeed, we are using a 64-bit assembler. Look at how msg is referenced. Because the memory location of msg is not known yet, it is referred to as [0000000000000000].

You will agree that assembler mnemonics and symbolic names for memory addresses are quite a bit easier to remember than hexadecimal values, knowing that there are hundreds of mnemonics, with a multitude of operands, each resulting in even more hexadecimal instructions. In the early days of computers, programmers used machine language, the first-generation programming language. Assembly language, with its "easier to remember" mnemonics, is a second-generation programming language.

Summary

In this chapter, you learned about the following:

- The basic structure of an assembly program, with the different sections

- Memory, with symbolic names for addresses

- Registers

- An assembly instruction: mov

- How to use a syscall

- The difference between machine code and assembly code

CHAPTER 2

Binary Numbers, Hexadecimal Numbers, and Registers

In current computers, *bits* are the smallest piece of information; a bit can have a value of 1 or 0. In this chapter, we will investigate how bits are combined to represent data, such as integers or floating-point values. The decimal representation of values, which is so intuitive to humans, is not ideal for computers to work with. When you have a binary system, with only two possible values (1 or 0), it is much more efficient to work with powers of 2. When we talk about historical computer generations, you had 8-bit CPUs (2^3), 16-bit CPUs (2^4), 32-bit CPUs (2^5), and currently mostly 64-bit CPUs (2^6). However, for humans, dealing with long strings of 1s and 0s is impractical or even impossible. In this chapter, we will show how to convert bits into decimal or hexadecimal values that we can more easily work with. After that, we will discuss *registers*, data storage areas that assist the processor in executing logical and arithmetic instructions.

A Short Course on Binary Numbers

Computers use binary digits (0s and 1s) to do the work. Eight binary digits grouped together are called a *byte*. However, binary numbers are too long for humans to work with, let alone to remember. Hexadecimal numbers are more user-friendly (only slightly), not in the least because every 8-bit byte can be represented by only two hexadecimal numbers.

J. Van Hoey, *Beginning x64 Assembly Programming*, https://doi.org/10.1007/978-1-4842-5076-1_2

When you want to view a binary, decimal, or hexadecimal value in a different display format, you need to use a converter. The Internet has plenty of conversion calculators. Here are some that are easy to use:

- `www.binaryconvert.com`

- `https://www.binaryhexconverter.com`

- `https://babbage.cs.qc.cuny.edu/IEEE-754/`

Here is the basic conversion table; it would be helpful to memorize this table:

Decimal	Hexadecimal	Binary
0	0	0000
1	1	0001
2	2	0010
3	3	0011
4	4	0100
5	5	0101
6	6	0110
7	7	0111
8	8	1000
9	9	1001
10	a	1010
11	b	1011
12	c	1100
13	d	1101
14	e	1110
15	f	1111

Integers

There are two kinds of integers, signed and unsigned. Signed integers have the leftmost bit set to 1 if negative and 0 if positive. Unsigned integers are 0 or positive; there is no room for a sign bit. To be able to do integer arithmetic, negative integers are used in what is called a *two's complement* representation. You obtain the binary representation of a negative number as follows:

1. Write the binary of the absolute value.

2. Take the complement (change all the 1s to 0s and the 0s to 1s).

3. Add 1.

Here is an example using 16-bit numbers, instead of 64-bit numbers (to keep the example manageable):

```
decimal number =        17
binary number =         0000    0000    0001    0001
hexadecimal number =    0       0       1       1     = 11
decimal number =                        -17
binary number absolute value =          0000    0000    0001    0001
complement =                            1111    1111    1110    1110
add 1 =                                 1111    1111    1110    1111
hexadecimal =                           f       f       e       f       = ffef

Verify:    -17      11111111 11101111
add:       +17      00000000 00010001
equals:      0      00000000 00000000
```

Hexadecimal numbers are normally preceded with 0x in order to distinguish them from decimal numbers, so -17 in hexadecimal is 0xffef. If you investigate a machine language listing, a .lst file, and you see the number 0xffef, you have to find out from the context if it is a signed or unsigned integer. If it is a signed integer, it means -17 in decimal. If it is an unsigned integer, it means 65519. Of course, if it is a memory address, it is unsigned (you get that, right?). Sometimes you will see other notations in assembler code, such as 0800h, which is also a hexadecimal number; 10010111b, a binary number; or 420o, an octal number. Yes, indeed, octal numbers can also be used. We will use octal numbers when we write our code for file I/O. If you need to convert integer numbers, don't sweat it; use the previously mentioned websites.

Floating-Point Numbers

Floating-point numbers are written in binary or hexadecimal according to the IEEE-754 standard. The process is even more complicated than with integers; if you want to know the details, here is a good place to start:

`http://mathcenter.oxford.emory.edu/site/cs170/ieee754/`

Again, if you need to convert floating-point numbers, use the previously mentioned web sites; we will not go into further detail here.

A Short Course on Registers

The CPU, the brain of the computer, executes the program instructions by making extensive use of the registers and memory of the computer, doing mathematical and logical operations on these registers and memory. Therefore, it is important to have a basic knowledge of registers and memory and how they are used. Here we give a short overview of the registers; more details about the usage of registers will become clear in later chapters. Registers are storage locations, used by the CPU to store data, instructions, or memory addresses. There are only a small number of registers, but the CPU can read and write them extremely quickly. You can consider registers as sort of a scratchpad for the processor to store temporary information. One rule to keep in mind if speed is important is that the CPU can access registers much faster than it can access memory.

Do not worry if this section is above your head; things will start making sense when we use registers in the upcoming chapters.

General-Purpose Registers

There are 16 general-purpose registers, and each register can be used as a 64-bit, 32-bit, 16-bit, or 8-bit register. In the following table, you can see the names of each register in different sizes. Four registers—rax, rbx, rcx, and rdx—can have two kinds of 8-bit registers: low 8-bit, which is the lower half of the 16-bit register, and high 8-bit, which is the higher half of the 16-bit register.

64-bit	32-bit	16-bit	low 8-bit	high 8-bit	comment
rax	eax	ax	al	ah	
rbx	ebx	bx	bl	bh	
rcx	ecx	cx	cl	ch	
rdx	edx	dx	dl	dh	
rsi	esi	si	sil	-	
rdi	edi	di	dil	-	
rbp	ebp	bp	bpl	-	Base pointer
rsp	esp	sp	spl	-	Stack pointer
r8	r8d	r8w	r8b	-	
r9	r9d	r9w	r9b	-	
r10	r10d	r10w	r10b	-	
r11	r11d	r11w	r11b	-	
r12	r12d	r12w	r12b	-	
r13	r13d	r13w	r13b	-	
r14	r14d	r14w	r14b	-	
r15	r15d	r15w	r15b	-	

Although rbp and rsp are called *general-purpose registers,* they should be handled with care, as they are used by the processor during the program execution. We will use rbp and rsp quite a bit in the more advanced chapters.

A 64-bit register contains a set of 64 bits, 0s and/or 1s, that is, 8 bytes. When we put 60 in rax in our hello, world program, rax contained the following:

00000000 00000000 00000000 00000000 00000000 00000000 00000000 00111100

This is the binary representation of the number 60 in a 64-bit register.

A 32-bit register is the set of the 32 lower (rightmost) bits of a 64-bit register. Similarly, a 16-bit register and an 8-bit register consist of the lowest 16 and lowest 8 bits, respectively, of the 64-bit register.

Remember, the "lower" bits are always the rightmost bits.

Bit number 0 is the rightmost bit; we start counting from the right and start with index 0, not 1. Thus, the leftmost bit of a 64-bit register has index 63, not 64.

So, when rax has the value 60, we could also say that eax now contains the following:

00000000 00000000 00000000 00111100

or that ax contains the following:

00000000 00111100

or that al contains the following:

00111100

Instruction Pointer Register (rip)

The processor keeps track of the next instruction to be executed by storing the address of the next instruction in rip. You can change the value in rip to whatever you want at your own peril; you have been warned. A safer way of changing the value in rip is by using jump instructions. This will be discussed in a later chapter.

Flag Register

Here is the layout of rflags, the flag register. After executing an instruction, a program can check whether a certain flag is set (e.g., ZF=1) and then act accordingly.

Name	Symbol	Bit	Content
Carry	CF	0	Previous instruction had a carry
Parity	PF	2	Last byte has even number of 1s
Adjust	AF	4	BCD operations
Zero	ZF	6	Previous instruction resulted a zero
Sign	SF	8	Previous instruction resulted in most significant bit equal to 1
Direction	DF	10	Direction of string operations (increment or decrement)
Overflow	OF	11	Previous instruction resulted in overflow

We will explain and use flags quite a bit in this book.

There is another flag register, called MXCSR, that will be used in the single instruction, multiple data (SIMD) instruction chapters; we will explain MXCSR there in more detail.

xmm and ymm Registers

These registers are used for floating-point calculations and SIMD. We will use the xmm and corresponding ymm registers extensively later, starting with the floating-point instructions.

In addition to the previously explained registers, there are more registers, but we will not use the others in this book.

Put the theory aside for now; it's time for the real work!

Summary

In this chapter, you learned the following:

- How to display values in decimal, binary, and hexadecimal formats

- How to use registers and flags

CHAPTER 3

Program Analysis with a Debugger: GDB

In this chapter, we will introduce you to debugging an assembly program. Debugging is an important skill, because with a debugger you can investigate the content of registers and memory in hexadecimal, binary, or decimal representation. You already know from the previous chapter that the CPU is intensively using registers and memory, and a debugger allows you to execute the instructions step-by-step, while looking at how the content of the registers, memory, and flag changes. Maybe you have experienced already your first assembly program crashing upon execution with an unfriendly message such as "Memory Segmentation Fault." With a debugger you can step through your program and find out exactly where and why things went wrong.

Start Debugging

Once you have assembled and linked your `hello, world` program, without errors, you obtain an executable file. With a debugger tool you can load an executable program into the computer memory and execute it line by line while examining various registers and memory places. There are several free and commercial debuggers available. In Linux, the mother of all debuggers is GDB; it is a command-line program, with very cryptic commands. So much fun! In future chapters, we will use SASM, a tool with a graphical user interface, that is based on GDB. But having a basic knowledge of GDB itself can be useful, because not all GDB functionality is available in SASM.

In your further career as an assembly programmer, you will certainly look at various debuggers with nice user interfaces, each one targeted at a specific platform, such as Windows, Mac, or Linux. These GUI debuggers will help you debug long and complex programs with much more ease as compared to a CLI debugger. But GDB is a comprehensive and "quick and dirty way" to do Linux debugging. GDB is installed on most

© Jo Van Hoey 2019
J. Van Hoey, *Beginning x64 Assembly Programming*, https://doi.org/10.1007/978-1-4842-5076-1_3

Linux development systems, and if not, it can be easily installed for troubleshooting without much overhead for the system. We will use GDB for now to give you some essentials and turn to other tools in later chapters. One note, GDB seems to be developed for debugging higher-level languages; some features will not be of any help when debugging assembly.

Debugging a program with a CLI debugger can be overwhelming the first time. Do not despair when reading this chapter; you will see that things get easier as we progress.

To start debugging the hello program, in the CLI navigate to the directory where you saved the hello program. At the command prompt, type the following:

```
gdb hello
```

GDB will load the executable hello into memory and answer with its own prompt (gdb), waiting for your instructions. If you type the following:

```
list
```

GDB will show a number of lines of your code. Type list again, and GDB will show the next lines, and so on. To list a specific line, for example, the start of your code, type list 1. Figure 3-1 shows an example.

```
jo@UbuntuDesktop:~/Desktop/linux64/gcc/01 hello $ gdb hello
GNU gdb (Ubuntu 7.11.1-0ubuntu1~16.5) 7.11.1
Copyright (C) 2016 Free Software Foundation, Inc.
License GPLv3+: GNU GPL version 3 or later <http://gnu.org/licenses/gpl.html>
This is free software: you are free to change and redistribute it.
There is NO WARRANTY, to the extent permitted by law.  Type "show copying"
and "show warranty" for details.
This GDB was configured as "x86_64-linux-gnu".
Type "show configuration" for configuration details.
For bug reporting instructions, please see:
<http://www.gnu.org/software/gdb/bugs/>.
Find the GDB manual and other documentation resources online at:
<http://www.gnu.org/software/gdb/documentation/>.
For help, type "help".
Type "apropos word" to search for commands related to "word"...
Reading symbols from hello...done.
(gdb) list
1         section .data
2            msg db        "hello, world",0
3         section .bss
4         section .text
5            global main
6       main:
7            mov      rax, 1         ; 1 = write
8            mov      rdi, 1         ; 1 = to stdout
9            mov      rsi, msg       ; string to display in rsi
10           mov      rdx, 12        ; length of the string, without 0
(gdb) █
```

Figure 3-1. *GDB list output*

If the output on your screen is different from our screen, containing lots of % signs, then your GDB is configured to use the AT&T syntax flavor. We will use the Intel syntax flavor, which is more intuitive (to us). We will show how to change the flavor in a minute.

If you type the following:

```
run
```

GDB will run your hello program, printing hello, world, and return to its prompt (gdb). Figure 3-2 shows the results on our screen.

```
jo@UbuntuDesktop:~/Desktop/linux64/gcc/01 hello $ gdb hello
GNU gdb (Ubuntu 7.11.1-0ubuntu1~16.5) 7.11.1
Copyright (C) 2016 Free Software Foundation, Inc.
License GPLv3+: GNU GPL version 3 or later <http://gnu.org/licenses/gpl.html>
This is free software: you are free to change and redistribute it.
There is NO WARRANTY, to the extent permitted by law.  Type "show copying"
and "show warranty" for details.
This GDB was configured as "x86_64-linux-gnu".
Type "show configuration" for configuration details.
For bug reporting instructions, please see:
<http://www.gnu.org/software/gdb/bugs/>.
Find the GDB manual and other documentation resources online at:
<http://www.gnu.org/software/gdb/documentation/>.
For help, type "help".
Type "apropos word" to search for commands related to "word"...
Reading symbols from hello...done.
(gdb) run
Starting program: /home/jo/Desktop/linux64/gcc/01 hello /hello
hello, world[Inferior 1 (process 4698) exited normally]
(gdb) █
```

Figure 3-2. *GDB run output*

To quit GDB, type quit.

Let's do some interesting stuff with GDB!

But first we will change the disassembly flavor; do this only if you had the % signs in the previous exercise. Load the executable hello into GDB if it is not already there.

Type the following:

```
set disassembly-flavor intel
```

This will put the disassembled code in a format that is already familiar. You can make Intel the default flavor for GDB by using the appropriate setting in your Linux shell profile. See the documentation of your Linux distribution. In Ubuntu 18.04, create a `.gdbinit` file in your home directory, containing the previous set instruction. Log out and log in, and you should be using GDB with the Intel flavor from now on.

Start GDB with `hello` to begin your analysis. As you learned before, the `hello, world` program first initializes some data in `section.data` and `section.bss` and then proceeds to the `main` label. That is where the action starts, so let's begin our examination there.

At the `(gdb)` prompt, type the following:

```
disassemble main
```

GDB returns your source code, more or less. The returned source code is not exactly the same as the source you wrote originally. Strange, isn't it? What happened here? Some analysis is needed.

Figure 3-3 shows what GDB returned on our computer.

```
(gdb) disassemble main
Dump of assembler code for function main:
   0x00000000004004e0 <+0>:     mov     eax,0x1
   0x00000000004004e5 <+5>:     mov     edi,0x1
   0x00000000004004ea <+10>:    movabs  rsi,0x601030
   0x00000000004004f4 <+20>:    mov     edx,0xc
   0x00000000004004f9 <+25>:    syscall
   0x00000000004004fb <+27>:    mov     eax,0x3c
   0x0000000000400500 <+32>:    mov     edi,0x0
   0x0000000000400505 <+37>:    syscall
   0x0000000000400507 <+39>:    nop     WORD PTR [rax+rax*1+0x0]
End of assembler dump.
(gdb) ▮
```

Figure 3-3. *GDB disassemble output*

The long numbers on the left, starting with `0x00...`, are memory addresses; they are the places where the machine instructions of our program are stored. As you can see, from the addresses and the `<+5>` in the second line, the first instruction, `mov eax,0x1`, needs five bytes of memory. But wait a minute, in our source code we wrote `mov rax,1`. What is the deal with the `eax`?

Well, if you look in the register table from Chapter 2, you will see that `eax` is the low 32-bit part of the `rax` register. The assembler is smart enough to figure out that a 64-bit register is far too much waste of resources for storing the number 1, so it uses a 32-bit register. The same is true for the use of `edi` and `edx` instead of `rdi` and `rdx`.

The 64-bit assembler is an extension of the 32-bit assembler, and you will see that whenever possible the assembler will use 32-bit instructions.

The 0x1 is the hexadecimal representation of the decimal number 1, 0xd is decimal 13, and 0x3c is decimal 60.

The nop instruction means "no operation" and is inserted there by the assembler for memory management reasons.

What happened to our msg? The instruction mov rsi, msg got replaced by movabs rsi,0x601030. Do not worry about movabs for now; it is there because of 64-bit addressing, and it is used to put an immediate (value) in a register. The 0x601030 is the memory address where msg is stored on our computer. This can be a different address in your case.

At the (gdb) prompt, type the following:

```
x/s 0x601030 (or x/s 'your_memory_address')
```

GDB answers with the output shown in Figure 3-4.

```
(gdb) x/s 0x601030
0x601030 <msg>: "hello, world"
(gdb) 
```

Figure 3-4. *GDB output*

The x stands for "examine," and the s stands for "string." GDB answered that 0x601030 is the start of the string msg and tries to show the whole string up until a string-terminating 0. Now you know one of the reasons why we put a terminating 0 after hello, world.

You can also type the following:

```
x/c 0x601030
```

to get the output shown in Figure 3-5.

```
(gdb) x/c 0x601030
0x601030 <msg>: 104 'h'
(gdb) 
```

Figure 3-5. *GDB output*

With c you ask for a character. Here GDB returns the first character of msg, preceded by the decimal ASCII code of that character. Do a Google search for a table of ASCII codes to verify, and keep that table handy for future use; there's no need to memorize it. Or open an additional terminal window and type man ascii at the CLI.

Let's look at some other examples.

Use this to show 13 characters starting at a memory address (see Figure 3-6):

```
x/13c 0x601030
```

```
(gdb) x/13c 0x601030
0x601030 <msg>: 104 'h' 101 'e' 108 'l' 108 'l' 111 'o' 44 ','  32 ' '  119 'w'
0x601038:       111 'o' 114 'r' 108 'l' 100 'd' 0 '\000'
(gdb) ▮
```

Figure 3-6. *GDB output*

Use the following to show 13 characters starting at a memory address in decimal representation (see Figure 3-7):

```
x/13d 0x601030
```

```
(gdb) x/13d 0x601030
0x601030 <msg>: 104      101      108      108      111      44       32       119
0x601038:       111      114      108      100      0
(gdb) ▮
```

Figure 3-7. *GDB output*

Use the following to show 13 characters starting at a memory address in hexadecimal representation (see Figure 3-8):

```
x/13x 0x601030
```

```
(gdb) x/13x 0x601030
0x601030 <msg>: 0x68     0x65     0x6c     0x6c     0x6f     0x2c     0x20     0x77
0x601038:       0x6f     0x72     0x6c     0x64     0x00
(gdb) ▮
```

Figure 3-8. *GDB output*

Use the following to show msg (see Figure 3-9):

    x/s &msg

```
(gdb) x/s &msg
0x601030 <msg>:  "hello, world"
(gdb) █
```

Figure 3-9. *GDB output*

Let's return to the disassemble listing. Type the following:

    x/2x 0x004004e0

This shows in hexadecimal the content of the two memory addresses starting at 0x004004e0 (see Figure 3-10).

```
(gdb) x/2x 0x004004e0
0x4004e0 <main>:         0xb8     0x01
(gdb) ▯
```

Figure 3-10. *GDB output*

This is our first instruction, mov eax,0x1, in machine language. We saw that same instruction when we examined the hello.lst file.

Step It Up!

Let's step through the program with the debugger. Load your program again in GDB if it is not there yet.

First, we will put a break in the program, pausing the execution and allowing us to examine a number or things. Type the following:

    break main

In our case, GDB answers with the output in Figure 3-11.

```
(gdb) break main
Breakpoint 1 at 0x4004e0: file hello.asm, line 7.
(gdb) ▌
```

Figure 3-11. *GDB output*

Then type the following:

```
run
```

Figure 3-12 shows the output.

```
(gdb) run
Starting program: /home/jo/Desktop/linux64/gcc/01 hello /hello

Breakpoint 1, main () at hello.asm:8
8           mov     rax, 1              ; 1 = write
(gdb) ▌
```

Figure 3-12. *GDB output*

The debugger stops at the break and shows the next instruction that will be executed. That is, mov rax,1 is **not executed yet**.

Type the following:

```
info registers
```

GDB returns the output shown in Figure 3-13.

```
(gdb) info registers
rax            0x4004e0 4195552
rbx            0x0      0
rcx            0x0      0
rdx            0x7fffffffddd8   140737488346584
rsi            0x7fffffffddc8   140737488346568
rdi            0x1      1
rbp            0x400510 0x400510 <__libc_csu_init>
rsp            0x7fffffffdce8   0x7fffffffdce8
r8             0x400580 4195712
r9             0x7ffff7de7ab0   140737351940784
r10            0x846    2118
r11            0x7ffff7a2d740   140737348032320
r12            0x4003e0 4195296
r13            0x7fffffffddc0   140737488346560
r14            0x0      0
r15            0x0      0
rip            0x4004e0 0x4004e0 <main>
eflags         0x246    [ PF ZF IF ]
cs             0x33     51
ss             0x2b     43
ds             0x0      0
es             0x0      0
fs             0x0      0
---Type <return> to continue, or q <return> to quit---
```

Figure 3-13. *GDB registers output*

The content of the registers is not important now, except for `rip`, the instruction pointer. Register `rip` has the value 0x4004e0, which is the memory address of the next instruction to execute. Check your disassemble listing; 0x4004e0 (in our case) points to the first instruction, `mov rax,1`. GDB stops just before that instruction and waits for your commands. **It is important to remember that the instruction pointed to by `rip` is not yet executed**.

In your case, GDB may show something different than 0x4004e0. That's okay; it is the address of that particular line in memory, which may be different depending on your computer configuration.

Type the following to advance one step:

```
step
```

The type the following, which is the abbreviation for `info registers`:

```
i r
```

Figure 3-14 shows the output.

```
(gdb) step
9          mov      rdi, 1                    ; 1 = to stdout
(gdb) i r
rax              0x1        1
rbx              0x0        0
rcx              0x0        0
rdx              0x7fffffffddd8    140737488346584
rsi              0x7fffffffddc8    140737488346568
rdi              0x1        1
rbp              0x400510 0x400510 <__libc_csu_init>
rsp              0x7fffffffdce8    0x7fffffffdce8
r8               0x400580 4195712
r9               0x7ffff7de7ab0    140737351940784
r10              0x846      2118
r11              0x7ffff7a2d740    140737348032320
r12              0x4003e0 4195296
r13              0x7fffffffddc0    140737488346560
r14              0x0        0
r15              0x0        0
rip              0x4004e5 0x4004e5 <main+5>
eflags           0x246      [ PF ZF IF ]
cs               0x33       51
ss               0x2b       43
ds               0x0        0
es               0x0        0
fs               0x0        0
gs               0x0        0
(gdb) ▮
```

Figure 3-14. *GDB registers output*

Indeed, rax contains now 0x1, and rip contains the address of the next instruction to execute.

Step further through the program and notice how rsi receives the address of msg, prints hello, world on the screen, and exits. Notice also how rip points every time to the next instruction to execute.

Some Additional GDB Commands

break or **b**: Set a breakpoint as we have done before.

> **disable breakpoint** *number*
>
> **enable breakpoint** *number*
>
> **delete breakpoint** *number*

continue or **c**: Continue execution until next breakpoint.

step or **s**: Step into the current line, eventually jumping into the called function.

next or **n**: Step over the current line and stop at the next line.

help or **h**: Show help.

tui enable: Enable a simple text user interface; to disable, use **tui disable**.

print or **p**: Print the value of a variable, register, and so on.

Here are some examples:

Print rax: p $rax.

Print rax in binary: p/t $rax.

Print rax in hexadecimal: p/x $rax.

One important remark about GDB: to properly use it, you must insert a *function prologue* and a *function epilogue* in your code. We will show in the next chapter how to do that, and in a later chapter we will discuss function prologues and function epilogues when we talk about stack frames. For short programs such as our hello, world program, there is no problem. But with longer programs, GDB will show unexpected behavior if there is no prologue or epilogue.

Play around with GDB, refer to the online manual (type man gdb at the CLI), and get familiar with GDB, because even when you use a GUI debugger, some functionality may not be available. Or you may not want to install a GUI debugger on your system at all.

A Slightly Improved Version of hello, world

You noticed that after printing hello, world, the command prompt appeared on the same line. We want to have hello, world printed on its own line, with the command prompt on a new line.

Listing 3-1 shows the code to do that.

Listing 3-1. A Better Version of hello,world

```
;hello2.asm
section .data
     msg     db      "hello, world",0
     NL      db      0xa  ; ascii code for new line
section .bss
section .text
    global main
main:
    mov     rax, 1      ; 1 = write
    mov     rdi, 1      ; 1 = to stdout
    mov     rsi, msg    ; string to display
    mov     rdx, 12     ; length of string, without 0
    syscall             ; display the string
    mov     rax, 1      ; 1 = write
    mov     rdi, 1      ; 1 = to stdout
    mov     rsi, NL     ; display new line
    mov     rdx, 1      ; length of the string
    syscall             ; display the string
    mov     rax, 60     ; 60 = exit
    mov     rdi, 0      ; 0 = success exit code
    syscall             ; quit
```

Type this code in your editor and save it as hello2.asm in a new directory. Copy the previous makefile to this new directory; in this makefile, change every instance of hello into hello2 and save the file.

We added a variable, NL, containing hexadecimal 0xa, which is the ASCII code for new line, and print this NL variable just after we print msg. That's it! Go ahead—assemble and run it (see Figure 3-15).

```
jo@UbuntuDesktop:~/Desktop/linux64/gcc/02 hello2$ make
nasm -f elf64 -g -F dwarf hello2.asm -l hello2.lst
gcc -o hello2 hello2.o
jo@UbuntuDesktop:~/Desktop/linux64/gcc/02 hello2$ ./hello2
hello, world
jo@UbuntuDesktop:~/Desktop/linux64/gcc/02 hello2$ █
```

Figure 3-15. *A better version of hello, world*

Another way to accomplish this is by changing our msg, as shown here:

```
msg    db        "hello, world",10,0
```

The 10 is the decimal representation of a new line (0xa in hexadecimal). Try it! Do not forget to increase rdx to 13 for the additional 10 character.

Listing 3-2 shows the code. Save this as hello3.asm in a separate directory, copy and a modify a makefile appropriately, and build and run.

Listing 3-2. Another Version of hello,world

```
;hello3.asm
section .data
     msg        db        "hello, world",10,0
section .bss
section .text
     global main
main:
     mov       rax, 1            ; 1 = write
     mov       rdi, 1            ; 1 = to stdout
     mov       rsi, msg          ; string to display
     mov       rdx, 13           ; length of string, without 0
     syscall                     ; display the string
     mov       rax, 60           ; 60 = exit
     mov       rdi, 0            ; 0 = success exit code
     syscall                     ; quit
```

Using this version, however, means that the new line is part of our string, and that is not always desired, because a new line is a formatting instruction that you may only intend to use when displaying a string, not when executing other string-handling functions. On the other hand, it makes your code simpler and shorter. It's your decision!

Summary

In this chapter, you learned the following:

- How to use GDB, a CLI debugger

- How to print a new line

CHAPTER 4

Your Next Program: Alive and Kicking!

Now that you have a firm grasp of GDB and know what an assembly program looks like, let's add some complexity. In this chapter, we will show how to obtain the length of a string variable. We will show how to print integer and floating-point values using `printf`. And we will expand your knowledge of GDB commands.

Listing 4-1 contains the example code that we will use to show how we can find the length of a string and how numeric values are stored in memory.

Listing 4-1. alive.asm

```
;alive.asm
section .data
    msg1    db      "Hello, World!",10,0        ; string with NL and 0
    msg1Len         equ     $-msg1-1     ; measure the length, minus the 0
    msg2    db      "Alive and Kicking!",10,0  ; string with NL and 0
    msg2Len         equ     $-msg2-1     ; measure the length, minus the 0
    radius dq       357                        ; no string, not displayable?
    pi      dq      3.14                       ; no string, not displayable?
section .bss
section .text
    global main
main:
    push            rbp             ; function prologue
    mov             rbp,rsp         ; function prologue
    mov             rax, 1          ; 1 = write
    mov             rdi, 1          ; 1 = to stdout
    mov             rsi, msg1       ; string to display
```

© Jo Van Hoey 2019
J. Van Hoey, *Beginning x64 Assembly Programming*, https://doi.org/10.1007/978-1-4842-5076-1_4

```
mov             rdx, msg1Len    ; length of the string
syscall                         ; display the string
mov             rax, 1          ; 1 = write
mov             rdi, 1          ; 1 = to stdout
mov             rsi, msg2       ; string to display
mov             rdx, msg2Len    ; length of the string
syscall                         ; display the string
mov             rsp,rbp         ; function epilogue
pop             rbp             ; function epilogue
mov             rax, 60         ; 60 = exit
mov             rdi, 0          ; 0 = success exit code
syscall                         ; quit
```

Type this program into your favorite editor and save it as alive.asm. Create the makefile containing the lines in Listing 4-2.

Listing 4-2. makefile for alive.asm

```
#makefile for alive.asm
alive: alive.o
       gcc -o alive alive.o -no-pie
alive.o: alive.asm
        nasm -f elf64 -g -F dwarf alive.asm -l alive.lst
```

Save this file and quit the editor.

At the command prompt, type make to assemble and build the program and then run the program by typing ./alive at the command prompt. If you see the output shown in Figure 4-1 displayed at the prompt, then everything worked as planned; otherwise, you made some typo or other error. Happy debugging!

```
jo@UbuntuDesktop:~/Desktop/linux64/gcc/04 alive$ make
nasm -f elf64 -g -F dwarf alive.asm -l alive.lst
gcc -o alive alive.o -ggdb -no-pie
jo@UbuntuDesktop:~/Desktop/linux64/gcc/04 alive$ ./alive
Hello, World!
Alive and Kicking!
jo@UbuntuDesktop:~/Desktop/linux64/gcc/04 alive$ █
```

Figure 4-1. *alive.asm output*

Analysis of the Alive Program

In our first program, hello.asm, we put the length of msg, 13 characters, in rdx in order to display msg. In alive.asm, we use a nice feature to calculate the length of our variables, as shown here:

```
msg1Len equ $-msg1-1
```

The $-msg1-1 part means this: take this memory location ($) and subtract the memory location of msg1. The result is the length of msg1. That length, -1 (minus the string-terminating zero), is stored in the constant msg1Len.

Note the use of a *function prologue* and *function epilogue* in the code. These are needed for GDB to function correctly, as pointed out in the previous chapter. The prologue and epilogue code will be explained in a later chapter.

Let's do some memory digging with GDB! Type the following:

```
gdb alive
```

Then at the (gdb) prompt, type the following:

```
disassemble main
```

Figure 4-2 shows the output.

```
(gdb) disass main
Dump of assembler code for function main:
   0x00000000004004e0 <+0>:     push   rbp
   0x00000000004004e1 <+1>:     mov    rbp,rsp
   0x00000000004004e4 <+4>:     mov    eax,0x1
   0x00000000004004e9 <+9>:     mov    edi,0x1
   0x00000000004004ee <+14>:    movabs rsi,0x601030
   0x00000000004004f8 <+24>:    mov    edx,0xe
   0x00000000004004fd <+29>:    syscall
   0x00000000004004ff <+31>:    mov    eax,0x1
   0x0000000000400504 <+36>:    mov    edi,0x1
   0x0000000000400509 <+41>:    movabs rsi,0x60103f
   0x0000000000400513 <+51>:    mov    edx,0x13
   0x0000000000400518 <+56>:    syscall
   0x000000000040051a <+58>:    mov    rsp,rbp
   0x000000000040051d <+61>:    pop    rbp
   0x000000000040051e <+62>:    mov    eax,0x3c
   0x0000000000400523 <+67>:    mov    edi,0x0
   0x0000000000400528 <+72>:    syscall
   0x000000000040052a <+74>:    nop    WORD PTR [rax+rax*1+0x0]
End of assembler dump.
(gdb) █
```

Figure 4-2. *alive disassemble*

So, on our computer, it seems that variable msg1 sits at memory location 0x601030; you can check that with this:

```
x/s 0x601030
```

Figure 4-3 shows the output.

```
(gdb) x/s 0x601030
0x601030 <msg1>:         "Hello, World!\n"
(gdb) █
```

Figure 4-3. *Memory location of msg1*

The \n stands for "new line." Another way to verify variables in GDB is as follows:

```
x/s &msg1
```

Figure 4-4 shows the output.

```
(gdb) x/s &msg1
0x601030 <msg1>:         "Hello, World!\n"
(gdb) █
```

Figure 4-4. *Memory location of msg1*

How about the numeric values?

```
x/dw        &radius
x/xw        &radius
```

Figure 4-5 shows the output.

```
(gdb) x/dw &radius
0x601053 <radius>:       357
(gdb) x/xw &radius
0x601053 <radius>:       0x00000165
(gdb) █
```

Figure 4-5. *Numeric values*

So, you get the decimal and hexadecimal values stored at memory location `radius`. For a floating-point variable, use the following:

```
x/fg &pi
x/fx &pi
```

Figure 4-6 shows the output.

```
(gdb) x/fg &pi
0x60105b <pi>:   3.1400000000000001
(gdb) x/fx &pi
0x60105b <pi>:   0x40091eb851eb851f
(gdb) ▮
```

Figure 4-6. *Floating-point values*

(Notice the floating-point error?)

There is a subtlety that you should be aware of here. To demonstrate, open the `alive.lst` file that was generated. See Figure 4-7.

```
 1    1                           ; alive.asm
 2    2                           section .data
 3    3 00000000 48656C6C6F2C20576F-    msg1 db    "Hello, World!",10,0     ; string with NL and 0
 4    3 00000009 726C64210A00
 5    4                           msg1Len   equ  $-msg1-1          ; measure the length, minus the 0
 6    5 0000000F 416C69766520616E64-    msg2 db    "Alive and Kicking!",10,0   ; string with NL and 0
 7    5 00000018 204B69636B696E6721-
 8    5 00000021 0A00
 9    6                           msg2Len   equ  $-msg2-1          ; measure the length, minus the 0
10    7 00000023 6501000000000000  radius    dq   357              ; no string, not displayable?
11    8 0000002B 1F85EB51B81E0940  pi        dq   3.14             ; no string, not displayable?
12    9                           section .bss
13   10                           section .text
14   11                               global main
15   12                           main:
16   13 00000000 55                   push  rbp                    ; function prologue
17   14 00000001 4889E5               mov   rbp,rsp                ; function prologue
18   15 00000004 B801000000           mov        rax, 1            ; 1 = write
19   16 00000009 BF01000000           mov        rdi, 1            ; 1 = to stdout
20   17 0000000E 48BE-                mov        rsi, msg1         ; string to display
21   17 00000010 [0000000000000000]
22   18 00000018 BA0E000000           mov        rdx, msg1Len      ; length of the string
23   19 0000001D 0F05             syscall                          ; display the string
24   20 0000001F B801000000           mov        rax, 1            ; 1 = write
25   21 00000024 BF01000000           mov        rdi, 1            ; 1 = to stdout
26   22 00000029 48BE-                mov        rsi, msg2         ; string to display
27   22 0000002B [0F00000000000000]
28   23 00000033 BA13000000           mov        rdx, msg2Len      ; length of the string
29   24 00000038 0F05             syscall                          ; display the string
30   25 0000003A 4889EC               mov   rsp,rbp                ; function epilogue
31   26 0000003D 5D                   pop   rbp                    ; function epilogue
32   27 0000003E B83C000000           mov        rax, 60           ; 60 = exit
33   28 00000043 BF00000000           mov        rdi, 0            ; 0 = success exit code
34   29 00000048 0F05             syscall                          ; quit
```

Figure 4-7. *alive.lst*

Look at lines 10 and 11, where on the left you can find the hexadecimal representation of radius and pi. Instead of 0165, you find 6501, and instead of 40091EB851EB851F, you find 1F85EB51B81E0940. So, the **bytes** (1 byte is two hex numbers) are in reverse order!

This characteristic is called *endianness*. The big-endian format stores numbers the way we are used to seeing them, with the *most* significant digits starting at the left. The little-endian format stores the *least* significant numbers starting at the left. Intel processors use little-endian, and that can be very confusing when looking at hexadecimal code.

Why do they have such strange names like big-endian and little-endian?

In 1726, Jonathan Swift wrote a famous novel, *Gulliver's Travels*. In that novel appear two fictional islands, Lilliput and Blefuscu. Inhabitants of Lilliput are at war with the people of Blefuscu about how to break eggs: on the smaller end or on the bigger end. Lilliputs are little endians, preferring to break their eggs on the smaller end. Blefuscus are big endians. Now you see that modern computing has traditions rooted in the distant past!

Take the time to single-step through the program (break main, run, next, next, next...). You can see that GDB steps over the function prologue. Edit the source code, delete the function prologue and epilogue, and re-make the program. Single-step again with GDB. In our case, GDB does refuse to single-step and completely executes the program. When assembling with YASM, another assembler based on NASM, we can safely omit the prologue and epilogue code and step through the code with GDB. Sometimes it is necessary to experiment, tinker, and Google around!

Printing

Our alive program prints these two strings:

```
Hello, World!
Alive and Kicking!
```

However, there are two other variables that were not defined as strings: radius and pi. Printing these variables is a bit more complex than printing strings. To print these variables in a similar way as we did with msg1 and msg2, we would have to convert the values radius and pi into strings. It is perfectly doable to add code for this conversion into our program, but it would make our small program too complicated at this point in time, so we are going to cheat a little bit. We will borrow printf, a common function, from the program language C and include it in our program. If this is upsetting you, have patience. When you become a more advanced assembler programmer, you can write your own function for converting/printing numbers. Or you could conclude that writing you own `printf` function is too much waste of time....

To introduce `printf` in assembler, we will start with a simple program. Modify the first program, `hello.asm`, as shown in Listing 4-3.

Listing 4-3. hello4.asm

```
; hello4.asm
extern      printf     ; declare the function as external
section .data
      msg    db    "Hello, World!",0
      fmtstr db    "This is our string: %s",10,0 ; printformat
section .bss
section .text
      global main
main:
      push  rbp
      mov   rbp,rsp
      mov   rdi, fmtstr      ; first argument for printf
      mov   rsi, msg         ; second argument for printf
      mov   rax, 0           ; no xmm registers involved
      call  printf           ; call the function
      mov   rsp,rbp
      pop   rbp
      mov   rax, 60          ; 60 = exit
      mov   rdi, 0           ; 0 = success exit code
      syscall                ; quit
```

So, we start by telling the assembler (and the linker) that we are going to use an external function called `printf`. We created a string for formatting how `printf` will display `msg`. The syntax for the format string is similar to the syntax in C; if you have any experience with C, you will certainly recognize the format string. `%s` is a placeholder for the string to be printed.

Do not forget the function prologue and epilogue. Move the address of msg into rsi, and move the address of the fmtstr into rdi. Clear rax, which in this case means there are no floating-point numbers in the xmm registers to be printed. Floating-point numbers and xmm registers will be explained later in Chapter 11.

Listing 4-4 shows the makefile.

Listing 4-4. makefile for hello4.asm

```
#makefile for hello4.asm
hello4: hello4.o
        gcc -o hello4 hello4.o -no-pie
hello4.o: hello4.asm
        nasm -f elf64 -g -F dwarf hello4.asm -l hello4.lst
```

Make sure the -no-pie flag is added in the makefile; otherwise, the use of printf will cause an error. Remember from Chapter 1 that the current gcc compiler generates position-independent executable (pie) code to make it more hacker-safe. One of the consequences is that we cannot simply use external functions anymore. To avoid this complication, we use the flag -no-pie.

Build and run the program. Google the C printf function to get an idea of the possible formats. As you will see, with printf we have the flexibility of formatting the output as print integers, floating-point values, strings, hexadecimal data, and so on. The printf function requires that a string is terminated with 0 (NULL). If you omit the 0, printf will display everything until it finds a 0. Terminating a string with a 0 is not a requirement in assembly, but it is necessary with printf, GDB, and also some SIMD instructions (SIMD will be covered in Chapter 26).

Figure 4-8 shows the output.

```
jo@UbuntuDesktop:~/Desktop/linux64/gcc/05  hello4$ make
nasm -f elf64 -g -F dwarf hello4.asm -l hello4.lst
gcc -o hello4 hello4.o
jo@UbuntuDesktop:~/Desktop/linux64/gcc/05  hello4$ ./hello4
This is our string: Hello, World!
jo@UbuntuDesktop:~/Desktop/linux64/gcc/05  hello4$ ▮
```

Figure 4-8. alive.lst

Back to our alive program! With printf we can now print the variables radius and pi. Listing 4-5 shows the source code. By now you know what to do: create the source code, copy or create/modify a makefile, and there you go.

Listing 4-5. makefile for alive2.asm

```
; alive2.asm
section .data
     msg1          db      "Hello, World!",0
     msg2          db      "Alive and Kicking!",0
     radius        dd      357
     pi            dq      3.14
     fmtstr        db      "%s",10,0 ;format for printing a string
     fmtflt        db      "%lf",10,0 ;format for a float
     fmtint        db      "%d",10,0 ;format for an integer
section .bss
section .text
extern     printf
     global main
main:
   push    rbp
   mov     rbp,rsp

; print msg1
   mov     rax, 0              ; no floating point
   mov     rdi, fmtstr
   mov     rsi, msg1
   call    printf
; print msg2
   mov     rax, 0              ; no floating point
   mov     rdi, fmtstr
   mov     rsi, msg2
   call    printf
; print radius
   mov     rax, 0              ; no floating point
   mov     rdi, fmtint
   mov     rsi, [radius]
```

```
    call    printf
; print pi
    mov     rax, 1              ; 1 xmm register used
    movq    xmm0, [pi]
    mov     rdi, fmtflt
    call    printf

    mov     rsp,rbp
    pop     rbp
ret
```

We added three strings for formatting the printout. Put the format string in rdi, point rsi to the item to be printed, put 0 into rax to indicate that no floating-point numbers are involved, and then call printf. For printing a floating-point number, move the floating-point value to be displayed in xmm0, with the instruction movq. We use one xmm register, so we put 1 into rax. In later chapters, we will talk more about XMM registers for floating-point calculations and about SIMD instructions.

Note the square brackets, [ ], around radius and pi.

```
    mov rsi, [radius]
```

This means: take the content at address radius and put it in rsi. The function printf wants a memory address for strings, but for numbers it expects a value, not a memory address. Keep that in mind.

The exit of our program is something new. Instead of the familiar code shown here:

```
    mov   rax, 60     ; 60 = exit
    mov   rdi, 0      ; 0 = success exit code
    syscall           ; quit
```

we use the equivalent:

```
    ret
```

A warning about printf: printf takes a format string, and that format string can take different forms and can convert the nature of values printed (integer, double, float, etc.). Sometimes this conversion is unintentional and can be confusing. If you really want to know the value of a register or variable (memory location) in your program, use a debugger and examine the register or memory location.

Figure 4-9 shows the output of the alive2 program.

```
jo@UbuntuDesktop:~/Desktop/linux64/gcc/06 alive2$ make
nasm -f elf64 -g -F dwarf alive2.asm -l alive2.lst
gcc -o alive2 alive2.o -no-pie
jo@UbuntuDesktop:~/Desktop/linux64/gcc/06 alive2$ ./alive2
Hello, World!
Alive and Kicking!
357
3.140000
jo@UbuntuDesktop:~/Desktop/linux64/gcc/06 alive2$ █
```

Figure 4-9. *alive2 output*

Summary

In this chapter, you learned about the following:

- Additional GDB functionality

- Function prologue and epilogue

- Big endian versus small endian

- Using the C library function printf for printing strings, integers, and floating-point numbers

CHAPTER 5

Assembly Is Based on Logic

It's time to rehearse some logic theory. Don't panic, because we will look at only what we need: NOT, OR, XOR, and AND.

In this chapter, 0 means false, and 1 means true.

NOT

A	0	1
NOT A	1	0

Convert every 0 into 1 and every 1 into 0.

Here's an example:

```
A     =      11001011
NOT A =      00110100
```

OR

A	0	1	0	1
B	0	0	1	1
A OR B	0	1	1	1

If there is a 1 in A or B or in both, the outcome is a 1.

© Jo Van Hoey 2019
J. Van Hoey, *Beginning x64 Assembly Programming*, https://doi.org/10.1007/978-1-4842-5076-1_5

Here's an example:

```
A =          11001011
B =          00011000
A OR B =     11011011
```

XOR

A	0	1	0	1
B	0	0	1	1
A XOR B	0	1	1	0

Exclusive OR: If there is a 1 in A or B, the outcome is a 1. If A and B are both 1 or 0, the outcome is 0.

Here's an example:

```
A =          11001011
B =          00011000
A XOR B =    11010011
```

XOR as an assembly instruction that can be used to clear a register.

```
A =          11001011
A =          11001011
A XOR A =    00000000
```

Hence, xor rax, rax is the same is mov rax,0. But xor executes faster than mov. You can also use xor to modify the sign of a floating-point number.

Here's a 32-bit floating-point example:

```
A          = 17.0  = 0x41880000 = 01000001 10001000 00000000 00000000
B          = -0.0  = 0x80000000 = 10000000 00000000 00000000 00000000
A XOR B    = -17.0 = 0xC1880000 = 11000001 10001000 00000000 00000000
```

Use the tool at www.binaryconvert.com/result_float.html to verify this.

Note that if you want to change the sign of an integer, subtract it from zero or use the neg instruction.

AND

A	0	1	0	1
B	0	0	1	1
A AND B	0	0	0	1

If there is a 1 in A and in B, the outcome is a 1; otherwise, it's 0.

Here's an example:

```
A  =         11001011
B  =         00011000
A  AND  B  = 00001000
```

The AND instruction can be used as a mask to select and investigate bits.

In this example, B is used as a mask to select bits 3 and 6 from A (the lowest, rightmost bit has index 0):

```
A  =         11000011
B  =         01001000
A  AND  B  = 01000000
```

Here we conclude that bit 6 is set and bit 3 is not set. I'll talk more about that later.

The AND instruction can also be used to round down numbers, and it is especially useful to round down addresses on a 16-byte boundary. We will use this later to align stacks.

16 and multiples of 16 in hexadecimal all end with 0 or 0000 in binary.

```
address =    0x42444213 = 01000010010001000100001000010011
mask =       0xfffffff0 = 11111111111111111111111111110000
rounded =    0x42444210 = 01000010010001000100001000010000
```

Here we rounded down the lowest byte of the address. If the address already ends in a zero byte, the and instruction would not change anything. Verify that the rounded address is divisible by 16. Use an online utility to do the conversion (e.g., www.binaryconvert.com/convert_unsigned_int.html).

Summary

In this chapter, you learned about the following:

- Logical operators

- How to use logical operators as assembly instructions

CHAPTER 6

Data Display Debugger

Data Display Debugger (DDD) is a debugging tool with a graphical user interface for Linux. Install it now (using `sudo apt install ddd`) because we will use it later in this chapter. The program we will write in this chapter has no output; we will be investigating the code execution and register the content with DDD.

Working with DDD

Listing 6-1 shows the sample code.

Listing 6-1. move.asm

```
; move.asm
section .data
        bNum    db      123
        wNum    dw      12345
        dNum    dd      1234567890
        qNum1   dq      1234567890123456789
        qNum2   dq      123456
        qNum3   dq      3.14
section .bss
section .text
        global main
main:
push    rbp
mov     rbp,rsp
```

© Jo Van Hoey 2019
J. Van Hoey, *Beginning x64 Assembly Programming*, https://doi.org/10.1007/978-1-4842-5076-1_6

```
    mov rax, -1            ; fill rax with 1s
    mov al, byte [bNum]    ; does NOT clear upper bits of rax
    xor rax,rax            ; clear rax
    mov al, byte [bNum]    ; now rax has the correct value

    mov rax, -1            ; fill rax with 1s
    mov ax, word [wNum]    ; does NOT clear upper bits of rax
    xor rax,rax            ; clear rax
    mov ax, word [wNum]    ; now rax has the correct value

    mov rax, -1            ; fill rax with 1s
    mov eax, dword [dNum]  ; does clear upper bits of rax

    mov rax, -1            ; fill rax with 1s
    mov rax, qword [qNum1] ; does clear upper bits of rax
    mov qword [qNum2], rax ; one operand always a register
    mov rax, 123456        ; source operand an immediate value

    movq xmm0, [qNum3]     ; instruction for floating point
mov rsp,rbp
pop rbp

ret
```

Save the source file as move.asm, and build and run it to see if works. It should not display anything when you run it. At the command prompt, type the following:

```
ddd move
```

You will see a GUI with a rather dated layout (see Figure 6-1). DDD is an old open source tool, and apparently nobody is willing to adapt it to the GUI standards we are used to today.

You have a window with your source code displayed and a window where you can type GDB commands. There is also a floating panel where you can click Run, Step, Stepi, and so on. Click Source in the menu and choose to display line numbers. In that same menu, you can choose to have a window with the assembled code.

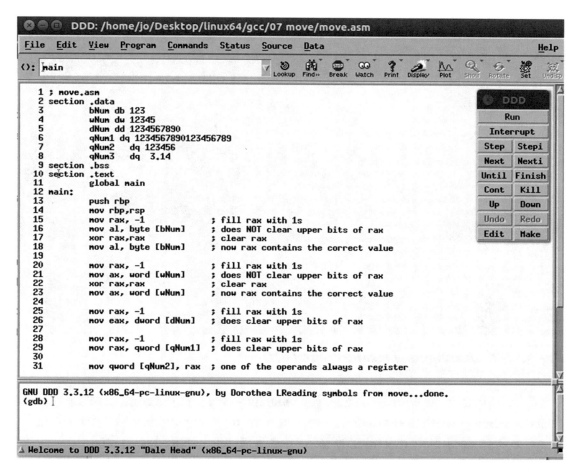

Figure 6-1. *DDD screen*

Place the cursor in front of main:, right-click and choose Break, or choose the Stop icon on the top menu. Click Run on the floating panel, and the debugging starts. Click Status in the menu bar at the top and choose Registers. Click Step to execute the instruction. Now you can follow how the registers change when you step through the program. If you want to examine memory addresses such as qNum1 or bNum, you can use the Data menu item on the top. First go to View to make a data window visible. Then click Memory under the Data menu item. Refer to Figure 6-2 for an example of how to investigate memory. Since the interface of DDD is arcane, using the GDB input window is sometimes much faster than using the menus.

DDD is built on top of GDB, so we need to use a function prologue and epilogue in order to avoid problems. Note that when stepping through the program, DDD just ignores the prologue.

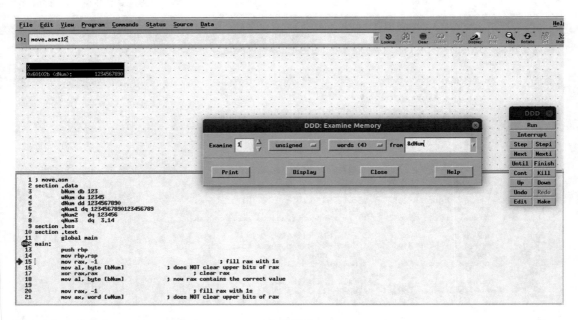

Figure 6-2. Investigating memory with DDD

The purpose of the code is to show you what happens with the content of the registers when you use the mov command. Open the Registers window in DDD (select Status ➤ Registers). Note that initially rax contains -1; this means that all bits in rax are 1. Go back to the chapter on binary numbers if you do not understand why. You will see that if we move a number into al or ax, the upper bits in rax are **not cleared** to 0, and as a result, the rax register does not contain the same value as al or ax. In our example, if rax contains 0xffffffffffffff7b, this is large negative number. But al contains 0x7b, 123 in decimal, as we expected. This may or may not be your intention. If you mistakenly used rax instead of al in a calculation, the result would be very wrong! However, as you continue to step through the code, you will see that when you move a 32-bit value to a 64-bit register, the higher bits in the 64-bit register will be cleared. When you move a value into eax, then the upper bits of rax are cleared. **This is important to remember!**

To conclude the exercise, we move a value from a register to qNum2. Note the square brackets to tell the assembler that qNum2 is an address in memory. Finally, we put an "immediate value" into a register.

Summary

In this chapter, you learned the following:

- DDD, although outdated, can be used as a debugger and is based on GDB.

- Copying a value in an 8-bit or 16-bit register does not clear the higher part of a 64-bit register.

- However, copying a value in a 32-bit register does clear the higher part of a 64-bit register.

CHAPTER 7

Jumping and Looping

You will agree that a visual debugger such as DDD is quite useful, especially for investigating large programs. In this chapter, we will introduce SASM (for **S**imple**ASM**). It is an open source, cross-platform integrated development environment (IDE). It features syntax highlighting and graphical debugging. It's a fantastic tool for an assembler programmer!

Installing SimpleASM

Go to `https://dman95.github.io/SASM/english.html`, select the version for your OS, and install it. For Ubuntu 18.04, go into the directory `xUbuntu_18.04/amd64/` and download and install the `sasm_3.10.1_amd64.deb` package with the following command:

`sudo dpkg -i sasm_3.10.1_amd64.deb`

If you get an error message about dependency problems, install the missing packages and retry the installation of SASM. You can also try the following:

`sudo apt --fix-broken install`

This will normally install all the required missing packages.

Using SASM

Start SASM by typing `sasm` at the CLI and choose your language. SASM starts, and if you see an error on the CLI such as `Failed to load module "canberra-gtk-module"`, install the following packages:

```
sudo apt install libcanberra-gtk*
```

© Jo Van Hoey 2019
J. Van Hoey, *Beginning x64 Assembly Programming*, https://doi.org/10.1007/978-1-4842-5076-1_7

A bunch of files will be installed, and you won't see the error anymore.

In SASM, go to the Settings dialog, as shown in Figure 7-1. On the Common tab, select Yes for "Show all registers in debug."

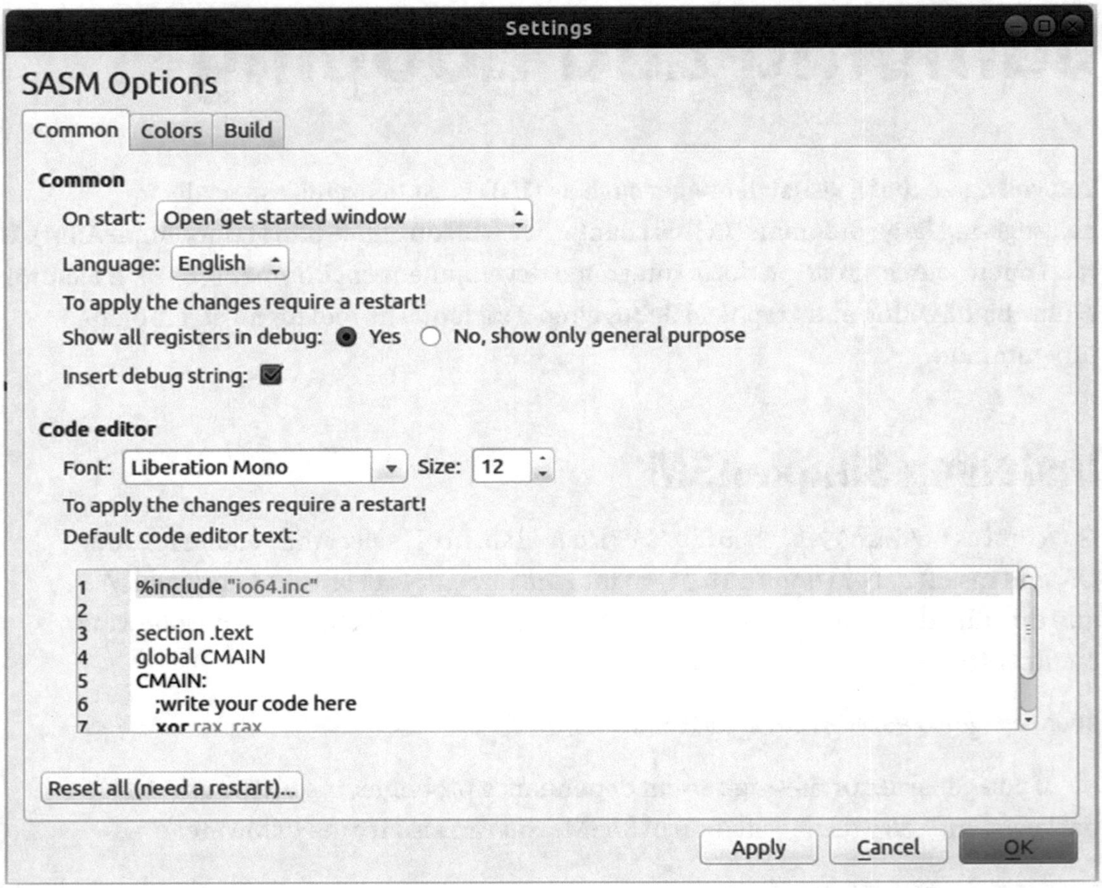

Figure 7-1. *SASM Settings dialog, Common tab*

On the Build tab, modify the settings as shown in Figure 7-2.

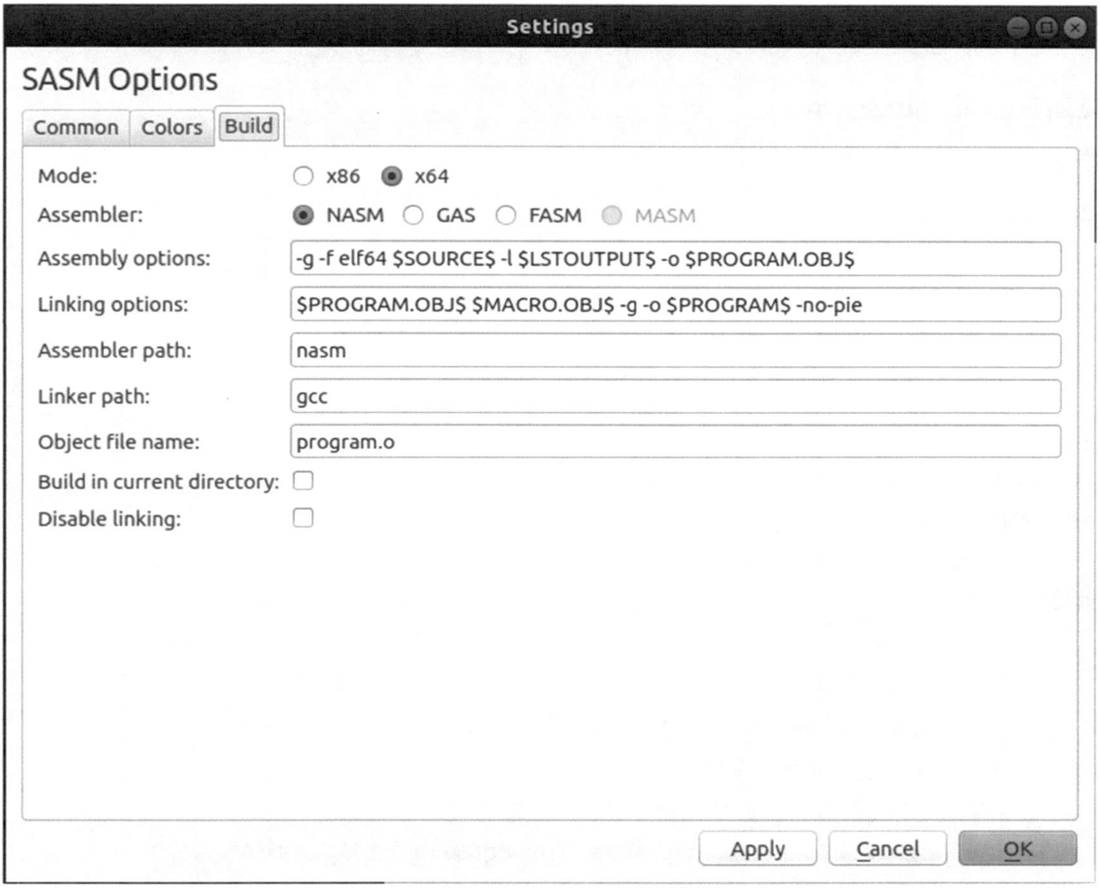

Figure 7-2. *SASM Settings dialog, Build tab*

Be very careful here, because the settings have to be exactly as shown in the figure; one space too many, even hidden at the end of a line, and SASM will not do what you want. When you are ready, click the OK button and restart SASM.

When you start a new project with SASM, you will find some default code already in the editor window. We will not use that code, so you can delete it. At the CLI, type the following:

```
sasm jump.asm
```

If jump.asm does not exist, SASM will start with a new editor window; just delete the default code. If the file exists, it will open in the editor window.

Listing 7-1 shows the code for jump.asm.

Listing 7-1. jump.asm

```
; jump.asm
extern printf
section .data
        number1     dq      42
        number2     dq      41
        fmt1    db      "NUMBER1 > = NUMBER2",10,0
        fmt2    db      "NUMBER1 < NUMBER2",10,0

section .bss
section .text
        global      main
main:
        push    rbp
        mov     rbp,rsp
        mov     rax, [number1]    ; move the numbers into registers
        mov     rbx, [number2]
        cmp     rax,rbx     ; compare rax and rbx
        jge     greater     ; rax greater or equal go to greater:
mov     rdi,fmt2            ; rax is smaller, continue here
mov     rax,0              ; no xmm involved
        call    printf      ; display fmt2
        jmp     exit        ; jump to label exit:
greater:
        mov     rdi,fmt1    ; rax is greater
        mov     rax,0       ; no xmm involved
        call    printf      ; display fmt1
exit:
        mov     rsp,rbp
        pop     rbp
        ret
```

Copy the code into the SASM editor window; by default SASM will use syntax highlighting. When you are finished typing, hit the green triangle icon at the top, which means "run." If everything goes correctly, you will see your output in the Output area, as shown in Figure 7-3.

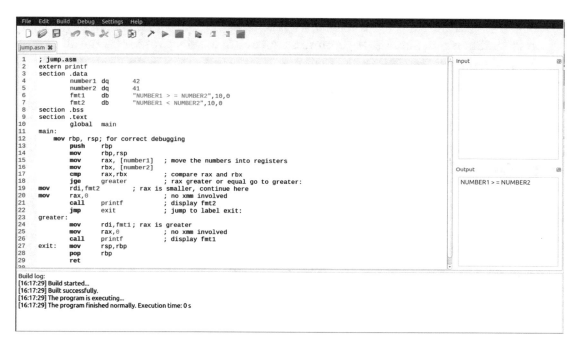

Figure 7-3. *SASM output*

When you save a file in SASM, the source code will be saved. If you want to save the executable, you need to choose Save.exe in the File menu.

To start debugging, click in the numbered left margin to the left of the `main:` label. This will put a red circle between the `main:` label and its line number. This is a breakpoint. Then at the top click the green triangle with the bug on it. In the top menu, choose Debug and select Show Registers and Show Memory. A number of additional windows will appear on your screen: Registers, Memory, and also a GDB command-line widget.

With the Step icons, you can now walk through the code and see how the register values change. To investigate how a variable changes, right-click the variable declaration in `section .data` and choose Watch. The variable will be added in the Memory window, and SASM tries to guess the type. If the value displayed by SASM is not as expected, change the type manually to the proper format. When debugging with SASM, the following line of code is added for correct debugging:

```
mov rbp, rsp; for correct debugging
```

This line can confuse other debuggers such as GDB, so **make sure to remove it from the code before you run GDB separately from the CLI**.

In the SASM menu Settings ➤ Common, make sure to select Yes for "Show all registers in debug." When debugging in SASM, scroll down in the register window. At the bottom you will see 16 ymm registers, each with two values between parentheses. The first value is the corresponding xmm register. We will explain these registers in more detail when we talk about SIMD.

By the way, Figure 7-4 shows the output on the screen after building and running the program as we did before.

```
jo@UbuntuDesktop:~/Desktop/linux64/gcc/08 jump$ make
nasm -f elf64 -g -F dwarf jump.asm -l jump.lst
gcc -o jump jump.o
jo@UbuntuDesktop:~/Desktop/linux64/gcc/08 jump$ ./jump
NUMBER1 > = NUMBER2
jo@UbuntuDesktop:~/Desktop/linux64/gcc/08 jump$ ▮
```

Figure 7-4. *Output from jump.asm*

In the program we use a compare instruction cmp and two jump instructions, jge and jmp. The cmp instruction is what is called a *conditional instruction*. Here cmp compares two operands, in this case two registers. One of the two operands can also be a memory operand, and the second operand can be an immediate value. In any case, the size of the two operands must be the same (byte, word, and so on). The cmp instruction will set or clear flags in the flag register.

The flags are bits located in the rflags register that can be set to 1 or cleared to 0, depending on a number of conditions. Important in our case are the zero flag (ZF), the overflow flag (OF), and the sign flag (SF). You can use your debugger to examine these and other flags. With SASM you can easily see what is happing to all the registers, including the flag register, called eflags in SASM. Different values in the cmp operands will result in different flags being set or cleared. Experiment a little bit with the values to see what is happening with the flags.

If you want to use the flags, you have to evaluate them immediately after the cmp instruction. If you execute other instructions before you evaluate rflags, the flags may have been changed. In our program we evaluate the flags with jge, meaning "jump if greater than or equal." If the condition is met, the execution jumps to the label following the jge instruction. If the condition is not met, execution continues with the instruction just after the jge instruction. Table 7-1 lists some of the usual conditions, but you can hunt for more details in the Intel manuals.

Table 7-1. *Jump Instructions and Flags*

Instruction	Flags	Meaning	Use
je	ZF=1	Jump if equal	Signed, unsigned
jne	ZF=0	Jump if not equal	Signed, unsigned
jg	((SF XOR OF) OR ZF) = 0	Jump if greater	Signed
jge	(SF XOR OF) = 0	Jump if greater or equal	Signed
jl	(SF XOR OF) = 1	Jump if lower	Signed
jle	((SF XOR OF) OR ZF) = 1	Jump if lower or equal	Signed
ja	(CF OR ZF) = 0	Jump if above	Unsigned
jae	CF=0	Jump if above or equal	Unsigned
jb	CF=1	Jump if lesser	Unsigned
jbe	(CF OR ZF) = 1	Jump if lesser or equal	Unsigned

In our program we have also an unconditional jump instruction, jmp. If the program execution hits this instruction, the program jumps to the label specified after jmp, regardless of flags or conditions.

A more complicated form of jumping is *looping*, which means repeating a set of instructions until a condition is met (or is not met). Listing 7-2 shows an example.

Listing 7-2. jumploop.asm

```
; jumploop.asm
extern printf
section .data
    number      dq      5
```

```
        fmt             db      "The sum from 0 to %ld is %ld",10,0
section .bss
section .text
        global main
main:
        push  rbp
        mov   rbp, rsp
        mov   rbx,0               ; counter
        mov   rax,0               ; sum will be in rax
jloop:
        add   rax, rbx
        inc   rbx
        cmp   rbx,[number]        ; number already reached?
        jle   jloop               ; number not reached yet, loop
                                  ; number reached, continue here
        mov   rdi,fmt             ; prepare for displaying
        mov   rsi, [number]
        mov   rdx,rax
        mov   rax,0
        call  printf
        mov   rsp,rbp
        pop   rbp
        ret
```

The program adds all the numbers from 0 to the value in number. We use rbx as a counter and rax to keep track of the sum. We created a loop, which is the code between jloop: and jle jloop. In the loop, we add the value in rbx to rax, increase rbx with 1, and then compare if we have reached the end (number). If we have in rbx a value lower than or equal to number, we restart the loop; otherwise, we continue with the instruction after the loop and get ready to print the result. We used an arithmetic instruction, inc, to increase rbx. We will discuss arithmetic instructions in later chapters.

Listing 7-3 shows another way to write a loop.

Listing 7-3. betterloop.asm

```
; betterloop
extern printf
section .data
        number      dq      5
        fmt         db      "The sum from 0 to %ld is %ld",10,0
section .bss
section .text
        global main
main:
        push    rbp
        mov     rbp,rsp
        mov     rcx,[number]    ; initialize rcx with number
        mov     rax, 0
bloop:
        add     rax,rcx         ; add rcx to sum
        loop    bloop           ; loop while decreasing rcx with 1
                                ; until rcx = 0
        mov     rdi,fmt         ; rcx = 0, continue here
        mov     rsi, [number]   ; sum to be displayed
        mov     rdx, rax
        mov     rax,0           ; no floating point
        call    printf          ; display
        mov     rsp,rbp
        pop     rbp
        ret
```

Here you see that there is a special loop instruction that uses rcx as a decreasing loop counter. With every pass through the loop, rcx is decreased automatically, and as long as rcx is not equal to 0, the loop is executed again. That's less code to type.

An interesting experiment is to put 1000000000 (a one and nine zeros) in number and then rebuild and run the two previous programs. You can time the speed with the Linux time command, as shown here:

```
time ./jumploop
time ./betterloop
```

Note that betterloop is slower than jumploop (see Figure 7-5)! Using the loop instruction is convenient but comes at a price in terms of execution performance. We used the Linux time instruction to measure the performance; later we will show more appropriate ways to investigate and tune program code.

```
jo@UbuntuDesktop:~/Desktop/linux64/gcc/09 loopcompare$ time ./betterloop_long
The sum from 0 to 1000000000 is 500000000500000000

real    0m1.731s
user    0m1.726s
sys     0m0.004s
jo@UbuntuDesktop:~/Desktop/linux64/gcc/09 loopcompare$ time ./jumploop_long
The sum from 0 to 1000000000 is 500000000500000000

real    0m0.404s
user    0m0.391s
sys     0m0.008s
jo@UbuntuDesktop:~/Desktop/linux64/gcc/09 loopcompare$ █
```

Figure 7-5. *Looping versus jumping*

You may wonder why we bothered to use DDD when there is a tool such as SASM. Well, you will see Iater that in SASM you cannot investigate the stack, but you can with DDD. We will return to DDD later.

Summary

In this chapter, you learned the following:

- How to use SASM

- How to use jump instructions

- How to use the cmp instruction

- How to use the loop instruction

- How to evaluate flags

CHAPTER 8

Memory

Memory is used by the processor as a storage room for data and instructions. We have already discussed registers, which are high-speed access storage places. Accessing memory is a lot slower than accessing registers. But the number of registers is limited. The memory size has a theoretical limit of 2^{64} addresses, which is 18,446,744,073,709,551,616, or 16 exabytes. You cannot use that much memory because of practical design issues! It is time to investigate memory in more detail.

Exploring Memory

Listing 8-1 shows an example we will use during our discussion of memory.

Listing 8-1. memory.asm

```
; memory.asm
section .data
        bNum        db      123
        wNum        dw      12345
        warray      times       5 dw 0      ; array of 5 words
                                            ; containing 0

        dNum        dd      12345
        qNum1       dq      12345
        text1       db      "abc",0
        qNum2       dq      3.141592654
        text2       db      "cde",0
section .bss
        bvar    resb    1
        dvar    resd    1
        wvar    resw    10
```

© Jo Van Hoey 2019
J. Van Hoey, *Beginning x64 Assembly Programming*, https://doi.org/10.1007/978-1-4842-5076-1_8

```
        qvar   resq  3
section .text
        global main
main:
        push   rbp
        mov    rbp, rsp
        lea    rax, [bNum]      ;load address of bNum in rax
        mov    rax, bNum        ;load address of bNum in rax
        mov    rax, [bNum]      ;load value at bNum in rax
        mov    [bvar], rax      ;load from rax at address bvar
        lea    rax, [bvar]      ;load address of bvar in rax
        lea    rax, [wNum]      ;load address of wNum in rax
        mov    rax, [wNum]      ;load content of wNum in rax
        lea    rax, [text1]     ;load address of text1 in rax
        mov    rax, text1       ;load address of text1 in rax
        mov    rax, text1+1     ;load second character in rax
        lea    rax, [text1+1]   ;load second character in rax
        mov    rax, [text1]     ;load starting at text1 in rax
        mov    rax, [text1+1]   ;load starting at text1+1 in rax
        mov    rsp,rbp
        pop    rbp
        ret
```

Make this program. There is no output for this program; use a debugger to step through each instruction. SASM is helpful here.

We defined some variables of different sizes, including an array of five double words filled with zeros. We also defined some items in section .bss. Look in your debugger for rsp, the stack pointer; it is a very high value. The *stack pointer* refers to an address in high memory. The *stack* is an area in memory used for temporarily storing data. The stack will grow as more data is stored in it, and it will grow in the downward direction, from higher addresses to lower addresses. The stack pointer rsp will decrease every time you put data on the stack. We will discuss the stack in a separate chapter, but remember already that the stack is a place somewhere in high memory. See Figure 8-1.

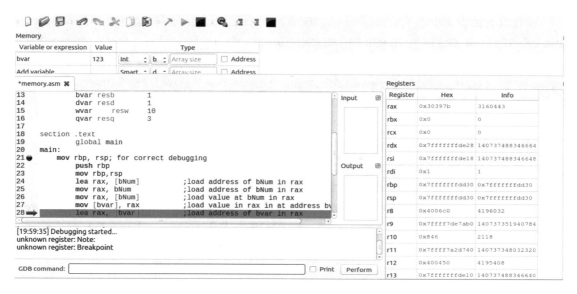

Figure 8-1. *rsp contains an address in high memory*

We used the lea instruction, which means "load effective address," to load the memory address of bNum into rax. We can obtain the same result with mov, without the square brackets around bNum. If we use the square brackets, [ ], with the mov instruction, we are loading the value, not the address at bNum into rax. But we are not loading only bNum into rax. Because rax is a 64-bit (or 8-byte) register, more bytes are loaded into rax. Our bNum is the rightmost byte in rax (little endian); here we are only interested in the register al. When you require rax to contain only the value 123, you would first have to clear rax, as shown here:

    xor rax, rax

Then instead of this:

    mov rax, [bNum]

use this:

    mov al, [bNum]

Be careful about the sizes of data you are moving to and from memory. Look, for instance, at the following:

    mov [bvar],rax

With this instruction, you are moving the 8 bytes in rax to the address bvar. If you only intended to write 123 to bvar, you can check with your debugger that you overwrite another 7 bytes in memory (choose type d for bvar in the SASM memory window)! This can introduce nasty bugs in your program. To avoid that, replace the instruction with the following:

```
mov [bvar],al
```

When loading content from memory address text1 into rax, note how the value in rax is in little-endian notation. Step through the program to investigate the different instructions, and change values and sizes to see what happens.

There are two ways to load a memory address: mov and lea. Using lea can make your code more readable, as everybody can immediately see that you are handling addresses here. You can also use lea to speed up calculations, but we will not use lea for that purpose here.

Start gdb memory and then disass main and look at the left column with memory addresses (Figure 8-2). Do not forget to first delete the line added by SASM for correct debugging, as we explained in the previous chapter. In our case, the first instruction is located at address 0x4004a0.

```
(gdb) disass main
Dump of assembler code for function main:
   0x00000000004004a0 <+0>:      mov     rbp,rsp
   0x00000000004004a3 <+3>:      push    rbp
   0x00000000004004a4 <+4>:      mov     rbp,rsp
   0x00000000004004a7 <+7>:      lea     rax,ds:0x601028
   0x00000000004004af <+15>:     movabs  rax,0x601028
   0x00000000004004b9 <+25>:     mov     rax,QWORD PTR ds:0x601028
   0x00000000004004c1 <+33>:     mov     QWORD PTR ds:0x601058,rax
   0x00000000004004c9 <+41>:     lea     rax,ds:0x601058
   0x00000000004004d1 <+49>:     lea     rax,ds:0x601029
   0x00000000004004d9 <+57>:     mov     rax,QWORD PTR ds:0x601029
   0x00000000004004e1 <+65>:     lea     rax,ds:0x601041
   0x00000000004004e9 <+73>:     movabs  rax,0x601041
   0x00000000004004f3 <+83>:     movabs  rax,0x601042
   0x00000000004004fd <+93>:     lea     rax,ds:0x601042
   0x0000000000400505 <+101>:    mov     rax,QWORD PTR ds:0x601041
   0x000000000040050d <+109>:    mov     rax,QWORD PTR ds:0x601042
   0x0000000000400515 <+117>:    mov     rsp,rbp
   0x0000000000400518 <+120>:    pop     rbp
   0x0000000000400519 <+121>:    ret
   0x000000000040051a <+122>:    nop     WORD PTR [rax+rax*1+0x0]
End of assembler dump.
(gdb) █
```

Figure 8-2. *GDB disassemble main*

Now we will use `readelf` at the command line. Remember that we asked NASM to assemble using the ELF format (see the `makefile`). `readelf` is a CLI tool used to obtain more information about the executable file. If you feel the irresistible urge to know more about linkers, here is an interesting source of information:

> *Linkers and Loaders*, John R. Levine, 1999, The Morgan Kaufmann
> Series in Software Engineering and Programming

Here is a shorter treatment of the ELF format:

> `https://linux-audit.com/elf-binaries-on-linux-`
> `understanding-and-analysis/`

or

> `https://www.cirosantilli.com/elf-hello-world/`

As you probably guessed, at the CLI you can also type the following:

```
man elf
```

For our purposes, at the CLI type the following:

```
readelf --file-header ./memory
```

You will get some general information about our executable `memory`. Look at `Entry point address: 0x4003b0`. That is the memory location of the start of our program. So, between the program entry and the start of the code, as shown in GDB (`0x4004a0`), there is some overhead. The header provides us with additional information about the OS and the executable code. See Figure 8-3.

```
jo@ubuntu18:~/Desktop/linux64/gcc/10 memory$ readelf --file-header ./memory
ELF Header:
  Magic:   7f 45 4c 46 02 01 01 00 00 00 00 00 00 00 00 00
  Class:                             ELF64
  Data:                              2's complement, little endian
  Version:                           1 (current)
  OS/ABI:                            UNIX - System V
  ABI Version:                       0
  Type:                              EXEC (Executable file)
  Machine:                           Advanced Micro Devices X86-64
  Version:                           0x1
  Entry point address:               0x4003b0
  Start of program headers:          64 (bytes into file)
  Start of section headers:          7192 (bytes into file)
  Flags:                             0x0
  Size of this header:               64 (bytes)
  Size of program headers:           56 (bytes)
  Number of program headers:         9
  Size of section headers:           64 (bytes)
  Number of section headers:         34
  Section header string table index: 33
jo@ubuntu18:~/Desktop/linux64/gcc/10 memory$ █
```

Figure 8-3. *readelf header*

readelf is convenient for exploring a binary executable. Figure 8-4 shows some more examples.

```
jo@ubuntu18:~/Desktop/linux64/gcc/10 memory$ readelf --symbols ./memory |grep main
     1: 0000000000000000     0 FUNC    GLOBAL DEFAULT  UND __libc_start_main@GLIBC_2.2.5 (2)
    64: 0000000000000000     0 FUNC    GLOBAL DEFAULT  UND __libc_start_main@@GLIBC_
    74: 00000000004004a0     0 NOTYPE  GLOBAL DEFAULT   11 main
jo@ubuntu18:~/Desktop/linux64/gcc/10 memory$ █
```

Figure 8-4. *readelf symbols*

With grep we specify that we are looking for all lines with the word main in it. Here you see that the main function starts at 0x4004a0, as we saw in GDB. In the following example, we look in the symbols table for every occurrence of the label start. We see the start addresses of section .data, section .bss, and the start of the program itself. See Figure 8-5.

```
jo@ubuntu18:~/Desktop/linux64/gcc/10 memory$ readelf --symbols ./memory |grep start
     1: 0000000000000000     0 FUNC    GLOBAL DEFAULT  UND __libc_start_main@GLIBC_2.2.5 (2)
     2: 0000000000000000     0 NOTYPE  WEAK   DEFAULT  UND __gmon_start__
    57: 0000000000600e50     0 NOTYPE  LOCAL  DEFAULT   16 __init_array_start
    61: 0000000000601018     0 NOTYPE  WEAK   DEFAULT   21 data_start
    64: 0000000000000000     0 FUNC    GLOBAL DEFAULT  UND __libc_start_main@@GLIBC_
    65: 0000000000601018     0 NOTYPE  GLOBAL DEFAULT   21 __data_start
    66: 0000000000000000     0 NOTYPE  WEAK   DEFAULT  UND __gmon_start__
    72: 00000000004003b0    43 FUNC    GLOBAL DEFAULT   11 _start
    73: 0000000000601051     0 NOTYPE  GLOBAL DEFAULT   22 __bss_start
jo@ubuntu18:~/Desktop/linux64/gcc/10 memory$
```

Figure 8-5. *readelf symbols*

Let's see what we have in memory with the instruction, as shown here:

```
readelf --symbols ./memory |tail +10|sort -k 2 -r
```

The `tail` instruction ignores some lines that are not interesting to us right now. We sort on the second column (the memory addresses) in reverse order. As you see, some basic knowledge of Linux commands comes in handy!

The start of the program is at some low address, and the start of `main` is at 0x004004a0. Look for the start of `section .data`, (0x00601018), with the addresses of all its variables and the start of `section .bss`, (0x00601051), with the addresses reserved for its variables.

Let's summarize our findings: we found at the beginning of this chapter that the stack is in high memory (see `rsp`). With `readelf`, we found that the executable code is at the lower side of memory. On top of the executable code, we have `section .data` and on top of that `section .bss`. The stack in high memory can grow; it grows in the downward direction toward `section .bss`. The available free memory between the stack and the other sections is called the *heap*.

The memory in `section .bss` is assigned at runtime; you can easily check that. Take note of the size of the executable, and then change, for example, the following:

```
qvar        resq        3
```

to the following:

```
qvar        resq        30000
```

Rebuild the program and look again at the size of the executable. The size will be the same, so no additional memory is reserved at assembly/link time. See Figure 8-6.

```
jo@ubuntu18:~/Desktop/linux64/gcc/10 memory$ readelf --symbols ./memory |tail +10|sort -k 2 -r
    70: 0000000000601090     0 NOTYPE  GLOBAL DEFAULT   22 _end
    51: 0000000000601071     1 OBJECT  LOCAL  DEFAULT   22 qvar
Files  000000000060105d     1 OBJECT  LOCAL  DEFAULT   22 wvar
    49: 0000000000601059     1 OBJECT  LOCAL  DEFAULT   22 dvar
    48: 0000000000601058     1 OBJECT  LOCAL  DEFAULT   22 bvar
    75: 0000000000601058     0 OBJECT  GLOBAL HIDDEN    21 __TMC_END__
    35: 0000000000601054     1 OBJECT  LOCAL  DEFAULT   22 completed.7696
    22: 0000000000601054     0 SECTION LOCAL  DEFAULT   22
    73: 0000000000601051     0 NOTYPE  GLOBAL DEFAULT   22 __bss_start
    62: 0000000000601051     0 NOTYPE  GLOBAL DEFAULT   21 _edata
    47: 000000000060104d     1 OBJECT  LOCAL  DEFAULT   21 text2
    46: 0000000000601045     8 OBJECT  LOCAL  DEFAULT   21 qNum2
    45: 0000000000601041     1 OBJECT  LOCAL  DEFAULT   21 text1
    44: 0000000000601039     8 OBJECT  LOCAL  DEFAULT   21 qNum1
    43: 0000000000601035     4 OBJECT  LOCAL  DEFAULT   21 dNum
    42: 000000000060102b     2 OBJECT  LOCAL  DEFAULT   21 warray
    41: 0000000000601029     2 OBJECT  LOCAL  DEFAULT   21 wNum
    40: 0000000000601028     1 OBJECT  LOCAL  DEFAULT   21 bNum
    67: 0000000000601020     0 OBJECT  GLOBAL HIDDEN    21 __dso_handle
    21: 0000000000601018     0 SECTION LOCAL  DEFAULT   21
    61: 0000000000601018     0 NOTYPE  WEAK   DEFAULT   21 data_start
    65: 0000000000601018     0 NOTYPE  GLOBAL DEFAULT   21 __data_start
    20: 0000000000601000     0 SECTION LOCAL  DEFAULT   20
    59: 0000000000601000     0 OBJECT  LOCAL  DEFAULT   20 _GLOBAL_OFFSET_TABLE_
    19: 0000000000600ff0     0 SECTION LOCAL  DEFAULT   19
    18: 0000000000600e60     0 SECTION LOCAL  DEFAULT   18
    56: 0000000000600e60     0 OBJECT  LOCAL  DEFAULT   18 _DYNAMIC
    17: 0000000000600e58     0 SECTION LOCAL  DEFAULT   17
    36: 0000000000600e58     0 OBJECT  LOCAL  DEFAULT   17 __do_global_dtors_aux_fin
    55: 0000000000600e58     0 NOTYPE  LOCAL  DEFAULT   16 __init_array_end
    16: 0000000000600e50     0 SECTION LOCAL  DEFAULT   16
    38: 0000000000600e50     0 OBJECT  LOCAL  DEFAULT   16 __frame_dummy_init_array_
    57: 0000000000600e50     0 NOTYPE  LOCAL  DEFAULT   16 __init_array_start
    53: 0000000000400684     0 OBJECT  LOCAL  DEFAULT   15 __FRAME_END__
    15: 00000000004005d0     0 SECTION LOCAL  DEFAULT   15
    14: 00000000004005a4     0 SECTION LOCAL  DEFAULT   14
    58: 00000000004005a4     0 NOTYPE  LOCAL  DEFAULT   14 __GNU_EH_FRAME_HDR
    68: 00000000004005a0     4 OBJECT  GLOBAL DEFAULT   13 _IO_stdin_used
    13: 00000000004005a0     0 SECTION LOCAL  DEFAULT   13
    12: 0000000000400594     0 SECTION LOCAL  DEFAULT   12
    63: 0000000000400594     0 FUNC    GLOBAL DEFAULT   12 _fini
    60: 0000000000400590     2 FUNC    GLOBAL DEFAULT   11 __libc_csu_fini
    69: 0000000000400520   101 FUNC    GLOBAL DEFAULT   11 __libc_csu_init
    74: 00000000004004a0     0 NOTYPE  GLOBAL DEFAULT   11 main
    37: 0000000000400490     0 FUNC    LOCAL  DEFAULT   11 frame_dummy
    34: 0000000000400460     0 FUNC    LOCAL  DEFAULT   11 __do_global_dtors_aux
    33: 0000000000400420     0 FUNC    LOCAL  DEFAULT   11 register_tm_clones
    32: 00000000004003f0     0 FUNC    LOCAL  DEFAULT   11 deregister_tm_clones
    71: 00000000004003e0     2 FUNC    GLOBAL HIDDEN    11 _dl_relocate_static_pie
    72: 00000000004003b0    43 FUNC    GLOBAL DEFAULT   11 _start
    11: 00000000004003b0     0 SECTION LOCAL  DEFAULT   11
```

Figure 8-6. *Output of readelf --symbols ./memory |tail +10|sort -k 2 -r*

To summarize, Figure 8-7 shows how the memory looks when an executable is loaded.

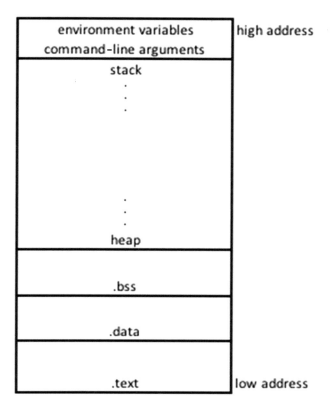

Figure 8-7. Memory map

Why is it important to know about memory structure? It is important to know that the stack grows in the downward direction. When we exploit the stack later in this book, you will need this knowledge. Also, if you are into forensics or malware investigation, being able to analyze memory is an essential skill. We only touched on some basics here; if you want to know more, refer to the previously mentioned sources.

Summary

In this chapter, you learned about the following:

- The structure of the process memory

- How to avoid overwriting memory unintentionally

- How to use `readelf` to analyze binary code

CHAPTER 9

Integer Arithmetic

In this chapter, you'll see a number of arithmetic instructions for integers. Floating-point arithmetic will be covered in a later chapter. Now is a good time to quickly review Chapter 2 on binary numbers.

Starting with Integer Arithmetic

Listing 9-1 shows the example code we will analyze.

Listing 9-1. icalc.asm

```
; icalc.asm
extern printf
section .data
        number1     dq      128     ; the numbers to be used to
        number2     dq      19      ; show the arithmetic
        neg_num     dq      -12     ; to show sign extension
        fmt         db      "The numbers are %ld and %ld",10,0
        fmtint      db      "%s %ld",10,0
        sumi   db   "The sum is",0
        difi   db   "The difference is",0
        inci   db   "Number 1 Incremented:",0
        deci   db   "Number 1 Decremented:",0
        sali   db   "Number 1 Shift left 2 (x4):",0
        sari   db   "Number 1 Shift right 2 (/4):",0
        sariex db   "Number 1 Shift right 2 (/4) with "
            db      "sign extension:",0
        multi db    "The product is",0
        divi   db   "The integer quotient is",0
```

© Jo Van Hoey 2019
J. Van Hoey, *Beginning x64 Assembly Programming*, https://doi.org/10.1007/978-1-4842-5076-1_9

```
        remi  db    "The modulo is",0
section .bss
        resulti  resq  1
        modulo   resq  1
section .text
        global main
main:
        push  rbp
        mov   rbp,rsp
; displaying the numbers
            mov   rdi, fmt
            mov   rsi, [number1]
            mov   rdx, [number2]
            mov   rax, 0
            call printf
; adding-----------------------------------------------------------
        mov   rax, [number1]
        add   rax, [number2]            ; add number2 to rax
        mov   [resulti], rax            ; move sum to result
        ; displaying the result
            mov   rdi, fmtint
            mov   rsi, sumi
            mov   rdx, [resulti]
            mov   rax, 0
            call printf
; substracting----------------------------------------------------
        mov   rax, [number1]
        sub   rax, [number2]            ; subtract number2 from rax
        mov   [resulti], rax
        ; displaying the result
            mov   rdi, fmtint
            mov   rsi, difi
            mov   rdx, [resulti]
            mov   rax, 0
            call printf
; incrementing----------------------------------------------------
```

```
        mov    rax, [number1]
        inc    rax                  ; increment rax with 1
        mov    [resulti], rax
        ; displaying the result
                mov    rdi, fmtint
                mov    rsi, inci
                mov    rdx, [resulti]
                mov    rax, 0
                call printf
; decrementing--------------------------------------------------------
        mov    rax, [number1]
        dec    rax                  ; decrement rax with 1
          mov [resulti], rax
        ; displaying the result
                mov    rdi, fmtint
                mov    rsi, deci
                mov    rdx, [resulti]
                mov    rax, 0
                call printf
; shift arithmetic left----------------------------------------------
        mov    rax, [number1]
        sal    rax, 2                   ; multiply rax by 4
        mov    [resulti], rax
        ; displaying the result
                mov    rdi, fmtint
                mov    rsi, sali
                mov    rdx, [resulti]
                mov    rax, 0
                call printf
; shift arithmetic right---------------------------------------------
        mov    rax, [number1]
        sar    rax, 2                   ; divide rax by 4
        mov    [resulti], rax
        ; displaying the result
                mov    rdi, fmtint
```

```
        mov    rsi, sari
        mov    rdx, [resulti]
        mov    rax, 0
        call   printf
; shift arithmetic right with sign extension ----------------------
    mov    rax, [neg_num]
    sar    rax, 2                 ; divide rax by 4
    mov    [resulti], rax
    ; displaying the result
        mov    rdi, fmtint
        mov    rsi, sariex
        mov    rdx, [resulti]
        mov    rax, 0
        call   printf
; multiply-----------------------------------------------------------
    mov        rax, [number1]
    imul   qword [number2]        ; multiply rax with number2
    mov        [resulti], rax
    ; displaying the result
        mov    rdi, fmtint
        mov    rsi, multi
        mov    rdx, [resulti]
        mov    rax, 0
        call   printf
; divide-------------------------------------------------------------
    mov        rax, [number1]
    mov    rdx, 0                 ; rdx needs to be 0 before idiv
    idiv   qword [number2]        ; divide rax by number2, modulo in rdx
    mov        [resulti], rax
    mov    [modulo], rdx   ; rdx to modulo
    ; displaying the result
      mov rdi, fmtint
        mov    rsi, divi
        mov    rdx, [resulti]
        mov    rax, 0
```

```
        call   printf
        mov    rdi, fmtint
        mov    rsi, remi
        mov    rdx, [modulo]
        mov    rax, 0
        call   printf
mov rsp,rbp
pop rbp
ret
```

Figure 9-1 shows the output.

```
jo@UbuntuDesktop:~/Desktop/linux64/gcc/11 icalc$ make
nasm -f elf64 -g -F dwarf icalc.asm -l icalc.lst
gcc -o icalc icalc.o -no-pie
jo@UbuntuDesktop:~/Desktop/linux64/gcc/11 icalc$ ./icalc
The numbers are 128 and 19
The sum is 147
The difference is 109
Number 1 Incremented: 129
Number 1 Decremented: 127
Number 1 Shift left 2 (x4): 512
Number 1 Shift right 2 (/4): 32
Number 1 Shift right 2 (/4) with sign extension: -3
The product is 2432
The integer quotient is 6
The modulo is 14
jo@UbuntuDesktop:~/Desktop/linux64/gcc/11 icalc$ █
```

Figure 9-1. *Integer arithmetic*

Examining Arithmetic Instructions

Many arithmetic instructions are available; we are going to show a selection of them, and the others are similar to what you'll learn here. Before we investigate the arithmetic instructions, note that we use printf with more than two arguments, so we need an additional register: the first argument goes into rdi, the second into rsi, and the third into rdx. That is how printf expects us to provide the arguments in Linux. You'll learn more about that later, when we talk about calling conventions.

Here are some arithmetic instructions:

- The first instruction is add, which can be used to add signed or unsigned integers. The second operand (source) is added to the first operand (destination), and the result is placed in the first operand (destination). The destination operand can be a register or a memory location. The source can be an immediate value, a register, or a memory location. The source and destination cannot be a memory location in the same instruction. When the resulting sum is too large to fit in the destination, the CF flag is set for signed integers. For unsigned integers, the OF flag is then set. When the result is 0, the ZF flag is set to 1, and when the result is negative, the SF flag is set.

- The subtraction with sub is similar to the add instruction.

- To increment a register or value in a memory location with 1, use the inc instruction. Similarly, dec can be used to decrement a register or value in a memory location with 1.

- The arithmetic shift instructions are a special breed. The shift left, sal, is in fact multiplying; if you shift left one position, you are multiplying by 2. Every bit is shifted one place to the left, and a 0 is added to the right. Take the binary number 1. Shift left one place, and you obtain binary 10 or 2 in decimal representation. Shift left one place again, and you have binary 100 or 4 in decimal representation. If you shift left two positions, you multiply by 4. What if you want to multiply by 6? You shift left two times and then the add two times the original source, in that order.

- Shift right, sar, is similar to shift left, but it means dividing by 2. Every bit is shifted one place to the right, and an additional bit is added to the left. Here there is a complication, however: if the original value was negative, the leftmost bit would be 1; if the shift instruction added a 0 bit at the left, the value would become positive, and the result would be wrong. So, in the case of a negative value, a sar will add a 1 bit to the left, and in the case of a positive value, 0 bits will be added to the left. This is called *sign extension*. By the way, a quick way to see if a hexadecimal number is negative is to look at byte 7 (the leftmost byte, counting from byte 0, which is the rightmost byte). The number is negative if byte 7 starts with an 8, 9, A, B, C, D, E, or F. But you need to take into account all 8 bytes. For example, 0xd12 is still a positive number because the leftmost byte, which is not shown, is a 0.

•   There are also nonarithmetic shift instructions; they will be discussed in Chapter 16.

•   Next, we multiply integers. For multiplying unsigned integers, you can use mul for unsigned multiplication and imul for signed multiplication. We will use imul, signed multiplication, which offers more flexibility: imul can take one, two, or three operands. In our example, we use one operand; the operand following the imul instruction is multiplied with the value in rax. You may expect that the resulting product is stored in rax, but that is not entirely correct. Let's illustrate with an example: you can verify that when you multiply, for example, a two-digit number with a three-digit number, the product has four or five digits. When you multiply a 48-bit digit with a 30-bit digit, you will obtain a 77-bit digit or a 78-bit digit, and that value does not fit in a 64-bit register. To cope with this, the instruction imul will store the lower 64 bits of the resulting product in rax and the upper 64 bits in rdx. And this can be very deceptive!

Let's experiment a little bit: go back to the source code in SASM. Modify number1 so that it contains 12345678901234567 and modify number2 so that it contains 100. The product will just fit in rax; you can check that in SASM debug mode. Put a break before the imul instruction. Restart debugging mode and step through the program. The result of the multiplication will be 1234567890123456700, as you can see in rax after the imul instruction is executed. Now modify number2 into 10000. Restart debugging. Look at rax after executing imul. You see that the product is a large negative number! That is because the most significant bit in rax is a 1 and SASM concludes that this must be a negative number. Also, printf thinks that rax contains a negative number because rax contains a 1 bit in the leftmost position, so it is assumed to be negative. So, be careful with printf!

We will dig somewhat deeper: as soon as the imul instruction is executed, rax contains 0xb14e9f812f364970. In binary, this is 10 11000101001110100111111000000100101111001101100100100100 with a 1 in the most significant position and hence is negative.

And rdx contains 0x6. That is 0000000000000000000000000000000 0000000000000000000000000110 with a 0 in the most significant position and hence is positive.

The actual product is 0x6b14e9f812f364970 and can be found by combining rdx and rax, in this order: rdx:rax. If you convert this hexadecimal number to decimal, you will find the product you expect: 123456789012345670000. See Figure 9-2.

On the Internet you can find hexadecimal to decimal conversion apps; see https://www.rapidtables.com/convert/number/hex-to-decimal.html

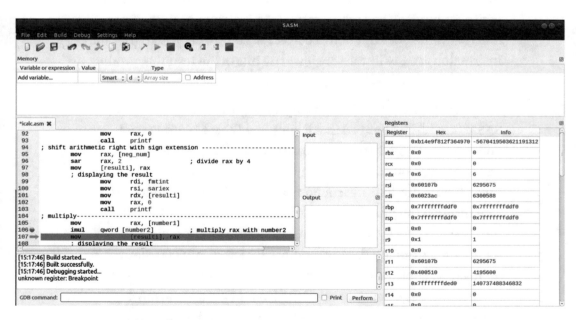

Figure 9-2. *Content of rax and rdx*

- Let's continue with integer division, `idiv`. This is in fact the reverse of multiplication (well, what did you expect?). Divide the dividend in `rdx:rax` by the divisor in the source operand and store the **integer** result in `rax`. The **modulo** can be found in `rdx`. It's important and easy to forget: make sure to set `rdx` to zero every time before you use `idiv` or the resulting quotient may be wrong.

64-bit integer multiplication and division have some subtleties for which you can find more details in the Intel manuals. Here we just gave an overview that serves as a general introduction to integer arithmetic. In the Intel manuals, not only will you find more details about the instructions, but you will find a large number of other arithmetic instructions that can be used in specific situations.

Summary

In this chapter, you learned the following:

- How to do integer arithmetic.

- How to do arithmetic shift left and shift right.

- Multiplication uses `rax` and `rdx` for storing the product.

- Division uses `rax` and `rdx` for the dividend.

- Be careful when using `printf` when printing values.

CHAPTER 10

The Stack

We have already discussed registers, the type of fast temporary storage that can be used to store values or addresses to be used during execution of instructions. There is also the slower storage, *memory*, where the processor can store values for a longer time. Then there is the *stack*, a contiguous array of memory locations.

Understanding the Stack

As discussed in Chapter 8, the stack segment starts in high memory, and when it grows, it grows in the downward direction, like an icicle grows downward when it grows larger. Items are placed on the stack with the push instruction and removed from the stack with the pop instruction. Every time you push, the stack grows; every time you pop, the stack shrinks. You can verify this stack behavior by monitoring rsp, the stack pointer, which points to the top (thus actually the bottom, because it grows downward) of the stack.

The stack can be used as temporary storage to save values in registers and call them back later or, more importantly, to transfer values to functions. Functions or procedures will be treated in detail later.

In the example code in Listing 10-1, we will use the stack to reverse a string.

Listing 10-1. stack.asm

```
; stack.asm
extern printf
section .data
        strng       db      "ABCDE",0
        strngLen    equ     $ - strng-1 ; stringlength without 0
        fmt1        db      "The original string: %s",10,0
        fmt2        db      "The reversed string: %s",10,0
section .bss
```

© Jo Van Hoey 2019
J. Van Hoey, *Beginning x64 Assembly Programming*, https://doi.org/10.1007/978-1-4842-5076-1_10

```nasm
section .text
      global main
main:
push  rbp
mov   rbp,rsp

; Print the original string
    mov     rdi, fmt1
    mov     rsi, strng
    mov     rax, 0
    call    printf

;push the string char per char on the stack
    xor    rax, rax
    mov    rbx, strng ; address of strng in rbx
    mov    rcx, strngLen   ; length in rcx counter
    mov    r12, 0          ; use r12 as pointer
    pushLoop:
        mov    al, byte [rbx+r12] ; move char into rax
        push   rax         ;push rax on the stack
        inc    r12         ; increase char pointer with 1
        loop   pushLoop    ; continue loop

;pop the string char per char from the stack
;this will reverse the original string
    mov    rbx, strng ; address of strng in rbx
    mov    rcx, strngLen   ; length in rcx counter
    mov    r12, 0          ; use r12 as pointer
    popLoop:
        pop    rax         ; pop a char from the stack
        mov    byte [rbx+r12], al   ;move the char into strng
        inc    r12         ; increase char pointer with 1
        loop   popLoop                ; continue loop
        mov    byte [rbx+r12],0 ; terminate string with 0

; Print the reversed string
    mov     rdi, fmt2
```

```
    mov    rsi, strng
    mov    rax, 0
    call   printf

mov    rsp,rbp
pop    rbp
ret
```

Figure 10-1 shows the output.

```
jo@UbuntuDesktop:~/Desktop/linux64/gcc/12 stack$ make
nasm -f elf64 -g -F dwarf stack.asm -l stack.lst
gcc -o stack stack.o
jo@UbuntuDesktop:~/Desktop/linux64/gcc/12 stack$ ./stack
The original string: ABCDE
The reversed string: EDCBA
jo@UbuntuDesktop:~/Desktop/linux64/gcc/12 stack$ █
```

Figure 10-1. *Reversing a string*

First, note that to calculate the string length, we decreased the length of the string by 1, ignoring the terminating 0. Otherwise, the reversed string would start with a 0. Then the original string is displayed followed by a new line. We will use rax to push the characters, so let's first initialize rax with zeros using xor. The address of the string goes into rbx, and we will use a loop instruction, so we set rcx to the string length. Then a loop is used to push character after character on the stack, starting with the first character. We move a character (byte) into al. Then we push rax onto the stack. Every time you use push, 8 bytes are moved to the stack. If we did not initialize rax before, it might well be that rax contains values in the upper bytes, and pushing these values to the stack may not be what we want. After that, the stack contains the pushed character plus the additional 0 bits in the bits above al.

When the loop is finished, the last character is at the "top" of the stack, which is in fact at the lowest address of the icicle because the stack grows in the downward direction. Another loop is started that pops character after character from the stack and stores them in memory in the original string, one after another. Note that we only want 1 byte, so we pop to rax and only use al.

Here is an overview of what is happening (see Figure 10-2): the original string is at the right, and the characters are pushed, sent one by one to the stack, where they are appended to the previous stack content. After that the characters are popped and sent back to the memory address of the string, and because of the "last in first out" working of the stack, the string is reversed.

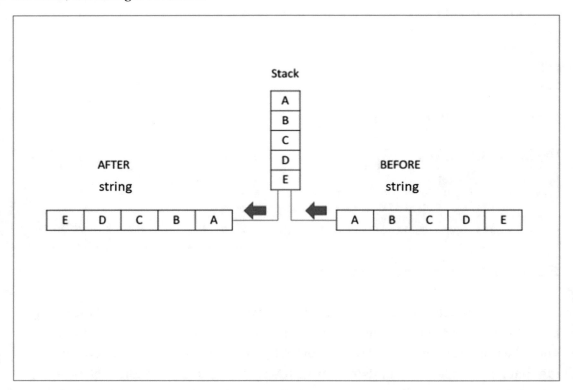

Figure 10-2. *Schema of reversing a string*

Somehow you have to keep track of what you pushed on the stack and in what order. For example, when you use the stack to temporarily store registers, be sure to pop the registers in the reverse correct order; otherwise, your program will be wrong or in the worst case will probably crash. That is, when you push the following sequence:

```
push rax
push rbx
push rcx
```

then you have to pop as follows, according to the "last in first out" principle:

```
pop rcx
pop rbx
pop rax
```

In addition to registers, you can push memory and immediate values. You can pop to a register or a memory location but not to an immediate value, which is quite evident.

That's good to know, but we will not use this here. If you want to push and pop the flag register to the stack, you can use the instructions pushf and use popf.

Keeping Track of the Stack

So, keeping track of the stack is important, and our old friend DDD has some easy features to do that. First open your editor to the source and delete the debug line that SASM added; then save the file and quit. At the CLI, make the program and then type the following:

```
ddd stack
```

Select Data ➤ Status Displays in the menu, and scroll down until you find "Backtrace of the stack" and enable it. Set a breakpoint at, for example, main: and then click Run in the floating panel. Now start debugging and step through the program with the Next button (you do not want to step line per line through the printf function). See how the stack is displayed and updated in the upper window. Do not worry about the initial stuff that is displayed. When you arrive at the instruction after the push instruction, you will see that characters are pushed onto the stack in ASCII decimal representation (41, 42, etc.). Watch how the stack decreases during the second loop. That is an easy way to see what is on the stack and in what order.

Figure 10-3 shows how it looks.

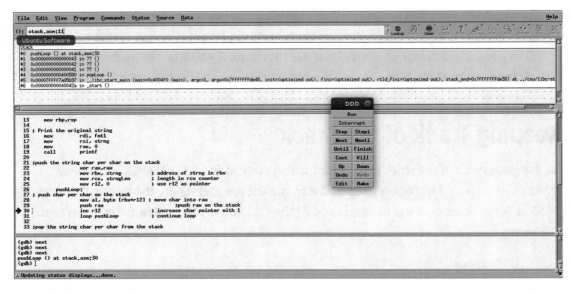

Figure 10-3. *The stack in DDD*

As we said before, DDD is open source and outdated. There is no guarantee that it will continue working as expected in the future, but for now it is not very elegant, but it will do.

In all fairness, you could force SASM to show the stack also, but that requires more manual work. Here is how it works: remember that you can show memory variables during debugging in SASM, and the stack is just a list of memory locations, with rsp pointing to the lowest location. Thus, we have to convince SASM to show us what is at address rsp and at the memory locations above. Figure 10-4 shows an example memory window in SASM showing the stack.

Variable or expression	Value	Type				
$rsp	{68'D',0'\000',0'\000',0'\000',0'\000',0'\000',0'\000',0'\000'}	Char	b	8		☑ Address
$rsp+8	{67'C',0'\000',0'\000',0'\000',0'\000',0'\000',0'\000',0'\000'}	Char	b	8		☑ Address
$rsp+16	{66'B',0'\000',0'\000',0'\000',0'\000',0'\000',0'\000',0'\000'}	Char	b	8		☑ Address
$rsp+24	{65'A',0'\000',0'\000',0'\000',0'\000',0'\000',0'\000',0'\000'}	Char	b	8		☑ Address
$rsp+32	{-8'370',-35'335',-1'\377',-1'377',-1'377',127'177',0'\000',0'\000'}	Char	b	8		☑ Address
Add variable...		Smart	d	Array size		☐ Address

Figure 10-4. *The stack in SASM*

We referred to `rsp` as `$rsp`. We increase the stack address every time with 8 (`$rsp + 8`), because at every `push`, 8 bytes are sent to the stack. As Type, we specified Char, bytes, 8 bytes, and Address. We chose Characters because we are pushing a string and then it is easy to read for us, and we chose bytes, because we are interested in byte values (`al` contains 1 byte every time), so 8 bytes are pushed every time. And `rsp` contains an Address. Step through the program and see how the stack changes.

It works, but you have to detail every stack memory place manually, which can be a burden if you are using a large stack and/or have a lot of additional memory variables you want to keep track of.

Summary

In this chapter, you learned the following:

- The stack starts at an address in high memory and grows to lower addresses.

- Push decreases the stack pointer (`rsp`).

- Pop increases the stack pointer (`rsp`).

- Push and pop work in reverse order.

- How to use DDD to examine the stack.

- How to use SASM to examine the stack.

CHAPTER 11

Floating-Point Arithmetic

You already know about integer arithmetic; now we will introduce some floating-point computations. There is nothing difficult here; a floating-point value has a decimal point in it and zero or more decimals. We have two kinds of floating-point numbers: single precision and double precision. Double precision is more accurate because it can handle more significant digits. With that information, you now know enough to run and analyze the sample program in this chapter.

Single vs. Double Precision

For those more curious, here is the story.

A single-precision number is stored in 32 bits: 1 sign bit, 8 exponent bits, and 23 fraction bits.

```
S       EEEEEEEE        FFFFFFFFFFFFFFFFFFFFFFF
0       1      8        9                     31
```

A double-precision number is stored in 64 bits: 1 sign bit, 11 exponent bits, and 52 fraction bits.

```
S       EEEEEEEEEEE       FFFFFFFFFFFF......FFFFFFFFFF
0       1        11       12                        63
```

The sign bit is simple. When the number is positive, it is 0; when the number is negative, the sign bit is 1.

The exponent bits are more complicated. Let's look at a decimal example.

$$200 = 2.0 \times 10^2$$

$$5000.30 = 5.0003 \times 10^3$$

© Jo Van Hoey 2019
J. Van Hoey, *Beginning x64 Assembly Programming*, https://doi.org/10.1007/978-1-4842-5076-1_11

Here is a binary example:

1101010.01011 = 1.0101001011 x 2^6 (we moved the point six places
to the left)

However, the exponent can be positive, negative, or zero. To make that distinction clear, in the case of single precision, 127 is added to a positive exponent before storing it. That means a zero exponent would be stored as 127. That 127 is called a *bias*. With double-precision values, the bias is 1023.

In the example above, the 1.0101001011 is called the significand or mantissa. The first bit of the significand is a 1 by assumption (it is 'normalized'), so it is not stored.

Here is a simple example to show how it works. Use, for example, `https://babbage.cs.qc.cuny.edu/IEEE-754/` to verify and experiment:

Single precision, decimal number 10:

- Decimal 10 is 1010 as a binary integer.

- Sign bit 0, because the number is positive.

- Obtain a number in the format `b.bbbb`. 1.010 is the significand with a leading 1 as required. The leading 1 will not be stored.

- Hence, the exponent is 3 because we moved the point three places. We add 127 because the exponent is positive, so we obtain 130, which in binary is 10000010.

- Thus, the decimal single-precision number 10 will be stored as:

```
0  10000010       01000000000000000000000
S  EEEEEEEE       FFFFFFFFFFFFFFFFFFFFFFF
```

or 41200000 in hexadecimal.

Note that the hexadecimal representation of the same value is different in single precision than in double precision. Why not always use double precision and benefit from the higher precision? Double-precision calculations are slower than single-precision calculations, and the operands use more memory.

If you think this is complicated, you are right. Find an appropriate tool on the Internet to do or at least verify the conversions.

You can encounter 80-bit floating-point numbers in older programs, and these numbers have their own instructions, called *FPU instructions*. This functionality is a legacy from the past and should not be used in new developments. But you will find FPU instructions in articles on the Internet from time to time.

Let's do some interesting things.

Coding with Floating-Point Numbers

Listing 11-1 shows the example program.

Listing 11-1. fcalc.asm

```
; fcalc.asm
extern printf
section .data
        number1         dq      9.0
        number2         dq      73.0
        fmt             db      "The numbers are %f and %f",10,0

        fmtfloat        db      "%s %f",10,0
        f_sum           db      "The float sum of %f and %f is %f",10,0
        f_dif           db      "The float difference of %f and %f is %f",10,0
        f_mul           db      "The float product of %f and %f is %f",10,0
        f_div           db      "The float division of %f by %f is %f",10,0
        f_sqrt          db      "The float squareroot of %f is %f",10,0
section .bss
section .text
        global main
main:
    push    rbp
    mov     rbp,rsp
; print the numbers
        movsd           xmm0, [number1]
        movsd           xmm1, [number2]
    mov     rdi,fmt
    mov     rax,2       ; two floats
    call    printf
```

```
; sum
    movsd    xmm2, [number1]    ; double precision float into xmm
    addsd    xmm2, [number2]    ; add doube precision to xmm
             ; print the result
             movsd xmm0, [number1]
             movsd xmm1, [number2]
             mov    rdi,f_sum
             mov    rax,3 ; three floats
             call   printf
; difference
    movsd    xmm2, [number1]       ; double precision float into xmm
    subsd    xmm2, [number2]       ; subtract from xmm
             ; print the result
             movsd xmm0, [number1]
             movsd xmm1, [number2]
             mov    rdi,f_dif
             mov    rax,3 ; three floats
             call   printf
; multiplication
    movsd    xmm2, [number1]       ; double precision float into xmm
    mulsd    xmm2, [number2]       ; multiply with xmm
             ; print the result
             mov    rdi,f_mul
             movsd xmm0, [number1]
             movsd xmm1, [number2]
             mov    rax,3 ; three floats
             call   printf
; division
    movsd    xmm2, [number1]       ; double precision float into xmm
    divsd    xmm2, [number2]       ; divide xmm0
             ; print the result
             mov    rdi,f_div
             movsd xmm0, [number1]
             movsd xmm1, [number2]
             mov    rax,1 ; one float
             call   printf
```

```
; squareroot
    sqrtsd  xmm1, [number1]        ; squareroot double precision in xmm
            ; print the result
            mov    rdi,f_sqrt
            movsd xmm0, [number1]
            mov    rax,2 ; two floats
            call   printf
; exit
            mov    rsp, rbp
            pop    rbp              ; undo the push at the beginning
            ret
```

This is a simple program; in fact, the printing takes more effort than the floating-point calculations.

Use a debugger to step through the program and investigate the registers and memory. Note, for example, how 9.0 and 73.0 are stored in memory addresses number1 and number2; these are the double-precision floating-point values.

Remember that when debugging in SASM, the xmm registers are at the bottom of the register window, in the leftmost part of the ymm registers.

movsd means "move a double precision-floating point value." There is also movss for single precision. Similarly, there are addss, subss, mulss, divss, and sqrtss instructions.

The rest should be pretty straightforward by now! Figure 11-1 shows the output.

```
jo@UbuntuDesktop:~/Desktop/linux64/gcc/13 fcalc$ make
nasm -f elf64 -g -F dwarf fcalc.asm -l fcalc.lst
gcc -o fcalc fcalc.o
jo@UbuntuDesktop:~/Desktop/linux64/gcc/13 fcalc$ ./fcalc
The numbers are 9.000000 and 73.000000
The float sum of 9.000000 and 73.000000 is 82.000000
The float difference of 9.000000 and 73.000000 is -64.000000
The float product of 9.000000 and 73.000000 is 657.000000
The float division of 9.000000 by 73.000000 is 0.123288
The float squareroot of 9.000000 is 3.000000
jo@UbuntuDesktop:~/Desktop/linux64/gcc/13 fcalc$ █
```

Figure 11-1. *fcalc.asm output*

Now that you know about the stack, try this: comment out push rbp at the beginning and pop rbp at the end. Make and run the program and see what happens: program crash! The cause for the crash will become clear later, but it has to do with stack alignment.

Summary

In this chapter, you learned the following:

- The basic use of xmm registers for floating-point calculations

- The difference between single precision and double precision

- The instructions `movsd`, `addsd`, `subsd`, `mulsd`, `divsd`, and `sqrtsd`

CHAPTER 12

Functions

Assembler is not a "structured language." Look at the multitude of `jmp` instructions and labels that allow the program execution to jump around and back and forth. Modern high-level programming languages have structures such as `do...while`, `while...do`, `case`, and so on. This is not so with assembly language.

But similar to modern program languages, assembly language has functions and procedures to help you give your code more structure. A little bit of nit-picking: a function executes instructions and returns a value. A procedure executes instructions and does not return a value.

In this book, we have already used functions; that is, we used an external function called `printf`, which is a C library function. In this chapter, we will introduce simple functions; in later chapters, we will cover important aspects of functions such as stack alignment, external functions, and calling conventions.

Writing a Simple Function

Listing 12-1 shows an example of an assembler program with a simple function to calculate the area of a circle.

Listing 12-1. function.asm

```
; function.asm
extern printf
section .data
        radius      dq      10.0
        pi          dq      3.14
        fmt         db      "The area of the circle is %.2f",10,0
```

© Jo Van Hoey 2019
J. Van Hoey, *Beginning x64 Assembly Programming*, https://doi.org/10.1007/978-1-4842-5076-1_12

```
section .bss
section .text
      global main
;-----------------------------------------------
main:
push  rbp
mov   rbp, rsp
      call  area              ; call the function
      mov   rdi,fmt           ; print format
      movsd xmm1, [radius]    ; move float to xmm1
      mov   rax,1             ; area in xmm0
      call  printf
leave
ret
;-----------------------------------------------
area:
push  rbp
mov   rbp, rsp
      movsd xmm0, [radius]    ; move float to xmm0
      mulsd xmm0, [radius]    ; multiply xmm0 by float
      mulsd xmm0, [pi]        ; multiply xmm0 by float
leave
ret
```

Figure 12-1 shows the output.

```
jo@UbuntuDesktop:~/Desktop/linux64/gcc/14 function$ make
nasm -f elf64 -g -F dwarf function.asm -l function.lst
gcc -o function function.o
jo@UbuntuDesktop:~/Desktop/linux64/gcc/14 function$ ./function
The area of the circle is 314.00
jo@UbuntuDesktop:~/Desktop/linux64/gcc/14 function$ ▮
```

***Figure 12-1.** function.asm output*

There is a main part, identified as before with the label main, and then there is a function, identified with the label area. In main, the function area is called, which calculates the area of a circle using radius and pi, which are variables stored in a location in memory. As you can see, functions must have a prologue and an epilogue, similar to main.

The computed area is stored in xmm0. Returning from the function to main, printf is called with rax containing the value 1, meaning there is one xmm register that needs to be printed. We introduce a new instruction here: leave. This instruction does the same as mov rsp, rbp, and pop rbp (the epilogue).

If you return a value from a function, you use xmm0 for floating-point values and use rax for other values, such as integers or addresses. The function arguments, pi and radius, are located in memory. That is okay for now, but it is better to use registers and the stack to store function arguments. Using memory variables to pass on values to functions can create naming conflicts between values used in main and in functions and can make your code less "portable."

More Functions

Let's discuss some more characteristics of functions using another example (see Listing 12-2).

Listing 12-2. function2.asm

```
; function2.asm
extern printf
section .data
     radius      dq      10.0
section .bss
section .text
;--------------------------------------------
area:
     section .data
          .pi  dq    3.141592654      ; local to area
     section .text
push  rbp
```

```
mov    rbp, rsp
       movsd       xmm0, [radius]
       mulsd       xmm0, [radius]
       mulsd       xmm0, [.pi]
leave
ret
;------------------------------------------------
circum:
section .data
       .pi  dq     3.14          ; local to circum
section .text
push   rbp
mov    rbp, rsp
       movsd       xmm0, [radius]
       addsd       xmm0, [radius]
       mulsd       xmm0, [.pi]
leave
ret
;------------------------------------------------
circle:
section .data
       .fmt_area   db     "The area is %f",10,0
       .fmt_circum         db      "The circumference is %f",10,0
section .text
push   rbp
mov    rbp, rsp
       call   area
       mov    rdi,.fmt_area
       mov    rax,1             ; area in xmm0
       call   printf
       call   circum
       mov    rdi,.fmt_circum
       mov    rax,1             ; circumference in xmm0
       call   printf
```

```
leave
ret
;--------------------------------------------
      global main
main:
push  rbp
mov   rbp, rsp
      call  circle
leave
ret
```

Here, we have `main` calling the function `circle`, which in turn calls the functions `area` and `circum`. So, functions can call other functions. In fact, `main` is just a function calling other functions. But beware that functions cannot be nested, which means functions cannot contain the code for other functions.

Also, functions can have their own sections, such as `.data`, `.bss`, and `.text`. What about the period before `pi` and the `fmt` variables? The period indicates a local variable, which means that the variable is known only inside the function where it is declared. In the function `area`, we used a value for `pi` that is different from the `pi` used in the function `circum`. The variable `radius`, declared in `section .data` of `main`, is known in every function in this source code listing, including `main`. It is always advisable to use local variables whenever possible; this reduces the risk of conflicting variable names.

Figure 12-2 shows the output for the program.

```
jo@UbuntuDesktop:~/Desktop/linux64/gcc/15 function2$ make
nasm -f elf64 -g -F dwarf function2.asm -l function2.lst
gcc -g -o function2 function2.o
jo@UbuntuDesktop:~/Desktop/linux64/gcc/15 function2$ ./function2
The area is 314.16
The circumference is 62.80
jo@UbuntuDesktop:~/Desktop/linux64/gcc/15 function2$ █
```

Figure 12-2. *function2.asm output*

Summary

In this chapter, you learned the following:

- How to use functions.

- Functions can have their own `section .data` and `section .bss`.

- Functions cannot be nested.

- Functions can call other functions.

- `main` is just another function.

- How to use local variables.

CHAPTER 13

Stack Alignment and Stack Frame

When your main program calls a function, it will push an 8-byte return address on the stack. That 8-byte address is the address of the instruction to be executed after the function. So, when the function ends, the program execution will find the return address from the stack and continue operation after the function call. Inside the function, we can also use the stack for different purposes. Every time you push something on the stack, the stack pointer will decrease by 8 bytes, and every time you pop something from the stack, the stack pointer will increase by 8 bytes. So, we have to make sure to "restore" the stack to the appropriate value before we leave the function. Otherwise, the executing program would have a wrong address for the instruction to be executed after the function call.

Stack Alignment

In the Intel manuals, you will find mention of a requirement that the **stack has to have a 16-byte alignment** when you call a function. This may sound a bit weird, as the stack is built in 8-byte (or 64-bit) memory. The reason is that there are SIMD instructions that perform parallel operations on larger blocks of data, and these SIMD instructions may require that these data are located in memory on addresses that are multiples of 16 bytes. In previous examples, when we used `printf` with xmm registers, we aligned the stack on 16 bytes, without explicitly telling you. Go back to Chapter 11 on floating-point arithmetic, where we crashed the program by commenting out `push rbp` and `pop rbp`. The program crashed because deleting these instructions caused the stack to be not aligned. If you use `printf` without xmm registers, you can get away without stack alignment, but if you do that, bugs are going to bite you someday.

© Jo Van Hoey 2019
J. Van Hoey, *Beginning x64 Assembly Programming*, https://doi.org/10.1007/978-1-4842-5076-1_13

We will discuss SIMD and alignment in later chapters, so don't worry if the previous explanation does not make sense to you. For now, keep in mind that when you call a function, you need to align the stack on an address that is a multiple of 16 bytes.

As far as the processor is concerned, main is just another function. Before your program starts execution, the stack is aligned. Just before main starts, an 8-byte return address is pushed onto the stack, which means the stack is not aligned upon the start of main. If the stack is not touched between the start of main and the call of a function, the stack pointer rsp is not 16-byte aligned. You can verify that by looking at rsp: if rsp ends with 0, it is 16-bit aligned. To make it zero, you push something onto the stack so that it becomes 16-bit aligned. Of course, do not forget the corresponding pop instruction later.

This alignment requirement is one of the reasons for using a prologue and an epilogue. The first instruction in main and in a function should push something onto the stack to align it. That's the reason for the prologue instruction push rbp. The rbp register is also called the *base pointer*.

Why are we using rbp? In the prologue, when using stack frames (explained later), rbp is modified, so before rbp is used in a stack frame, it is pushed onto the stack to preserve it when returning. Even when not building a stack frame, rbp is the ideal candidate to align the stack because it is not used for argument passing to a function. Argument passing will be discussed later in the chapter. In the prologue, we also use the instruction mov rbp,rsp. This instruction preserves rsp, which is our stack pointer containing the return address. The prologue instructions are reversed in the epilogue; needless to say, it is best to not meddle with rbp! In future chapters, you will see a number of other methods to align the stack.

Listing 13-1 shows some source code to play with. Keep an eye on rsp when debugging and stepping through the program with SASM. Comment out push rbp and pop rbp and see what happens. If the program execution arrives at printf with an unaligned stack, the program will crash. That is because printf definitely requires alignment.

In this program, we do not use complete prologues and epilogues; that is, we do not build stack frames. We only use push and pop to illustrate alignment.

Listing 13-1. aligned.asm

```
; aligned.asm
extern printf
section .data
      fmt   db      "2 times pi equals %.14f",10,0
```

```
      pi    dq      3.14159265358979
section .bss
section .text
;------------------------------------------------
func3:
      push  rbp
            movsd       xmm0, [pi]
            addsd       xmm0, [pi]
            mov   rdi,fmt
            mov   rax,1
            call  printf     ; print a float
      pop   rbp
      ret
;------------------------------------------------
func2:
      push  rbp
            call  func3 ; call the third function
      pop   rbp
      ret
;------------------------------------------------
func1:
      push  rbp
            call  func2 ; call the second function
      pop   rbp
      ret
;------------------------------------------------
      global main
main:
      push  rbp
            call  func1 ; call the first function
      pop   rbp
ret
```

Note that if you do a certain number of calls (even or odd, depending how you start), the stack will be 16-byte aligned even if you do not push/pop to align, and the program will not crash. Pure luck!

More on Stack Frames

You can distinguish two types of functions: branch functions and leaf functions. Branch functions contain calls to other functions, while leaf functions execute some commands and then return to the parent function without calling any other function.

In principle, every time you call a function, you need to build a stack frame. This is done as follows: in the called function, you first align the stack on a 16-byte border, that is, push rbp. Then you save stack pointer rsp into rbp. When leaving the function, restore rsp and pop rbp to restore rbp. That is the role of the function prologue and epilogue. Inside the function, register rbp now serves as an anchor point to the original stack location. Every time a function calls another function, the new function should build its own stack frame.

Inside a leaf function, you can in general ignore stack frame and stack alignment; it is not necessary as long as you don't mess with the stack. Note that when you call, for example, printf in your function, your function is not a leaf function. Similarly, if your function does not use SIMD instructions, you do not need to care about alignment.

Compilers have optimizing functionality, and sometimes when you look at code generated by compilers, you will find that there was no stack frame used. That happens when the compilers noticed during optimizing that a stack frame is not needed.

Anyway, it is a good habit to always include a stack frame and check the stack alignment; it can save you a lot of trouble later. A good reason to include a stack frame is the fact that GDB and GDB-based debuggers (such as DDD and SASM) expect to find a stack frame. If there is no stack frame in your code, the debugger will behave unpredictably, such as ignoring breakpoints or jumping over instructions. Take some code from a previous chapter (e.g., alife.asm), comment away the function prologue and epilogue, and then start GDB and see what happens.

As an additional exercise, look at the code from the previous chapter (function2.asm) with SASM or GDB and see how the stack remains aligned during the execution.

Here is an additional shortcut: you can substitute the function prologue for the instruction enter 0,0 and the function epilogue for the instruction leave. However, enter has poor performance, so you can just continue to use push rbp and mov rbp, rsp if you think performance is an issue. The instruction leave has no such performance problem.

Summary

In this chapter, you learned about the following:

- Stack alignment
- Using stack frames
- Using SASM to check the stack pointer
- Entering and leaving instructions

CHAPTER 14

External Functions

We already know how to create and use functions in our source code. But the functions do not have to reside in the same file as our main program. We can write and assemble these functions in a separate file and link them in when building the program. The function printf, which we already used several times, is an example of an external function. In the source file where you plan to use the external function, you declare it with the keyword extern, and the assembler knows it does not have to look for the source of the function. The assembler will assume that the function is already assembled in an object file. The external function will be inserted by the linker, provided it can find it in an object file.

Similar to using C functions such as printf, you can build your own set of functions and link them when you need them.

Building and Linking Functions

Listing 14-1 shows an example program, with three source files, to be saved as separate files: function4.asm, circle.asm, and rect.asm. There is also a new makefile. Study it carefully.

Listing 14-1. function4.asm

```
; function4.asm
extern printf
extern c_area
extern c_circum
extern r_area
extern r_circum
global pi
section .data
```

© Jo Van Hoey 2019
J. Van Hoey, *Beginning x64 Assembly Programming*, https://doi.org/10.1007/978-1-4842-5076-1_14

```
      pi          dq      3.141592654
      radius      dq      10.0
      side1       dq      4
      side2       dq      5
      fmtf   db   "%s %f",10,0
      fmti   db   "%s %d",10,0
      ca     db   "The circle area is ",0
      cc     db   "The circle circumference is ",0
      ra     db   "The rectangle area is ",0
      rc     db   "The rectangle circumference is ",0
section .bss
section .text
      global main
main:
push   rbp
mov    rbp,rsp

; circle area
      movsd   xmm0, qword [radius]     ; radius xmm0 argument
      call    c_area                   ; area returned in xmm0
      ; print the circle area
            mov    rdi, fmtf
            mov    rsi, ca
            mov    rax, 1
            call   printf
; circle circumference
      movsd      xmm0, qword [radius] ; radius xmm0 argument
      call   c_circum                 ; circumference in xmm0
      ; print the circle circumference
            mov    rdi, fmtf
            mov    rsi, cc
            mov    rax, 1
            call   printf

; rectangle area
      mov    rdi, [side1]
```

```
        mov    rsi, [side2]
        call   r_area               ; area returned in rax
        ; print the rectangle area
                mov    rdi, fmti
                mov    rsi, ra
                mov    rdx, rax
                mov    rax, 0
                call   printf
; rectangle circumference
        mov    rdi, [side1]
        mov    rsi, [side2]
        call   r_circum             ; circumference in rax
        ; print the rectangle circumference
                mov    rdi, fmti
                mov    rsi, rc
                mov    rdx, rax
                mov    rax, 0
                call   printf
mov rsp,rbp
pop rbp
ret
```

In the above source, we declared a number of functions as external, as we already did several times before when using printf. There's nothing new here. But we also declared the variable pi to be global. That means this variable will also be available to external functions.

Listing 14-2 and Listing 14-3 show separate files that contain only functions.

Listing 14-2. circle.asm

```
; circle.asm
extern pi
section .data
section .bss
section .text
;------------------------------------------------
global c_area
```

```
c_area:
      section .text
      push rbp
      mov rbp,rsp
          movsd xmm1, qword [pi]
          mulsd xmm0, xmm0        ;radius in xmm0
          mulsd xmm0, xmm1
      mov rsp,rbp
      pop rbp
      ret
;---------------------------------------------------
global c_circum
c_circum:
      section .text
      push rbp
      mov rbp,rsp
          movsd xmm1, qword [pi]
          addsd xmm0, xmm0        ;radius in xmm0
          mulsd xmm0, xmm1
      mov rsp,rbp
      pop rbp
      ret
```

Listing 14-3. rect.asm

```
; rect.asm
section .data
section .bss
section .text
;-----------------------------------------------
global r_area
r_area:
      section .text
      push rbp
      mov rbp,rsp
          mov   rax, rsi
```

```
        imul   rax, rdi
        mov    rsp,rbp
    pop rbp
    ret
;---------------------------------------------
global r_circum
r_circum:
    section .text
    push rbp
    mov rbp,rsp
        mov    rax, rsi
        add    rax, rdi
        add    rax, rax
    mov rsp,rbp
    pop rbp
    ret
```

In circle.asm we want to use the variable pi declared in the main source file as global, which is by the way not a good idea, but we are doing it here for demonstration purposes. Global variables such as pi are difficult to keep track of and could even lead to conflicting variables with the same names. It is best practice to use registers to pass values to a function. Here, we have to specify that pi is external. circle.asm and rect.asm each have two functions, one for computing the circumference and one for computing the area. We have to indicate that these functions are global, similar to the main program. When these functions are assembled, the necessary "overhead" is added, enabling the linker to add these functions to other object code.

Expanding the makefile

To make all this work, we need an expanded makefile, as shown in Listing 14-4.

Listing 14-4. makefile

```
# makefile for function4, circle and rect.
function4: function4.o circle.o rect.o
    gcc -g -o function4 function4.o circle.o rect.o -no-pie
function4.o: function4.asm
```

```
        nasm -f elf64 -g -F dwarf function4.asm -l function4.lst
circle.o: circle.asm
        nasm -f elf64 -g -F dwarf circle.asm -l circle.lst
rect.o: rect.asm
        nasm -f elf64 -g -F dwarf rect.asm -l rect.lst
```

You read the makefile from the bottom up: first the different assembly source files are assembled into object files, and then the object files are linked together in function4, the executable. You can see here the power of using make. When you modify one of the source files, make knows, thanks to the tree structure, which files to re-assemble and link. Of course, if your functions are stable and will not change anymore, there is no need to try to re-assemble them in every makefile. Just store the object file somewhere in a convenient directory and refer to that object file with its complete path in the gcc line of the makefile. An object file is the result of assembling or compiling source code. It contains machine code and also information for a linker about which global variables and external functions are needed in order to produce a valid executable. In our case, the object files all reside in the same directory as our main source, so no paths were specified here.

What about the printf function? Why is no reference made to printf in the makefile? Well, gcc is smart enough to also check C libraries for functions that are referenced in the source code. This means you should not use the names of C functions for naming your own functions! That will confuse everybody, not to mention your linker.

In the code, we used registers to transfer values from the main program to the functions, and vice versa, and that is best practice. For example, before calling r_area, we moved side1 to rdi and side2 to rsi. Then we returned the computed area in rax. To return the result, we could have used a global variable, similar to pi in the section .data section of main. But as we said before, that should be avoided. In the next chapter on calling conventions, we will discuss this more in detail.

Figure 14-1 shows the output of this program.

```
jo@UbuntuDesktop:~/Desktop/linux64/gcc/17 function4$ make
nasm -f elf64 -g -F dwarf function4.asm -l function4.lst
nasm -f elf64 -g -F dwarf circle.asm -l circle.lst
nasm -f elf64 -g -F dwarf rect.asm -l rect.lst
gcc -g -o function4 function4.o circle.o rect.o
jo@UbuntuDesktop:~/Desktop/linux64/gcc/17 function4$ ./function4
The circle area is   314.159265
The circle circumference is   62.831853
The rectangle area is   20
The rectangle circumference is   18
jo@UbuntuDesktop:~/Desktop/linux64/gcc/17 function4$ █
```

Figure 14-1. *Output of function4*

When using this example in SASM, you have to assemble the external functions first to obtain object files. Then on the SASM Settings dialog's Build tab, you need to add the location of these object files in the Linking Options line. The Linking Options line would look like the following in this case (be careful not to introduce unwanted spaces in this line!):

```
$PROGRAM.OBJ$ -g -o $PROGRAM$ circle.o rect.o -no-pie
```

Summary

In this chapter, you learned the following:

- How to use external functions

- How to global variables

- How to use the makefile and external functions

- How to transfer values to and from functions

CHAPTER 15

Calling Conventions

Calling conventions describe how you transfer variables to and from functions. If you will be using only functions that you have built yourself, you do not have to care about calling conventions. But when you are using C functions from the C library, you need to know in which registers you have to put the values to be used by that function. Also, if you write assembly functions for building a library that will be used by other developers, you'd better follow some convention for which registers to use for which function arguments. Otherwise, you will have lots of conflicts with arguments.

You already noticed that with the function `printf`, we put an argument in `rdi`, another in `rsi`, and yet another argument in `xmm0`. We were using a calling convention.

To avoid conflicts and the resulting crashes, smart developers designed *calling conventions*, a standardized way to call functions. It is a nice idea, but as you may expect, not everybody agrees with everybody else, so there are several different calling conventions. Up until now in this book we have used the System V AMD64 ABI calling convention, which is the standard on Linux platforms. But there is also another calling convention worth knowing: the Microsoft x64 calling convention to be used in Windows programming.

These calling conventions allow you to use external functions built with assembly, as well as functions compiled from languages such as C, without having access to the source code. Just put the correct arguments in the registers specified in the calling convention.

You can find out more about the System V AMD64 ABI calling convention at `https://software.intel.com/sites/default/files/article/402129/mpx-linux64-abi.pdf`. This Intel document has an overwhelming amount of detailed information about the System V application binary interface. In this chapter, we will show what you have to know to start calling functions in the standard way.

© Jo Van Hoey 2019
J. Van Hoey, *Beginning x64 Assembly Programming*, https://doi.org/10.1007/978-1-4842-5076-1_15

Function Arguments

Look back at the previous source files: for the circle calculations, we used xmm0 to transfer floating-point values from the main program to the circle function, and we used xmm0 to return the floating-point result of the function to the main program. For the rectangle calculation, we used rdi and rsi to transfer integer values to the function, and the integer result was returned in rax. This way of passing arguments and results is dictated by the calling convention.

Non-floating-point arguments, such as integers and addresses, are passed as follows:

The 1st argument goes into rdi.

The 2nd argument goes into rsi.

The 3rd argument goes into rdx.

The 4th argument goes into rcx.

The 5th argument goes into r8.

The 6th argument goes into r9.

Additional arguments are passed via the stack and in reverse order so that we can pop off in the right order. For instance, with 10 arguments, we have this:

The 10th argument is pushed first.

Then the 9th argument is pushed.

Then the 8th argument is pushed.

The 7th argument is pushed.

Once you are in the function, it is just a matter of getting the values from the registers. When popping the values from the stack, you have to be careful; remember that when a function is called, the return address is pushed on the stack, just after the arguments.

When you push the 10th argument, you decrease the stack pointer rsp by 8 bytes.

When you push the 9th argument, rsp decreases by 8 bytes.

When you push the 8th argument, rsp decreases by 8 bytes.

With the 7th argument, rsp decreases by 8 bytes.

Then the function is called; `rip` is pushed on the stack, and `rsp`
decreases by 8 bytes.

Then `rbp` is pushed at the beginning of the function; as part of the
prologue, `rsp` decreases by 8 bytes.

Then align the stack on a 16-byte boundary, so maybe another
push is needed to decrease `rsp` by 8 bytes.

Thus, after we pushed the function's arguments, at least two additional registers are
pushed on the stack, i.e., 16 additional bytes. So, when you are in the function, to access
the arguments, you have to skip the first 16 bytes on the stack, maybe more if you had to
align the stack.

Floating-point arguments are passed via xmm registers as follows:

The 1st argument goes into `xmm0`.

The 2nd argument goes into `xmm1`.

The 3rd argument goes into `xmm2`.

The 4th argument goes into `xmm3`.

The 5th argument goes into `xmm4`.

The 6th argument goes into `xmm5`.

The 7th argument goes into `xmm6`.

The 8th argument goes into `xmm7`.

Additional arguments are passed via the stack; this is not accomplished with a push
instruction as you might expect. We will show later how to do that, in the more advanced
SIMD chapters.

A function returns a floating-point result in `xmm0`, and an integer number or address
is returned in `rax`.

Complicated? Listing 15-1 shows an example that prints a number of arguments with
`printf`.

Listing 15-1. function5.asm

```
; function5.asm
extern printf
section .data
```

```
        first       db      "A",0
        second      db      "B",0
        third       db      "C",0
        fourth      db      "D",0
        fifth       db      "E",0
        sixth       db      "F",0
        seventh     db      "G",0
        eighth      db      "H",0
        ninth       db      "I",0
        tenth       db      "J",0
        fmt1    db      "The string is: %s%s%s%s%s%s%s%s%s%s",10,0
        fmt2    db      "PI = %f",10,0
        pi          dq      3.14
section .bss
section .text
        global main
main:
push    rbp
mov     rbp,rsp

        mov     rdi,fmt1    ;first use the registers
        mov     rsi, first
        mov     rdx, second
        mov     rcx, third
        mov     r8, fourth
        mov     r9, fifth

        push    tenth       ; now start pushing in
        push    ninth       ; reverse order
        push    eighth
        push    seventh
        push    sixth
        mov     rax, 0
        call    printf
        and     rsp, 0xfffffffffffffff0 ; 16-byte align the stack
        movsd       xmm0,[pi] ; now print a floating-point
        mov     rax, 1              ; 1 float to print
```

```
        mov    rdi, fmt2
        call   printf
leave
ret
```

In this example, we pass all arguments in the correct order to `printf`. Note the reverse order of pushing the arguments.

Use your debugger to check `rsp` just before the `call printf`. The stack is not 16-byte aligned! The program did not crash because we did not ask `printf` to print a floating-point number. But the next `printf` does exactly that. Thus, before using `printf`, we have to align the stack, so we use the following instruction:

```
        and       rsp, 0xfffffffffffffff0
```

This instruction leaves all the bytes in `rsp` intact, except the last one: the last four bits in `rsp` are changed to 0, thus decreasing the number in `rsp` and aligning `rsp` on a 16-byte boundary. If the stack had been aligned to start with, the and instruction would do nothing. Be careful, though. If you want to pop values from the stack after this and instruction, you have a problem: you have to find out if the and instruction changed `rsp` and eventually adjust `rsp` again to its value before the execution of the and instruction.

Figure 15-1 shows the output.

```
jo@UbuntuDesktop:~/Desktop/linux64/gcc/18 function5$ make
nasm -f elf64 -g -F dwarf function5.asm -l function5.lst
gcc -g -o function5 function5.o -no-pie
jo@UbuntuDesktop:~/Desktop/linux64/gcc/18 function5$ ./function5
The string is: ABCDEFGHIJ
PI = 3.140000
jo@UbuntuDesktop:~/Desktop/linux64/gcc/18 function5$ ▮
```

Figure 15-1. *Output of function5*

Stack Layout

Let's look at an example where we can see what happens on the stack when we push function arguments. Listing 15-2 shows a program that uses a function to build a string, and when the function returns, the string is printed.

Listing 15-2. function6.asm

```
; function6.asm
extern printf
section .data
        first       db      "A"
        second      db      "B"
        third       db      "C"
        fourth      db      "D"
        fifth       db      "E"
        sixth       db      "F"
        seventh     db      "G"
        eighth      db      "H"
        ninth       db      "I"
        tenth       db      "J"
        fmt         db      "The string is: %s",10,0
section .bss
        flist       resb 11     ;length of string + terminating 0
section .text
        global main
main:
push  rbp
mov   rbp, rsp
        mov   rdi, flist        ; length
        mov   rsi, first        ; fill the registers
        mov   rdx, second
        mov   rcx, third
        mov   r8, fourth
        mov   r9, fifth
        push  tenth        ; now start pushing in
        push  ninth        ; reverse order
        push  eighth
        push  seventh
        push  sixth
        call  lfunc             ;call the function
        ; print the result
```

```
        mov   rdi, fmt
        mov   rsi, flist
        mov   rax, 0
        call  printf
leave
ret
;----------------------------------------------
lfunc:
push  rbp
mov   rbp,rsp
        xor   rax,rax    ;clear rax (especially higher bits)
        mov   al,byte[rsi]     ; move content 1st argument to al
        mov   [rdi], al       ; store al to memory
        mov   al, byte[rdx]    ; move content 2nd argument to al
        mov   [rdi+1], al     ; store al to memory
        mov   al, byte[rcx]    ; etc for the other arguments
        mov   [rdi+2], al
        mov   al, byte[r8]
        mov   [rdi+3], al
        mov   al, byte[r9]
        mov   [rdi+4], al
; now fetch the arguments from the stack
        push  rbx               ; callee saved
        xor   rbx,rbx
        mov   rax, qword [rbp+16]   ; first value: initial stack
                                    ; + rip + rbp
        mov   bl, byte[rax]         ; extract the character
        mov   [rdi+5], bl      ; store the character to memory
        mov   rax, qword [rbp+24]   ; continue with next value
        mov   bl, byte[rax]
        mov   [rdi+6], bl
        mov   rax, qword [rbp+32]
        mov   bl, byte[rax]
        mov   [rdi+7], bl
        mov   rax, qword [rbp+40]
```

```
        mov    bl, byte[rax]
        mov    [rdi+8], bl
        mov    rax, qword [rbp+48]
        mov    bl, byte[rax]
        mov    [rdi+9], bl
        mov    bl,0
        mov    [rdi+10], bl
pop     rbx                        ; callee saved
mov     rsp,rbp
pop     rbp
ret
```

Here, instead of printing with printf immediately after we provide all the arguments, as we did in the previous section, we call the function lfunc. This function takes all the arguments and builds a string in memory (flist); that string will be printed after returning to main.

Look at the lfunc function. We take only the lower byte of the argument registers, which is where the characters are, using an instruction such as the following:

```
        mov        al,byte[rsi]
```

We store these characters one by one in memory, starting at the address in rdi, which is the address of flist, with the instruction: mov [rdi], al. Using the byte keyword is not necessary, but it improves the readability of the code.

It gets interesting when we start popping values from the stack. At the start of lfunc, the value of rsp, which is the stack address, is saved into rbp. However, between this instruction and the end of pushing the values in main, rsp was modified twice. First, when lfunc was called, the return address was pushed onto the stack. Then we pushed rbp as part of the prologue. In total, rsp was decreased by 16 bytes. To access our pushed values, we have to augment the value of the addresses by 16 bytes. That is why we used this to access the variable sixth:

```
        mov rax, qword [rbp+16]
```

The other variables are each 8 bytes higher than the previous one. We used rbx as a temporary register for building the string in flist. Before using rbx, we saved the content of rbx to the stack. You never know if rbx is used in main for other purposes, so we preserve rbx and restore it before leaving the function.

Figure 15-2 shows the output.

```
jo@UbuntuDesktop:~/Desktop/linux64/gcc/18 function6$ make
nasm -f elf64 -g -F dwarf function6.asm -l function6.lst
gcc -g -o function6 function6.o -no-pie
jo@UbuntuDesktop:~/Desktop/linux64/gcc/18 function6$ ./function6
The string is: ABCDEFGHIJ
jo@UbuntuDesktop:~/Desktop/linux64/gcc/18 function6$ █
```

Figure 15-2. *Output of function6*

Preserving Registers

We will now explain the instructions.

```
        push       rbx                    ; callee saved
```

and

```
        pop        rbx                    ; callee saved
```

It should be clear that you have to keep track of with happens with the registers during a function call. Some registers will be altered during the execution of a function, and some will be kept intact. You need to take precautions in order to avoid unexpected results caused by functions modifying registers you are using in the main (calling) program.

Table 15-1 shows an overview of what is specified in the calling convention.

Table 15-1. *Calling Conventions*

Register	Usage	Save
rax	Return value	Caller
rbx	Callee saved	Callee
rcx	4th argument	Caller
rdx	3rd argument	Caller
rsi	2nd argument	Caller

(*continued*)

Table 15-1. (*continued*)

Register	Usage	Save
rdi	1st argument	Caller
rbp	Callee saved	Callee
rsp	Stack pointer	Callee
r8	5th argument	Caller
r9	6th argument	Caller
r10	Temporary	Caller
r11	Temporary	Caller
r12	Callee saved	Callee
r13	Callee saved	Callee
r14	Callee saved	Callee
r15	Callee saved	Callee
xmm0	First arg and return	Caller
xmm1	Second arg and return	Caller
xmm2-7	Arguments	Caller
xmm8-15	Temporary	Caller

The function called is the *callee*. When a function uses a *callee-saved register*, the function needs to push that register on the stack before using it and pop it in the right order afterward. The caller expects that a callee-saved register should remain intact after the function call. The argument registers can be changed during execution of a function, so it is the responsibility of the caller to push/pop them if they have to be preserved. Similarly, the temporary registers can be changed in the function, so they need to be pushed/popped by the caller if needed. Needless to say, rax, the returning value, needs to be pushed/popped by the caller!

Problems can start popping up when you modify an existing function and start using a caller-saved register. If you do not add a push/pop of that register in the caller, you will have unexpected results.

Registers that are callee saved are also called nonvolatile. Registers that the caller has to save are also called *volatile*.

The xmm registers can all be changed by a function; the caller will be responsible for preserving them if necessary.

Of course, if you are sure you are not going to use the changed registers, you can skip the saving of these registers. However, if you change the code in the future, you may get in trouble if you start using these registers without saving them. Believe it or not, after a couple of weeks or months, assembly code is difficult to read, even if you coded everything yourself.

One last note: `syscall` is also a function and will modify registers, so keep an eye on what a `syscall` is doing.

Summary

In this chapter, you learned about the following:

- Calling conventions

- Stack alignment

- Callee/caller-saved registers

CHAPTER 16

Bit Operations

We have already done bit operations in Chapter 9 on integer arithmetic: shift arithmetic sar and sal are bit operations, shifting bits right or left. Also, the and instruction for aligning the stack covered in the previous chapter is a bit operation.

Basics

In the following example program, we are building a custom C function called printb to print a string of bits. For convenience, it separates the string of 64 bits into 8 bytes, with 8 bits each. As an exercise, after you finish this chapter, take a look at the C code, and you should be able to write an assembler program to build a string of bits.

Listing 16-1, Listing 16-2, and Listing 16-3 show the example code for the bit operations in assembly, the C printb program, and the makefile, respectively.

Listing 16-1. bits1.asm

```
; bits1.asm
extern printb
extern printf
section .data
        msgn1 db    "Number 1",10,0
        msgn2 db    "Number 2",10,0
        msg1  db    "XOR",10,0
        msg2  db    "OR",10,0
        msg3  db    "AND",10,0
        msg4  db    "NOT number 1",10,0
        msg5  db    "SHL 2 lower byte of number 1",10,0
        msg6  db    "SHR 2 lower byte of number 1",10,0
        msg7  db    "SAL 2 lower byte of number 1",10,0
```

© Jo Van Hoey 2019
J. Van Hoey, *Beginning x64 Assembly Programming*, https://doi.org/10.1007/978-1-4842-5076-1_16

```
        msg8   db      "SAR 2 lower byte of number 1",10,0
        msg9   db      "ROL 2 lower byte of number 1",10,0
        msg10  db      "ROL 2 lower byte of number 2",10,0
        msg11  db      "ROR 2 lower byte of number 1",10,0
        msg12  db      "ROR 2 lower byte of number 2",10,0
        number1     dq      -72
        number2     dq      1064
section .bss
section .text
        global main
main:
push   rbp
mov    rbp,rsp
; print number1
        mov    rsi, msgn1
        call   printmsg
        mov    rdi, [number1]
        call   printb
; print number2
        mov    rsi, msgn2
        call   printmsg
        mov    rdi, [number2]
        call   printb

; print XOR (exclusive OR)-----------------------
        mov    rsi, msg1
        call   printmsg
; xor and print
        mov    rax,[number1]
        xor    rax,[number2]
        mov    rdi, rax
        call   printb

; print OR --------------------------------------
        mov    rsi, msg2
        call   printmsg
```

```
; or and print
      mov    rax,[number1]
      or     rax,[number2]
      mov    rdi, rax
      call   printb

; print AND  -------------------------------------
      mov    rsi, msg3
      call   printmsg
; and and print
      mov    rax,[number1]
      and    rax,[number2]
      mov    rdi, rax
      call   printb

; print NOT  -------------------------------------
      mov    rsi, msg4
      call   printmsg
; not and print
      mov    rax,[number1]
      not    rax
      mov    rdi, rax
      call   printb

; print SHL  (shift left----------------------------
      mov    rsi, msg5
      call   printmsg
; shl and print
      mov    rax,[number1]
      shl    al,2
      mov    rdi, rax
      call   printb

; print SHR  (shift right)--------------------------
      mov    rsi, msg6
      call   printmsg
;shr and print
```

```
        mov     rax,[number1]
        shr     al,2
        mov     rdi, rax
        call    printb

; print SAL  (shift arithmetic left)----------------
        mov     rsi, msg7
        call    printmsg
; sal and print
        mov     rax,[number1]
        sal     al,2
        mov     rdi, rax
        call    printb

; print SAR  (shift arithmetic right)----------------
        mov     rsi, msg8
        call    printmsg
; sar and print
        mov     rax,[number1]
        sar     al,2
        mov     rdi, rax
        call    printb

; print ROL  (rotate left)--------------------------
        mov     rsi, msg9
        call    printmsg
; rol and print
        mov     rax,[number1]
        rol     al,2
        mov     rdi, rax
        call    printb
        mov     rsi, msg10
        call    printmsg
        mov     rax,[number2]
        rol     al,2
        mov     rdi, rax
        call    printb
```

```nasm
; print ROR   (rotate right)----------------------------
      mov    rsi, msg11
      call   printmsg
; ror and print
      mov    rax,[number1]
      ror    al,2
      mov    rdi, rax
      call   printb
      mov    rsi, msg12
      call   printmsg
      mov    rax,[number2]
      ror    al,2
      mov    rdi, rax
      call   printb
leave
ret

;-------------------------------------------------------
printmsg:    ; print the heading for every bit operation
section .data
      .fmtstr            db        "%s",0
section .text
      mov    rdi,.fmtstr
      mov    rax,0
      call   printf
      ret
```

Listing 16-2. *printb.c*

```c
// printb.c

#include <stdio.h>

void printb(long long n){
      long long s,c;
      for (c = 63; c >= 0; c--)
      {
      s = n >> c;
```

```
        // space after every 8th bit
        if ((c+1) % 8 == 0) printf(" ");

        if (s & 1)
                printf("1");
        else
                printf("0");
    }
    printf("\n");
}
```

Listing 16-3. makefile for bits1 and printb

```
# makefile for bits1 and printb
bits1: bits1.o printb.o
    gcc -g -o bits1 bits1.o printb.o -no-pie
bits1.o: bits1.asm
    nasm -f elf64 -g -F dwarf bits1.asm -l bits1.lst
printb: printb.c
    gcc -c printb.c
```

Build and run the program and study the output. If you are using SASM, do not forget to compile the printb.c file first and then add the object file in the Linking Options, as mentioned when discussing external functions in Chapter 14.

This is quite a long program. Fortunately, the code is not complicated. We'll show how the different bit operation instructions work. Use the output shown in Figure 16-1 to guide you through the code.

```
jo@UbuntuDesktop:~/Desktop/linux64/gcc/20_bits1$ make
nasm -f elf64 -g -F dwarf bits1.asm -l bits1.lst
cc    -c -o printb.o printb.c
gcc -g -o bits1 bits1.o printb.o
jo@UbuntuDesktop:~/Desktop/linux64/gcc/20_bits1$ ./bits1
Number 1
 11111111 11111111 11111111 11111111 11111111 11111111 11111111 10111000
Number 2
 00000000 00000000 00000000 00000000 00000000 00000000 00000100 00101000
XOR
 11111111 11111111 11111111 11111111 11111111 11111111 11111011 10010000
OR
 11111111 11111111 11111111 11111111 11111111 11111111 11111111 10111000
AND
 00000000 00000000 00000000 00000000 00000000 00000000 00000100 00101000
NOT number 1
 00000000 00000000 00000000 00000000 00000000 00000000 00000000 01000111
SHL 2 lower byte of number 1
 11111111 11111111 11111111 11111111 11111111 11111111 11111111 11100000
SHR 2 lower byte of number 1
 11111111 11111111 11111111 11111111 11111111 11111111 11111111 00101110
SAL 2 lower byte of number 1
 11111111 11111111 11111111 11111111 11111111 11111111 11111111 11100000
SAR 2 lower byte of number 1
 11111111 11111111 11111111 11111111 11111111 11111111 11111111 11101110
ROL 2 lower byte of number 1
 11111111 11111111 11111111 11111111 11111111 11111111 11111111 11100010
ROL 2 lower byte of number 2
 00000000 00000000 00000000 00000000 00000000 00000000 00000100 10100000
ROR 2 lower byte of number 1
 11111111 11111111 11111111 11111111 11111111 11111111 11111111 00101110
ROR 2 lower byte of number 2
 00000000 00000000 00000000 00000000 00000000 00000000 00000100 00001010
jo@UbuntuDesktop:~/Desktop/linux64/gcc/20_bits1$ █
```

Figure 16-1. *bits1.asm output*

First note the binary representation of number1 (-72); the 1 in the most significant bit indicates a negative number.

The instructions xor, or, and, and not are pretty simple; they work as explained in Chapter 5. Experiment with different values to see how it works.

For shl, shr, sal, and sar, we use the lower byte of rax to illustrate what is going on. With shl, bits are shifted to the left and zeros are added to the **right** of al; the bits are moved to the left, and the bits that move to the left of the 8th bit are simply discarded. With shr, bits are shifted to the right and zeros are added to the **left** of al. All bits are moved to the right, and bits that move to the right of the least significant bit are dropped. When you are stepping through the program, keep an eye on the flag registers, especially the sign register and the overflow register.

The arithmetic left shift, `sal`, is exactly the same as `shl`; it multiplies the value. The arithmetic shift right, `sar`, division, is different from `shr`. Here we have what is called *sign extension*. If the leftmost bit in `al` is a 1, `al` contains a negative value. To do the arithmetic correctly, when shifting right, 1s instead of 0s are added to the left in case of a negative value. This is called *sign extension*.

Rotate left, `rol`, removes the leftmost bit, shifts left, and adds the removed bits to the right. Rotate right, `ror`, works in a similar way.

Arithmetic

Let's do some deep dive into shifting arithmetic. Why are there two types of shift left and two types of shift right? When doing arithmetic with negative values, shift instructions can give you wrong results, because sign extension needs to be taken into account. That is why there are arithmetic shift instructions and logical shift instructions.

Study the example in Listing 16-4.

Listing 16-4. bits2.asm

```
; bits2.asm
extern printf
section .data
      msgn1 db    "Number 1 is = %d",0
      msgn2 db    "Number 2 is = %d",0
      msg1  db    "SHL 2 = OK multiply by 4",0
      msg2  db    "SHR 2 = WRONG divide by 4",0
      msg3  db    "SAL 2 = correctly multiply by 4",0
      msg4  db    "SAR 2 = correctly divide by 4",0
      msg5  db    "SHR 2 = OK divide by 4",0

      number1     dq    8
      number2     dq    -8
      result      dq    0

section .bss
section .text
      global main
```

```
main:
push  rbp
mov   rbp,rsp

;SHL------------------------------------------------

;positive number
      mov   rsi, msg1
      call  printmsg          ;print heading
      mov   rsi, [number1]
      call  printnbr          ;print number1
      mov   rax,[number1]
      shl   rax,2       ;multiply by 4 (logic)
      mov   rsi, rax
      call  printres
;negative number
      mov   rsi, msg1
      call  printmsg          ;print heading
      mov   rsi, [number2]
      call  printnbr          ;print number2
      mov   rax,[number2]
      shl   rax,2       ;multiply by 4 (logic)
      mov   rsi, rax
      call  printres
;SAL------------------------------------------------
;positive number
      mov   rsi, msg3
      call  printmsg          ;print heading
      mov   rsi, [number1]
      call  printnbr          ;print number1
      mov   rax,[number1]
      sal   rax,2       ;multiply by 4 (arithmetic)
      mov   rsi, rax
      call  printres
```

```
;negative number
      mov   rsi, msg3
      call  printmsg          ;print heading
      mov   rsi, [number2]
      call  printnbr          ;print number2
      mov   rax,[number2]
      sal   rax,2       ;multiply by 4 (arithmetic)
      mov   rsi, rax
      call  printres
;SHR--------------------------------------------------
;positive number
      mov   rsi, msg5
      call  printmsg          ;print heading
      mov   rsi, [number1]
      call  printnbr          ;print number1
      mov   rax,[number1]
      shr   rax,2       ;divide by 4 (logic)
      mov   rsi, rax
      call  printres
;negative number
      mov   rsi, msg2
      call  printmsg          ;print heading
      mov   rsi, [number2]
      call  printnbr          ;print number2
      mov   rax,[number2]
      shr   rax,2       ;divide by 4 (logic)
      mov   [result], rax
      mov   rsi, rax
      call  printres
;SAR--------------------------------------------------
;positive number
      mov   rsi, msg4
      call  printmsg          ;print heading
      mov   rsi, [number1]
      call  printnbr          ;print number1
```

```
        mov   rax,[number1]
        sar   rax,2      ;divide by 4 (arithmetic)
        mov   rsi, rax
        call  printres
;negative number
        mov   rsi, msg4
        call  printmsg         ;print heading
        mov   rsi, [number2]
        call  printnbr         ;print number2
        mov   rax,[number2]
        sar   rax,2      ;divide by 4 (arithmetic)
        mov   rsi, rax
        call  printres
leave
ret
;----------------------------------
printmsg:               ;print the title
        section .data
            .fmtstr db 10,"%s",10,0 ;format for a string
        section .text
            mov   rdi,.fmtstr
            mov   rax,0
            call  printf
        ret
;----------------------------------
printnbr:               ;print the number
        section .data
            .fmtstr db "The original number is %lld",10,0
        section .text
            mov   rdi,.fmtstr
            mov   rax,0
            call  printf
        ret
;----------------------------------
printres:               ;print the result
```

```
section .data
      .fmtstr db "The resulting number is %lld",10,0
section .text
      mov    rdi,.fmtstr
      mov    rax,0
      call   printf
ret
```

Use the output shown in Figure 16-2 to analyze the code.

```
jo@UbuntuDesktop:~/Desktop/linux64/gcc/21 bits2$ make
nasm -f elf64 -g -F dwarf bits2.asm -l bits2.lst
gcc -g -o bits2 bits2.o
jo@UbuntuDesktop:~/Desktop/linux64/gcc/21 bits2$ ./bits2

SHL 2 = OK multiply by 4
The original number is 8
The resulting number is 32

SHL 2 = OK multiply by 4
The original number is -8
The resulting number is -32

SAL 2 = correctly multiply by 4
The original number is 8
The resulting number is 32

SAL 2 = correctly multiply by 4
The original number is -8
The resulting number is -32

SHR 2 = OK divide by 4
The original number is 8
The resulting number is 2

SHR 2 = wrong divide by 4
The original number is -8
The resulting number is 4611686018427387902

SAR 2 = correctly divide by 4
The original number is 8
The resulting number is 2

SAR 2 = correctly divide by 4
The original number is -8
The resulting number is -2
jo@UbuntuDesktop:~/Desktop/linux64/gcc/21 bits2$ █
```

Figure 16-2. *bits2.asm output*

Notice that shl and sal give the same results, also with negative numbers. But be careful; if shl would put a 1 in the leftmost bit instead of a 0, the result would become negative and wrong.

The instructions shr and sar give the same result only when the numbers are positive. The arithmetic result when using shr with negative numbers is simply wrong; that is because there is no sign extension with shr.

Conclusion: when you are doing arithmetic, use sal and sar.

Why would you need shifting when there are straightforward instructions such as multiply and divide? It turns out the shifting is much faster than the multiplying or dividing instructions. In general, bit instructions are very fast; for example, xor rax, rax is faster than mov rax,0.

Summary

In this chapter, you learned about the following:

- Assembly instructions for bit operations

- Difference between logical and arithmetic shift instructions

CHAPTER 17

Bit Manipulations

You already know that you can set or clear bits using bit operations such as and, xor, or, and not. But there are other ways to modify individual bits: bts for setting bits to 1, btr for resetting bits to 0, and bt for testing if a bit is set to 1.

Other Ways to Modify Bits

Listing 17-1 shows the example code.

Listing 17-1. bits3.asm

```
; bits3.asm
extern printb
extern printf
section .data
     msg1  db   "No bits are set:",10,0
     msg2  db   10,"Set bit #4, that is the 5th bit:",10,0
     msg3  db   10,"Set bit #7, that is the 8th bit:",10,0
     msg4  db   10,"Set bit #8, that is the 9th bit:",10,0
     msg5  db   10,"Set bit #61, that is the 62nd bit:",10,0
     msg6  db   10,"Clear bit #8, that is the 9th bit:",10,0
     msg7  db   10,"Test bit #61, and display rdi",10,0
     bitflags  dq      0
section .bss
section .text
     global main
main:
push  rbp
mov   rbp,rsp
```

© Jo Van Hoey 2019
J. Van Hoey, *Beginning x64 Assembly Programming*, https://doi.org/10.1007/978-1-4842-5076-1_17

```
        ;print title
        mov    rdi, msg1
        xor    rax,rax
        call   printf

        ;print bitflags
        mov    rdi, [bitflags]
        call   printb

;set bit 4 (=5th bit)
        ;print title
        mov    rdi, msg2
        xor    rax,rax
        call   printf

        bts    qword [bitflags],4    ; set bit 4
        ;print bitflags
        mov    rdi, [bitflags]
        call   printb

;set bit 7 (=8th bit)
        ;print title
        mov    rdi, msg3
        xor    rax,rax
        call   printf

        bts    qword [bitflags],7    ; set bit 7
        ;print bitflags
        mov    rdi, [bitflags]
        call   printb

;set bit 8 (=9th bit)
        ;print title
        mov    rdi, msg4
        xor    rax,rax
        call   printf

        bts    qword [bitflags],8    ; set bit 8
        ;print bitflags
```

```nasm
        mov    rdi, [bitflags]
        call   printb
;set bit 61 (=62nd bit)
        ;print title
        mov    rdi, msg5
        xor    rax,rax
        call   printf

        bts    qword [bitflags],61    ; set bit 61
        ;print bitflags
        mov    rdi, [bitflags]
        call   printb
;clear bit 8 (=9th bit)
        ;print title
        mov    rdi, msg6
        xor    rax, rax
        call   printf

        btr    qword [bitflags],8     ; bit reset 8
        ;print bitflags
        mov    rdi, [bitflags]
        call   printb
; test bit 61 (will set carry flag CF if 1)
        ;print title
        mov    rdi, msg7
        xor    rax, rax
        call   printf
        xor    rdi,rdi
        mov    rax,61                 ; bit 61 to be tested
        xor    rdi,rdi                ; make sure all bits are 0
        bt     [bitflags],rax         ; bit test
        setc   dil                    ; set dil (=low rdi) to 1 if CF is set
        call   printb                 ; display rdi
leave
ret
```

We again use the `printb.c` program here; make sure to adapt your `makefile` or SASM build settings accordingly.

The variable `bitflags` is the object of study here; we will be manipulating bits in this variable.

The bitflags Variable

Remember that the bit count (the index) starts at 0. This means that in a byte, which has 8 bits, the first bit is at position 0, and the last bit is at position 7. Setting bits to 1 with the instruction `bts` and resetting bits to 0 with `btr` is simple: just specify the index of the bit to be changed as the second operand.

Testing a bit is a bit more complicated. Put the index of the bit to be tested in `rax` and use the instruction `bt`. If the bit is 1, the carry flag, `CF`, will be set to 1; otherwise, `CF` will be 0. Based on the value of the flag, you can direct your program to execute certain instructions or not. In this case, we use a special instruction `setc`, a conditional set. In this case, the instruction sets `dil` to 1 if the carry flag is 1. `dil` is the lower part of `rdi`; be careful to set `rdi` to 0 before using `setc` to set `dil`. It might well be that the higher bits of `rdx` are set during the execution of a previous instruction.

The `setc` instruction is an example of `setCC`. `setCC` sets a byte in the operand if the condition in `CC` is met, where `CC` is a flag, such as `CF` (abbreviated as `c`), `ZF CF` (abbreviated as `z`), `SF CF` (abbreviated as `s`), and so on. Take a look in the Intel manuals for more details.

Figure 17-1 shows the output of the program.

```
jo@UbuntuDesktop:~/Desktop/linux64/gcc/22 bits3$ make
nasm -f elf64 -g -F dwarf bits3.asm -l bits3.lst
cc     -c -o printb.o printb.c
gcc -g -o bits3 bits3.o printb.o
jo@UbuntuDesktop:~/Desktop/linux64/gcc/22 bits3$ ./bits3
No bits are set:
 00000000 00000000 00000000 00000000 00000000 00000000 00000000 00000000

Set bit #4, that is the 5th bit:
 00000000 00000000 00000000 00000000 00000000 00000000 00000000 00010000

Set bit #7, that is the 8th bit:
 00000000 00000000 00000000 00000000 00000000 00000000 00000000 10010000

Set bit #8, that is the 9th bit:
 00000000 00000000 00000000 00000000 00000000 00000000 00000001 10010000

Set bit #61, that is the 62nd bit:
 00100000 00000000 00000000 00000000 00000000 00000000 00000001 10010000

Clear bit #8, that is the 9th bit:
 00100000 00000000 00000000 00000000 00000000 00000000 00000000 10010000

Test bit #61, and display dl
 00000000 00000000 00000000 00000000 00000000 00000000 00000000 00000001
jo@UbuntuDesktop:~/Desktop/linux64/gcc/22 bits3$ █
```

Figure 17-1. *bits3.asm output*

Summary

In this chapter, you learned about the following:

- Setting bits, resetting bits, and examining bits, with btr, bts, and bt
- The setCC instruction

151

CHAPTER 18

Macros

When you use the same set of instructions several times in a program, you can create a function and call that function every time you need to execute the instructions. However, there is a performance penalty with functions: every time you call a function, the execution jumps to the function at some place in memory and, when finished, jumps back to the calling program. Calling and returning from a function takes time.

To avoid this performance issue, you can work with macros. Similar to functions, macros are a sequence of instructions. You assign a name to the macro, and when you need to execute the macro in your code, you just specify the macro name, eventually accompanied by arguments.

Here is the difference: at assembly time, everywhere in the code where you "call" the macro, NASM substitutes the macro name with the instructions in the definition of the macro. At execution time, there is no jumping back and forth; NASM has already inserted the machine code where it is needed.

Macros are not a functionality in the Intel assembly language but a functionality provided by NASM (or another version of assembler). Macros are created using preprocessor directives, and NASM uses a macro processor to convert macros to machine language and insert the machine languages at the appropriate places in the code.

Macros will improve the execution speed of your code but also will increase the size of your code, because at assembly time the instructions in the macro will be inserted every place where you use the macro.

For more information about NASM macros, look in the NASM manual, in Chapter 4, "The NASM Preprocessor" (for NASM version 2.14.02).

© Jo Van Hoey 2019
J. Van Hoey, *Beginning x64 Assembly Programming*, https://doi.org/10.1007/978-1-4842-5076-1_18

Writing Macros

Listing 18-1 shows some examples of macros.

Listing 18-1. macro.asm

```
; macro.asm
extern printf

%define    double_it(r)    sal r, 1    ; single line macro

%macro     prntf 2    ; multiline macro with 2 arguments
     section .data
             %%arg1    db    %1,0              ; first argument
             %%fmtint  db    "%s %ld",10,0   ; formatstring
     section .text                    ; the printf arguments
             mov    rdi,%%fmtint
             mov    rsi,%%arg1
             mov    rdx,[%2]        ; second argument
             mov    rax,0          ; no floating point
             call   printf
%endmacro

section .data
     number        dq     15
section .bss
section .text
     global main
main:
push   rbp
mov    rbp,rsp
     prntf      "The number is", number
     mov        rax, [number]
     double_it(rax)
     mov        [number],rax
     prntf      "The number times 2 is", number
leave
ret
```

154

There are two kinds of macros: single-line macros and multiline macros. A single-line macro starts with %define. A multiline macro is enclosed between the keywords %macro and %endmacro. The keywords %define, %macro, and %endmacro are called *assembler preprocessor directives*.

A single-line macro is quite simple: at assembly time the instruction double_it(rax) is substituted for the machine code for sal r, 1, where r is the value in rax.

A multiline macro is somewhat more complicated; prntf is called with two arguments. You can see that in the macro definition, prntf is followed by the number 2 to indicate the number of arguments. To use the arguments inside the macro, they are indicated with %1 for the first argument, %2 for the second, and so on. Note how we can use %1 for using a string but [%2] (with brackets) for a numeric value, similar to what would be required without using a macro.

You can use variables inside macros, and it is best to precede the names with %% as in %%arg1 and in %%fmtint. If you omit %%, NASM would happily create the macro variables on the first call of prntf but would throw an assembly error at the second call of prntf, complaining that you try to redefine arg1 and fmtint. The %% tells NASM to create new instances of variables for every call of the macro. (Do the exercise: delete the %% and try to assemble.)

There is one big problem with assembler macros: they complicate debugging! Try to debug your program with GDB or a GDB-based debugger such as SASM to see the behavior.

Figure 18-1 shows the output.

```
jo@UbuntuDesktop:~/Desktop/linux64/gcc/23 macro$ make
nasm -f elf64 -g -F dwarf macro.asm -l macro.lst
gcc -o macro macro.o
jo@UbuntuDesktop:~/Desktop/linux64/gcc/23 macro$ ./macro
The number is 15
The number times 2 is 30
jo@UbuntuDesktop:~/Desktop/linux64/gcc/23 macro$ █
```

Figure 18-1. *macro.asm output*

Using objdump

Let's verify that the assembled macro code is inserted at the appropriate places in the executable every time the macro is used. To do that we will use a CLI tool called objdump. If you installed the development tools as recommended at the beginning of this book, objdump is already installed. At the CLI, type the following:

```
objdump -M intel -d macro
```

The flag -M intel will give us the code in Intel syntax, and -d macro will disassemble our macro executable. Scroll in the code toward the <main> section.

As you can see in Figure 18-2, the code for prntf is inserted in main from memory address 4004f4 to 400515 and from 40052d to 40054e. The code for double_it is at address 400522. The assembler took the liberty to change the sal instruction into shl, and that is for performance reasons. As you remember from Chapter 16 on shifting instructions, this can be done without any problem in most cases. While you are at it, change the sal instruction into sar. You will see that the assembler will not change sar into shr, avoiding problems.

The CLI tool objdump is useful to investigate code, even code that you did not write yourself. You can find a lot of information about an executable using objdump, but we will not go into detail in this book. If you want to know more, type man objdump at the CLI or search the Internet.

```
00000000004004f0 <main>:
  4004f0:    55                        push   rbp
  4004f1:    48 89 e5                  mov    rbp,rsp
  4004f4:    48 bf 46 10 60 00 00      movabs rdi,0x601046
  4004fb:    00 00 00
  4004fe:    48 be 38 10 60 00 00      movabs rsi,0x601038
  400505:    00 00 00
  400508:    48 8b 14 25 30 10 60      mov    rdx,QWORD PTR ds:0x601030
  40050f:    00
  400510:    b8 00 00 00 00            mov    eax,0x0
  400515:    e8 d6 fe ff ff            call   4003f0 <printf@plt>
  40051a:    48 8b 04 25 30 10 60      mov    rax,QWORD PTR ds:0x601030
  400521:    00
  400522:    48 d1 e0                  shl    rax,1
  400525:    48 89 04 25 30 10 60      mov    QWORD PTR ds:0x601030,rax
  40052c:    00
  40052d:    48 bf 64 10 60 00 00      movabs rdi,0x601064
  400534:    00 00 00
  400537:    48 be 4e 10 60 00 00      movabs rsi,0x60104e
  40053e:    00 00 00
  400541:    48 8b 14 25 30 10 60      mov    rdx,QWORD PTR ds:0x601030
  400548:    00
  400549:    b8 00 00 00 00            mov    eax,0x0
  40054e:    e8 9d fe ff ff            call   4003f0 <printf@plt>
  400553:    c9                        leave
  400554:    c3                        ret
  400555:    66 2e 0f 1f 84 00 00      nop    WORD PTR cs:[rax+rax*1+0x0]
  40055c:    00 00 00
  40055f:    90                        nop
```

Figure 18-2. *objdump -M intel -d macro*

Summary

In this chapter, you learned about the following:

- When to use macros and when to use functions

- Single-line macros

- Multiline macros

- Passing arguments to multiline macros

- GDB's problems with assembly macros

- `objdump`

CHAPTER 19

Console I/O

We already know how to do console output using system calls or using `printf`. In this chapter, we will again use system calls, not only for display on the screen but also for accepting input from the keyboard.

Working with I/O

We could easily borrow functions from the C library, but that would spoil the assembly fun! So, Listing 19-1 shows the example source code.

Listing 19-1. console1.asm

```
; console1.asm
section .data
    msg1        db      "Hello, World!",10,0
    msg1len     equ     $-msg1
    msg2        db      "Your turn: ",0
    msg2len     equ     $-msg2
    msg3        db      "You answered: ",0
    msg3len     equ     $-msg3
    inputlen equ     10    ;length of inputbuffer
section .bss
    input resb inputlen+1 ;provide space for ending 0
section .text
    global main
main:
push  rbp
mov   rbp,rsp
    mov   rsi, msg1       ; print first string
```

159

```
        mov    rdx, msg1len
        call   prints
        mov    rsi, msg2        ; print second string, no NL
        mov    rdx, msg2len
        call   prints
        mov    rsi, input       ; address of inputbuffer
        mov    rdx, inputlen    ; length of inputbuffer
        call   reads            ; wait for input
        mov    rsi, msg3        ; print third string
        mov    rdx, msg3len
        call   prints
        mov    rsi, input       ; print the inputbuffer
        mov    rdx, inputlen    ; length of inputbuffer
        call   prints
leave
ret
;----------------------------------------------------
prints:
push   rbp
mov    rbp, rsp
; rsi contains address of string
; rdx contains length of string
        mov    rax, 1           ; 1 = write
        mov    rdi, 1           ; 1 = stdout
        syscall
leave
ret
;----------------------------------------------------
reads:
push   rbp
mov    rbp, rsp
; rsi contains address of the inputbuffer
; rdi contains length of the inputbuffer
        mov    rax, 0           ; 0 = read
        mov    rdi, 1           ; 1 = stdin
```

```
    syscall
leave
ret
```

This is not very complicated; we provide an input buffer called input to store the characters from the input. We also specify the length of the buffer in inputlen. After displaying some welcome messages, we call the function reads, which accepts all the characters from the keyboard and returns them to the caller when the Enter key is pressed. The calling program then uses the function prints to display the characters that were entered. Figure 19-1 shows the output.

```
jo@ubuntu18:~/Desktop/Book/24 console 1$ make
nasm -f elf64 -g -F dwarf console1.asm -l console1.lst
gcc -o console1 console1.o -no-pie
jo@ubuntu18:~/Desktop/Book/24 console 1$ ./console1
Hello, World!
Your turn: Hi There!
You answered: Hi There!
jo@ubuntu18:~/Desktop/Book/24 console 1$ █
```

Figure 19-1. *console1.asm output*

There are some issues, however! We reserved 10 bytes for the input buffer. What happens if the input is longer than 10 characters? Figure 19-2 shows our result.

```
jo@ubuntu18:~/Desktop/Book/24 console 1$ ./console1
Hello, World!
Your turn: Hi there, how are you?
You answered: Hi there, jo@ubuntu18:~/Desktop/Book/24 console 1$ how are you?

Command 'how' not found, did you mean:

  command 'show' from deb mailutils-mh
  command 'show' from deb mmh
  command 'show' from deb nmh
  command 'cow' from deb fl-cow
  command 'hoz' from deb hoz
  command 'sow' from deb ruby-hoe
  command 'hot' from deb hopenpgp-tools

Try: sudo apt install <deb name>

jo@ubuntu18:~/Desktop/Book/24 console 1$ █
```

Figure 19-2. *console1.asm with too many characters*

The program accepted only ten characters and doesn't know what to do with the surplus characters, so it throws them back to the operating system. The operating system tries to figure out and interpret the characters as CLI commands but cannot find corresponding commands. Errors!

That's not nice, but it's even worse than at first glance. This way of handling input can cause a security breach, where a hacker can break out of a program and gets access to the operating system!

Dealing with Overflows

Listing 19-2 shows another version, where we count the characters and just ignore surplus characters. As an additional tweak, we only allow lowercase alphabetic characters, *a* to *z*.

Listing 19-2. console2.asm

```
; console2.asm
section .data
      msg1   db      "Hello, World!",10,0
      msg2   db      "Your turn (only a-z): ",0
      msg3   db      "You answered: ",0
      inputlen    equ    10    ;length of inputbuffer
      NL     db      0xa
section .bss
      input resb inputlen+1      ;provide space for ending 0
section .text
      global main
main:
push   rbp
mov    rbp,rsp
      mov    rdi, msg1    ; print first string
      call   prints
      mov    rdi, msg2    ; print second string, no NL
      call   prints
      mov    rdi, input      ; address of inputbuffer
      mov    rsi, inputlen    ; length of inputbuffer
```

```
        call   reads            ; wait for input
        mov    rdi, msg3        ; print third string and add the input string
        call   prints
        mov    rdi, input       ; print the inputbuffer
        call   prints
        mov    rdi,NL           ; print NL
        call   prints
leave
ret
;------------------------------------------------------------
prints:
push   rbp
mov    rbp, rsp
push   r12       ; callee saved

; Count characters
        xor    rdx, rdx     ; length in rdx
        mov    r12, rdi
.lengthloop:
        cmp    byte [r12], 0
        je     .lengthfound
        inc    rdx
        inc    r12
        jmp    .lengthloop
.lengthfound:                ; print the string, length in rdx
        cmp    rdx, 0        ; no string (0 length)
        je     .done
        mov    rsi,rdi       ; rdi contains address of string
        mov    rax, 1        ; 1 = write
        mov    rdi, 1        ; 1 = stdout
        syscall
.done:
pop r12
leave
ret
;------------------------------------------------------------
```

```
reads:
section .data
section .bss
      .inputchar        resb        1
section .text
push  rbp
mov   rbp, rsp
      push  r12             ; callee saved
      push  r13             ; callee saved
      push  r14             ; callee saved
      mov   r12, rdi    ; address of inputbuffer
      mov   r13, rsi    ; max length in r13
      xor   r14, r14    ; character counter
.readc:
      mov   rax, 0          ; read
      mov   rdi, 1          ; stdin
      lea   rsi, [.inputchar]    ; address of input
      mov   rdx, 1         ; # of characters to read
      syscall
      mov   al, [.inputchar]    ; char is NL?
      cmp   al, byte[NL]
      je    .done          ; NL end
      cmp   al, 97         ; lower than a?
      jl    .readc         ; ignore it
      cmp   al, 122        ; higher than z?
      jg    .readc         ; ignore it
      inc   r14                  ; inc counter
      cmp   r14, r13
      ja    .readc         ; buffer max reached, ignore
      mov   byte [r12], al ; safe the char in the buffer
      inc   r12            ; point to next char in buffer
      jmp   .readc
.done:
      inc   r12
      mov   byte [r12],0   ; add end 0 to inputbuffer
```

```
        pop     r14                 ; callee saved
        pop     r13                 ; callee saved
        pop     r12                 ; callee saved
leave
ret
```

We modified the prints function so that it first counts the number of characters to display; that is, it counts until it finds a 0 byte. When the length is determined, prints displays the string with a syscall.

The reads function waits for one input character and checks whether it is a new line. If it's a new line, the character reading from the keyboard stops. Register r14 holds the count of the input characters. The function checks whether the number of characters is larger than inputlen; if not, the character is added to the buffer input. If inputlen is exceeded, the character is ignored, but the reading from the keyboard continues. We require the ASCII code of the character to be 97 or higher and 122 or lower. This will guarantee that only lowercase alphabetic characters are accepted. Note that we saved and restored the callee-saved registers; we used r12 in both functions, prints and reads. In this case, not saving the callee-saved register would not be a problem, but you can imagine that if one function calls another and that one calls yet another, problems could arise.

Figure 19-3 shows the output.

```
jo@ubuntu18:~/Desktop/Book/24 console 2$ make
nasm -f elf64 -g -F dwarf console2.asm -l console2.lst
gcc -o console2 console2.o -no-pie
jo@ubuntu18:~/Desktop/Book/24 console 2$ ./console2
Hello, World!
Your turn (only a-z): 123a{bcde}fghijklmnop
You answered: abcdefghij
jo@ubuntu18:~/Desktop/Book/24 console 2$ █
```

Figure 19-3. *console2.asm*

Debugging console input with SASM is complicated because we are providing input via a syscall. SASM provides its own functionality for I/O, but we didn't want to use it because we wanted to show how assembly and machine language work without hiding the details. If you get stuck with debugging in SASM, go back to our good old friend GDB.

Summary

In this chapter, you learned about the following:

- Keyboard input using `syscall`

- Validating keyboard input

- Debugging with keyboard input, which can be complicated

CHAPTER 20

File I/O

File manipulation can be complex in software development. Different operating systems have different methods for file management, each with a list of different options. In this chapter, we will discuss file I/O for Linux systems; you will see in Chapter 43 that file I/O in Windows is entirely different.

In Linux, file management is complex and involves creating and opening a file for read-only or read/write, writing to a new file or appending to a file, and deleting files... not to mention the security settings for 'user', 'group', and 'other'. Brush up your admin skills on the Linux filesystem if necessary, and dust off your Linux system administration manual to refresh your memory. In the code, we specified only the flags for the current 'user', but you can also add flags for 'group' and 'other'. If you have no clue what we are talking about, it is time to study a bit about basic Linux file management.

Using syscalls

Files are created, opened, closed, and so on, via a `syscall`. In this chapter, we will use a lot of `syscalls`, so we are going to simplify things a bit. At the beginning of our code, we will define constants that are easier to refer to than `syscall` numbers. You can recognize the `syscall` constants in the following code because they start with NR_. Using these NR_ `syscall` constants makes the code more readable. You can find a list of `syscall` symbol names in the following file on your system:

`/usr/include/asm/unistd_64.h`

We will use the same names in our program. Note that there is also a file named `unistd_32h` for 32-bit legacy compatibility.

© Jo Van Hoey 2019
J. Van Hoey, *Beginning x64 Assembly Programming*, https://doi.org/10.1007/978-1-4842-5076-1_20

We also created symbolic constants for create flags, status flags, and access mode flags. These flags indicate if a file is to be created or appended, read-only, write-only, and so on. You can find a list and description of these flags in the file on your system.

```
/usr/include/asm-generic/fcntl.h
```

There these flags are given in octal notation (e.g., O_CREAT = 00000100). A value that starts with 0x is a hexadecimal value, and a value that starts with 0 without an x is an octal value. For readability, you can append the character q to an octal number.

When creating a file, the file permission will have to be specified. Remember in Linux, you have read, write, and execute permissions for user, group, and other. You can get an overview and find out a lot of subtleties with the following CLI command:

```
man 2 open
```

The file permissions are also given in octal notation and are familiar to a Linux system administrator. For the sake of consistency, we will borrow the symbolic names used in these files.

The example program is quite lengthy, but we will analyze it step-by-step, which can be accomplished using *conditional assembly*. This gives you a chance to analyze the program piece by piece.

File Handling

In the program, we do the following:

1. Create a file and then write data in the file.

2. Overwrite part of the content of the file.

3. Append data to the file.

4. Write data at a certain position in the file.

5. Read data from the file.

6. Read data from a certain position in the file.

7. Delete the file.

Listing 20-1 shows the code.

Listing 20-1. file.asm

```
; file.asm
section .data
; expressions used for conditional assembly
      CREATE      equ    1
      OVERWRITE   equ    1
      APPEND      equ    1
      O_WRITE     equ    1
      READ        equ    1
      O_READ      equ    1
      DELETE      equ    1

; syscall symbols
      NR_read     equ    0
      NR_write    equ    1
      NR_open     equ    2
      NR_close    equ    3
      NR_lseek    equ    8
      NR_create   equ    85
      NR_unlink   equ    87

; creation and status flags
      O_CREAT     equ    00000100q
      O_APPEND    equ    00002000q

; access mode
      O_RDONLY    equ    000000q
      O_WRONLY    equ    000001q
      O_RDWR      equ    000002q

; create mode (permissions)
      S_IRUSR     equ    00400q        ;user read permission
      S_IWUSR     equ    00200q        ;user write permission

      NL          equ    0xa
      bufferlen         equ    64
```

```
    fileName    db      "testfile.txt",0
    FD          dq      0      ; file descriptor

    text1 db    "1. Hello...to everyone!",NL,0
    len1  dq    $-text1-1         ;remove 0
    text2 db    "2. Here I am!",NL,0
    len2  dq    $-text2-1         ;remove 0
    text3 db    "3. Alife and kicking!",NL,0
    len3  dq    $-text3-1         ;remove 0
    text4 db    "Adios !!!",NL,0
  len4      dq    $-text4-1

    error_Create db "error creating file",NL,0
    error_Close  db "error closing file",NL,0
    error_Write  db "error writing to file",NL,0
    error_Open   db "error opening file",NL,0
    error_Append db "error appending to file",NL,0
    error_Delete db "error deleting file",NL,0
    error_Read   db "error reading file",NL,0
    error_Print  db "error printing string",NL,0
    error_Position db "error positioning in file",NL,0

    success_Create    db "File created and opened",NL,0
    success_Close     db "File closed",NL,NL,0
    success_Write     db "Written to file",NL,0
    success_Open      db "File opened for R/W",NL,0
    success_Append    db "File opened for appending",NL,0
    success_Delete    db "File deleted",NL,0
    success_Read      db "Reading file",NL,0
    success_Position  db "Positioned in file",NL,0

section .bss
    buffer resb bufferlen
section .text
    global main
main:
    push rbp
    mov  rbp,rsp
```

```
%IF CREATE
;CREATE AND OPEN A FILE, THEN CLOSE --------------------
; create and open file
      mov    rdi, fileName
      call   createFile
      mov    qword [FD], rax ; save descriptor

; write to file #1
      mov    rdi, qword [FD]
      mov    rsi, text1
      mov    rdx, qword [len1]
      call   writeFile

; close file
      mov    rdi, qword [FD]
      call   closeFile
%ENDIF
%IF OVERWRITE
;OPEN AND OVERWRITE A FILE, THEN CLOSE -----------------
; open file
      mov    rdi, fileName
      call   openFile
      mov    qword [FD], rax ; save file descriptor

; write to file #2 OVERWRITE!
      mov    rdi, qword [FD]
      mov    rsi, text2
      mov    rdx, qword [len2]
      call   writeFile

; close file
      mov    rdi, qword [FD]
      call   closeFile
%ENDIF
%IF APPEND
;OPEN AND APPEND TO A FILE, THEN CLOSE ----------------
; open file to append
```

```
        mov    rdi, fileName
        call   appendFile
        mov    qword [FD], rax ; save file descriptor

; write to file #3 APPEND!
        mov    rdi, qword [FD]
        mov    rsi, text3
        mov    rdx, qword [len3]
        call   writeFile

; close file
        mov    rdi, qword [FD]
        call   closeFile
%ENDIF
%IF O_WRITE
;OPEN AND OVERWRITE AT AN OFFSET IN A FILE, THEN CLOSE ----
; open file to write
        mov    rdi, fileName
        call   openFile
        mov    qword [FD], rax ; save file descriptor

; position file at offset
        mov    rdi, qword[FD]
        mov    rsi, qword[len2] ;offset at this location
        mov    rdx, 0
        call   positionFile

; write to file at offset
        mov    rdi, qword[FD]
        mov    rsi, text4
        mov    rdx, qword [len4]
        call   writeFile

; close file
        mov    rdi, qword [FD]
        call   closeFile
%ENDIF
%IF READ
```

```
;OPEN AND READ FROM A FILE, THEN CLOSE ----------------
; open file to read
      mov   rdi, fileName
      call  openFile
      mov  qword [FD], rax ; save file descriptor

; read from file
      mov   rdi, qword [FD]
      mov   rsi, buffer
      mov   rdx, bufferlen
      call  readFile
      mov   rdi,rax
      call  printString

; close file
      mov  rdi, qword [FD]
      call  closeFile
%ENDIF
%IF O_READ
;OPEN AND READ AT AN OFFSET FROM A FILE, THEN CLOSE -----
; open file to read
      mov   rdi, fileName
      call  openFile
      mov   qword [FD], rax ; save file descriptor

; position file at offset
      mov   rdi, qword[FD]
      mov   rsi, qword[len2]      ;skip the first line
      mov   rdx, 0
      call  positionFile

; read from file
      mov   rdi, qword [FD]
      mov   rsi, buffer
      mov   rdx, 10     ;number of characters to read
      call  readFile
      mov   rdi,rax
      call  printString
```

```
; close file
     mov    rdi, qword [FD]
     call   closeFile
%ENDIF
%IF DELETE
;DELETE A FILE -----------------------------------
; delete file   UNCOMMENT NEXT LINES TO USE
     mov    rdi, fileName
     call   deleteFile
%ENDIF

leave
ret

; FILE MANIPULATION FUNCTIONS-------------------
;-------------------------------------------------
global readFile
readFile:
     mov    rax, NR_read
     syscall        ; rax contains # of characters read
     cmp    rax, 0
     jl     readerror
     mov    byte [rsi+rax],0 ; add a terminating zero
     mov    rax, rsi

     mov    rdi, success_Read
     push   rax          ; caller saved
     call   printString
     pop    rax          ; caller saved
     ret
readerror:
     mov    rdi, error_Read
     call   printString
     ret
;-------------------------------------------------
global deleteFile
deleteFile:
```

```
        mov     rax, NR_unlink
        syscall
        cmp     rax, 0
        jl      deleteerror
        mov     rdi, success_Delete
        call    printString
        ret
deleteerror:
        mov     rdi, error_Delete
        call    printString
        ret
;----------------------------------------------------
global appendFile
appendFile:
        mov     rax, NR_open
        mov     rsi,  O_RDWR|O_APPEND
        syscall
        cmp     rax, 0
        jl      appenderror
        mov     rdi, success_Append
        push    rax         ; caller saved
        call    printString
        pop     rax         ; caller saved
        ret
appenderror:
        mov     rdi, error_Append
        call    printString
        ret
;---------------------------------------------------
global openFile
openFile:
        mov     rax, NR_open
        mov     rsi, O_RDWR
        syscall
        cmp     rax, 0
        jl      openerror
```

```
        mov    rdi, success_Open
        push   rax         ; caller saved
        call   printString
        pop    rax         ; caller saved
        ret
openerror:
        mov    rdi, error_Open
        call   printString
        ret
;------------------------------------------------
global writeFile
writeFile:
        mov    rax, NR_write
        syscall
        cmp    rax, 0
        jl     writeerror
        mov    rdi, success_Write
        call   printString
        ret
writeerror:
        mov    rdi, error_Write
        call   printString
        ret
;------------------------------------------------
global positionFile
positionFile:
        mov    rax, NR_lseek
        syscall
        cmp    rax, 0
        jl     positionerror
        mov    rdi, success_Position
        call   printString
        ret
```

```
positionerror:
      mov    rdi, error_Position
      call   printString
      ret
;---------------------------------------------
global closeFile
closeFile:
      mov    rax, NR_close
      syscall
      cmp    rax, 0
      jl     closeerror
      mov    rdi, success_Close
      call   printString
      ret
closeerror:
      mov    rdi, error_Close
      call   printString
      ret
;-------------------------------------------------
global createFile
createFile:
      mov    rax, NR_create
      mov    rsi, S_IRUSR |S_IWUSR
      syscall
      cmp    rax, 0                   ; file descriptor in rax
      jl     createerror
      mov    rdi, success_Create
      push   rax         ; caller saved
      call   printString
      pop    rax         ; caller saved
      ret
createerror:
      mov    rdi, error_Create
      call   printString
```

```
        ret
; PRINT FEEDBACK
;-----------------------------------------------
global printString
printString:
; Count characters
        mov     r12, rdi
        mov     rdx, 0
strLoop:
        cmp     byte [r12], 0
        je      strDone
        inc     rdx                     ;length in rdx
        inc     r12
        jmp     strLoop
strDone:
        cmp     rdx, 0                  ; no string (0 length)
        je      prtDone
        mov     rsi,rdi
        mov     rax, 1
        mov     rdi, 1
        syscall
prtDone:
        ret
```

Conditional Assembly

Because this is quite a long program, to make it easier to analyze, we use *conditional assembly*. We created different constants such as CREATE, WRITE, APPEND, and so on. If you set such a variable to 1, then certain code, enclosed by %IF 'variable' and %ENDIF, will be assembled. If that variable is set to 0, the assembler will ignore the code. The %IF and %ENDIF parts are called *assembler preprocessor directives*. Start with the variable CREATE equ 1, and set the other variables equal to 0, assemble, run, and analyze the program. Gradually work your way down. Continue with CREATE equ 1 and OVERWRITE equ 1 and set the other variables equal to 0 on the second build, and so on.

NASM gives you a considerable collection of preprocessor directives; here we use conditional assembly. To define macros, as we explained before, we also used preprocessor directives. In Chapter 4 of the NASM manual, you will find a complete description of preprocessor directives.

The File-Handling Instructions

Let's begin with creating a file. Move the file name into `rdi`, and call `createFile`. In `createFile`, put the symbolic variable `NR_create` into `rax`, and specify in `rsi` the flags for creating the file. In this case, the user gets read and write permissions and then does a `syscall`.

When for some reason the file cannot be created, `createFile` returns a negative value in `rax`, and in this case we want an error message to be displayed. If you want more detail, the negative value in `rax` indicates what kind of error occurred. If the file is created, the function returns a file descriptor in `rax`. In the calling program, we save the file descriptor to the variable FD for further file manipulations. You can see that we have to be careful to preserve the content of `rax` before calling the `printString` function. A call to `printString` will destroy the content of `rax`, so we push `rax` to the stack before calling. According to the calling conventions, `rax` is a caller-saved register.

Next in the code, some text is written to the file, and then the file is closed. Note that when you create a file, a new file will be created; if a file exists with the same name, it will be deleted.

Build and run the program with `CREATE  equ  1`; the other conditional assembly variables equal 0. Then go to the command prompt and verify that a `testfile.txt` file is created and that it has the message in it. If you want to see the content of the file in hexadecimal, which is sometimes useful, use `xxd  testfile.txt` at the CLI prompt.

Continue by gradually putting the conditional assembly variables to 1, one at the time, and check in `testfile.txt` what happens.

Note that in this case we created and used functions without a function prologue and epilogue. Figure 20-1 shows the output, with all the conditional assembly variables set to 1.

```
jo@UbuntuDesktop:~/Desktop/linux64/gcc/25 file$ make
nasm -f elf64 -g -F dwarf file.asm -l file.lst
gcc -o file file.o -no-pie
jo@UbuntuDesktop:~/Desktop/linux64/gcc/25 file$ ./file
File created and opened
Written to file
File closed

File opened for reading/(over)writing/updating
Written to file
File closed

File opened for appending
Written to file
File closed

File opened for reading/(over)writing/updating
Positioned in file
Written to file
File closed

File opened for reading/(over)writing/updating
Reading file
2. Here I am!
Adios !!!
3. Alife and kicking!
File closed

File opened for reading/(over)writing/updating
Positioned in file
Reading file
Adios !!!
File closed

File deleted
jo@UbuntuDesktop:~/Desktop/linux64/gcc/25 file$ █
```

Figure 20-1. *file.asm output*

Summary

In this chapter, you learned about the following:

- File creation, opening, closing, deleting

- Writing to a file, appending to a file, and writing to a file at a specific position

- Reading from a file

- The different parameters for file handling

CHAPTER 21

Command Line

Sometimes you want to start a program at the command line using arguments that will be used by that program. This can be useful when developing your own CLI tools. System administrators use CLI tools all the time, because as a rule, CLI tools work faster for a knowledgeable user.

Accessing Command-Line Arguments

In the example program in Listing 21-1, we show how you can access command-line arguments within your assembly program. We keep it simple; we just find the arguments and print them.

Listing 21-1. cmdline.asm

```
;cmdline.asm
extern printf
section .data
    msg    db       "The command and arguments: ",10,0
    fmt    db       "%s",10,0
section .bss
section .text
    global main
main:
push rbp
mov   rbp,rsp
    mov    r12, rdi    ; number of arguments
    mov    r13, rsi    ; address of arguments array
;print the title
```

© Jo Van Hoey 2019
J. Van Hoey, *Beginning x64 Assembly Programming*, https://doi.org/10.1007/978-1-4842-5076-1_21

```
        mov    rdi, msg
        call   printf
        mov    r14, 0
;print the command and arguments
.ploop:                    ; loop through the array and print
        mov    rdi, fmt
        mov    rsi, qword [r13+r14*8]
        call   printf
        inc    r14
        cmp    r14, r12    ; number of arguments reached?
        jl     .ploop
leave
ret
```

When executing this program, the number of arguments, including the program name itself, is stored in rdi. The register rsi contains the **address** of an array in memory, containing the **addresses** of the command-line arguments, with the first argument being the program itself. The use of rdi and rsi agrees with the calling conventions. Remember that we are working here on Linux and using the System V AMD64 ABI calling conventions; on other platforms, such as Windows, other calling conventions are used. We copy this information because rdi and rsi will be used later for printf.

The code loops through the argument array until the total number of arguments is reached. In the loop .ploop, r13 points to the array of arguments. The register r14 is used as an argument counter. In every loop, the address of the next argument is calculated and stored in rsi. The 8 in qword [r13+r14*8] refers to the length of the addresses pointed to: 8 bytes × 8 bits = 64-bit address. The register r14 is compared in every loop with r12, containing the number of arguments.

Figure 21-1 shows the output with some random arguments.

```
jo@UbuntuDesktop:~/Desktop/linux64/gcc/26 cmdline$ make
nasm -f elf64 -g -F dwarf cmdline.asm -l cmdline.lst
gcc -o cmdline cmdline.o -no-pie
jo@UbuntuDesktop:~/Desktop/linux64/gcc/26 cmdline$ ./cmdline arg1 arg2 abc 5
The command and arguments:
./cmdline
arg1
arg2
abc
5
jo@UbuntuDesktop:~/Desktop/linux64/gcc/26 cmdline$ ▌
```

Figure 21-1. *cmdln.asm output*

Debugging the Command Line

Currently, SASM cannot be used for debugging programs with command-line arguments; you will have to use GDB. The following is one way to do that:

```
gdb --args ./cmdline arg1 arg2 abc 5
break main
run
info registers rdi rsi rsp
```

You can verify with the previous instructions that rdi contains the number of arguments (including the command itself) and that rsi points to an address in high memory, even higher than the stack, as already hinted at in Chapter 8 (see Figure 8-7). Figure 21-2 shows the output of GDB.

```
(gdb) break main
Breakpoint 1 at 0x4004a0: file cmdline.asm, line 9.
(gdb) run
Starting program: /home/jo/Desktop/linux64/gcc/26 cmdline/cmdline arg1 arg2 abc 5

Breakpoint 1, main () at cmdline.asm:9
9        push rbp
(gdb) info registers rdi rsi rsp
rdi              0x5        5
rsi              0x7fffffffde58    140737488346712
rsp              0x7fffffffdd78    0x7fffffffdd78
(gdb) ▮
```

Figure 21-2. *gdb cmdline output*

In Figure 21-2 the array with the addresses of the arguments starts at 0x7fffffffde58. Let's dig down more for the actual arguments. The address of the first arguments can be found with the following:

```
x/1xg 0x7fffffffde58
```

Here we are asking for one giant word (8 bytes) in hexadecimal at address 0x7fffffffde58. Figure 21-3 shows the answer.

```
(gdb) x/1xg 0x7fffffffde58
0x7fffffffde58: 0x00007fffffffe204
(gdb) ▮
```

Figure 21-3. *GDB address of the first argument*

Now let's find out what sits at that address (Figure 21-4).

```
x/s 0x7fffffffe204
```

```
(gdb) x/s 0x7fffffffe204
0x7fffffffe204: "/home/jo/Desktop/linux64/gcc/26 cmdline/cmdline"
(gdb) █
```

Figure 21-4. *GDB, the first argument*

This is indeed our first argument, the command itself. To find the second argument, augment 0x7fffffffde58 with 8 bytes to 0x7fffffffde60, find the address of the second argument, and so on. Figure 21-5 shows the result.

```
(gdb) x/1xg 0x7fffffffde60
0x7fffffffde60: 0x00007fffffffe234
(gdb) x/s 0x7fffffffe234
0x7fffffffe234: "arg1"
(gdb) █
```

Figure 21-5. *GDB, the second argument*

This is how you can debug and verify command-line arguments.

Summary

In this chapter, you learned about the following:

- How to access command-line arguments

- How to use registers for command-line arguments

- How to debug with command-line arguments

CHAPTER 22

From C to Assembler

In the previous chapters, we used C functions from time to time for convenience, such as the standard `printf` function or the version we developed, `printb`. In this chapter, we will show how to use assembler functions in the programming language C. The value of the calling conventions will become immediately evident. In this chapter, we use the System V AMD64 ABI calling conventions, because we are working on a Linux operating system. Windows has different calling conventions. If you have worked your way through the previous chapters and example code, this chapter will be an easy one.

Writing the C Source File

Most of the assembler code should be familiar to you from previous chapters. Just the C program is new. We compute the area and circumference of a rectangle and a circle. Then we take a string and reverse it, and finally we take the sum of the elements of an array, double the elements of the array, and take the sum of the elements of the doubled array. Let's look at the different source files.

Let's start with the C source file; see Listing 22-1.

Listing 22-1. fromc.c.asm

```
// fromc.c

#include <stdio.h>
#include <string.h>

extern int rarea(int, int);
extern int rcircum(int, int);
extern double carea( double);
extern double ccircum( double);
extern void sreverse(char *, int );
```

© Jo Van Hoey 2019
J. Van Hoey, *Beginning x64 Assembly Programming*, https://doi.org/10.1007/978-1-4842-5076-1_22

```c
extern void adouble(double [], int );
extern double asum(double [], int );
int main()
{
    char rstring[64];
    int side1, side2, r_area, r_circum;
    double radius, c_area, c_circum;
    double darray[] = {70.0, 83.2, 91.5, 72.1, 55.5};
    long int len;
    double sum;

// call an assembly function with int arguments
    printf("Compute area and circumference of a rectangle\n");
    printf("Enter the length of one side : \n");
    scanf("%d", &side1 );
    printf("Enter the length of the other side : \n");
    scanf("%d", &side2 );

    r_area = rarea(side1, side2);
    r_circum = rcircum(side1, side2);

    printf("The area of the rectangle = %d\n", r_area);
    printf("The circumference of the rectangle = %d\n\n", r_circum);

// call an assembly function with double (float) argument
    printf("Compute area and circumference of a circle\n");
    printf("Enter the radius : \n");
    scanf("%lf", &radius);

    c_area = carea(radius);
    c_circum = ccircum(radius);
    printf("The area of the circle = %lf\n", c_area);
    printf("The circumference of the circle = %lf\n\n", c_circum);

// call an assembly function with string argument
    printf("Reverse a string\n");
    printf("Enter the string : \n");
    scanf("%s", rstring);
```

```
        printf("The string is = %s\n", rstring);
        sreverse(rstring,strlen(rstring));
        printf("The reversed string is = %s\n\n", rstring);
// call an assembly function with array argument
        printf("Some array manipulations\n");
        len = sizeof (darray) / sizeof (double);

        printf("The array has %lu elements\n",len);
        printf("The elements of the array are: \n");
        for (int i=0;i<len;i++){
            printf("Element %d = %lf\n",i, darray[i]);
        }

        sum = asum(darray,len);
        printf("The sum of the elements of this array = %lf\n", sum);

        adouble(darray,len);
        printf("The elements of the doubled array are: \n");
        for (int i=0;i<len;i++){
            printf("Element %d = %lf\n",i, darray[i]);
        }

        sum = asum(darray,len);
        printf("The sum of the elements of this doubled array = %lf\n", sum);
        return 0;
}
```

Writing the Assembler Code

We start with the function declarations for the assembler functions. These are external functions, and we declare the datatypes of the return values and arguments.

The program will prompt the user for most of the data to be used, except for the array, where we provide some values for convenience.

Listing 22-2 through Listing 22-7 show the assembly functions.

Listing 22-2. rect.asm

```
;rect.asm
section .data
section .bss
section .text

global rarea
rarea:
        section .text
                push   rbp
                mov    rbp, rsp
                mov    rax, rdi
                imul   rsi
                leave
                ret
global rcircum
rcircum:
        section .text
                push   rbp
                mov    rbp, rsp
                mov    rax, rdi
                add    rax, rsi
                imul   rax, 2
                leave
                ret
```

Listing 22-3. circle.asm

```
;circle.asm
section .data
        pi   dq     3.141592654

section .bss
section .text
```

```
global carea
carea:
      section .text
            push   rbp
            mov    rbp, rsp
            movsd xmm1, qword [pi]
            mulsd xmm0,xmm0         ;radius in xmm0
            mulsd xmm0, xmm1
            leave
            ret
global ccircum
ccircum:
      section .text
            push   rbp
            mov    rbp, rsp
            movsd xmm1, qword [pi]
            addsd xmm0,xmm0         ;radius in xmm0
            mulsd xmm0, xmm1
            leave
            ret
```

Listing 22-4. sreverse.asm

```
;sreverse.asm
section .data
section .bss
section .text

global sreverse
sreverse:
push   rbp
mov    rbp, rsp
pushing:

      mov rcx, rsi
      mov rbx, rdi
      mov r12, 0
```

```
    pushLoop:
            mov rax, qword [rbx+r12]
            push rax
            inc r12
            loop pushLoop
popping:
        mov rcx, rsi
        mov rbx, rdi
        mov r12, 0
        popLoop:
            pop rax
            mov byte [rbx+r12], al
            inc r12
            loop popLoop
mov rax, rdi
leave
ret
```

Listing 22-5. asum.asm

```
; asum.asm
section .data
section .bss
section .text

global asum
asum:
        section .text
;calculate the sum
                mov    rcx, rsi    ;array length
                mov    rbx, rdi    ;address of array
                mov    r12, 0
                movsd xmm0, qword [rbx+r12*8]
                dec rcx    ; one loop less, first
                           ; element already in xmm0
```

```
sloop:
        inc r12
        addsd xmm0, qword [rbx+r12*8]
        loop sloop
ret             ; return sum in xmm0
```

Listing 22-6. adouble.asm

```
; adouble.asm
section .data
section .bss
section .text
global adouble
adouble:
      section .text
;double the elements
            mov   rcx, rsi       ;array length
            mov   rbx, rdi       ;address of array
            mov   r12, 0
      aloop:
            movsd xmm0, qword [rbx+r12*8]       ;take an
            addsd xmm0,xmm0                     ; double it
            movsd qword [rbx+r12*8], xmm0       ;move it to array
            inc r12
            loop aloop
ret
```

Listing 22-7. makefile

```
fromc: fromc.c rect.o circle.o sreverse.o adouble.o asum.o
      gcc -o fromc fromc.c rect.o circle.o sreverse.o \
      adouble.o asum.o -no-pie
rect.o: rect.asm
      nasm -f elf64 -g -F dwarf rect.asm -l rect.lst
circle.o: circle.asm
      nasm -f elf64 -g -F dwarf circle.asm -l circle.lst
```

```
sreverse.o: sreverse.asm
      nasm -f elf64 -g -F dwarf sreverse.asm -l sreverse.lst
adouble.o: adouble.asm
      nasm -f elf64 -g -F dwarf adouble.asm -l adouble.lst
asum.o: asum.asm
      nasm -f elf64 -g -F dwarf asum.asm -l asum.lst
```

In the assembly code, there is nothing special; just be careful about the datatypes of the variables received from the calling C program. The assembly functions take the arguments from the calling program and store them in the registers according to the calling conventions. Results are returned to the caller in rax (integer value) or xmm0 (floating-point value). Now you can develop your own libraries of functions to use in assembler or C, and because of the calling conventions, you do not have to worry about how to pass arguments. Just be careful about using the correct datatypes.

Note how we used a backslash (\) in the makefile for splitting a long line, and we used tabs to align the instructions.

Figure 22-1 shows the output.

```
jo@ubuntu18:~/Desktop/Book/27 fromc$ ./fromc
Compute area and circumference of a rectangle
Enter the length of one side :
2
Enter the length of the other side :
3
The area of the rectangle = 6
The circumference of the rectangle = 10

Compute area and circumference of a circle
Enter the radius :
10
The area of the circle = 314.159265
The circumference of the circle = 62.831853

Reverse a string
Enter the string :
abcde
The string is = abcde
The reversed string is = edcba

Double the elements of an array
The array has 5 elements
The elements of the array are:
Element 0 = 70.000000
Element 1 = 83.200000
Element 2 = 91.500000
Element 3 = 72.100000
Element 4 = 55.500000
The sum of the elements of this array = 372.300000
The elements of the doubled array are:
Element 0 = 140.000000
Element 1 = 166.400000
Element 2 = 183.000000
Element 3 = 144.200000
Element 4 = 111.000000
The sum of this doubled array = 744.600000
jo@ubuntu18:~/Desktop/Book/27 fromc$ █
```

Figure 22-1. *fromc.c output*

Summary

In this chapter, you learned about the following:

- Calling an assembly function from within a higher language source, in this case from within C

- The value of a calling convention

CHAPTER 23

Inline Assembly

We will use the C programming language in this chapter to explain inline assembler. It is possible to write assembly instructions in your C program. Most of the time this is not advisable, because the C compilers of today are so well-designed that you need to be a very skilled assembly programmer to improve upon the performance of C code. In fact, using inline assembly makes it more difficult for a C or C++ compiler to optimize the code containing your inline assembly.

Also, the C compiler will not do any error checking on your assembly instructions; you have to find out everything yourself. Furthermore, accessing memory and registers that are in use by the C program may bring its own risks. However, in many Internet articles, C with inline assembly is used to explain low-level functionality, so knowing how to read that code can be useful.

There are two kinds of inline assembly: basic and extended.

Basic Inline

Let's start with an example of basic inline assembly. See Listing 23-1 and Listing 23-2.

Listing 23-1. inline1.c

```
// inline1.c
#include <stdio.h>

int x=11, y=12, sum, prod;
int subtract(void);
void multiply(void);
```

© Jo Van Hoey 2019
J. Van Hoey, *Beginning x64 Assembly Programming*, https://doi.org/10.1007/978-1-4842-5076-1_23

```c
int main(void)
{
        printf("The numbers are %d and %d\n",x,y);
        __asm__(
            ".intel_syntax noprefix;"
            "mov rax,x;"
            "add rax,y;"
            "mov sum,rax"
            );
        printf("The sum is %d.\n",sum);
        printf("The difference is %d.\n",subtract());
        multiply();
        printf("The product is %d.\n",prod);

}

int subtract(void)
{
        __asm__(
            ".intel_syntax noprefix;"
            "mov rax,x;"
            "sub rax,y"              // return value in rax
            );
}
void multiply(void)
{
        __asm__(
            ".intel_syntax noprefix;"
            "mov rax,x;"
            "imul rax,y;"
            "mov prod,rax"   //no return value, result in prod
            );
}
```

Listing 23-2. makefile

```
# makefile inline1.c
inline1: inline1.c
    gcc -o inline1 inline1.c -masm=intel -no-pie
```

Note the additional parameter in the makefile, in other words, -masm=intel. This parameter is necessary when using inline assembly.

The previous example shows what is called a *basic* inline assembly program. In the main program, two variables are added; then a function is called to subtract two variables, and then another function is called to multiply two variables. If you want to access the variables in a basic inline assembly program, you need to declare them as global, that is, declare them outside any function. If the variables are not global, gcc will complain that it cannot find them. But global variables are prone to errors, such as naming conflicts. Also, when you modify registers in the assembly code, you may have to save them before calling the inline assembly and restore them to the original values upon leaving the inline assembly or you risk crashing the program. Registers that are modified by inline assembly are called *clobbered* registers.

In the assembly part, which is enclosed in __asm__(...), the first statement indicates that we want to use Intel syntax, without prefixes. (Remember the discussion on Intel syntax and the AT&T syntax flavor in Chapter 3.) Then we use assembly instructions like usual, terminated by a ; or \n. The last assembly does not have to be terminated with a ; or \n. Take note of the use of the global variables. We are lucky, because clobbering the registers does not crash the program. To avoid this clobbering of the registers and the use of global variables, you need to use extended inline assembly, as shown in the next section.

Figure 23-1 shows the output.

```
jo@UbuntuDesktop:~/Desktop/linux64/gcc/28  inline 1$ make
gcc -o inline1 inline1.c -masm=intel
jo@UbuntuDesktop:~/Desktop/linux64/gcc/28  inline 1$ ./inline1
The numbers are 11 and 12
The sum is 23.
The difference is -1.
The product is 132.
jo@UbuntuDesktop:~/Desktop/linux64/gcc/28  inline 1$ █
```

Figure 23-1. *inline1.c output*

Extended Inline

Listing 23-3 and Listing 23-4 show an example of extended inline assembly.

Listing 23-3. inline2.c

```
// inline2.c

#include <stdio.h>
        int a=12;     // global variables
        int b=13;
        int bsum;

int main(void)
{
printf("The global variables are %d and %d\n",a,b);
__asm__(
        ".intel_syntax noprefix\n"
        "mov rax,a \n"
        "add rax,b \n"
        "mov bsum,rax \n"
        :::"rax"
        );

        printf("The extended inline sum of global variables is %d.\n\n", bsum);

int x=14,y=16, esum, eproduct, edif;   // local variables

printf("The local variables are %d and %d\n",x,y);
```

```
__asm__(
    ".intel_syntax noprefix;"
    "mov rax,rdx;"
    "add rax,rcx;"
    :"=a"(esum)
    :"d"(x), "c"(y)
    );
    printf("The extended inline sum is %d.\n", esum);
__asm__(
    ".intel_syntax noprefix;"
    "mov rbx,rdx;"
    "imul rbx,rcx;"
    "mov rax,rbx;"
    :"=a"(eproduct)
    :"d"(x), "c"(y)
    :"rbx"
    );
    printf("The extended inline product is %d.\n", eproduct);

__asm__(
    ".intel_syntax noprefix;"
    "mov rax,rdx;"
    "sub rax,rcx;"
    :"=a"(edif)
    :"d"(x), "c"(y)
    );
    printf("The extended inline asm difference is %d.\n", edif);

}
```

Listing 23-4. makefile

```
# makefile inline2.c
inline2: inline2.c
    gcc -o inline2 inline2.c -masm=intel -no-pie
```

The assembler instructions look different; specifically, a template is used, as shown here:

```
asm (
    assembler code
    : output operands              /* optional */
    : input operands               /* optional */
    : list of clobbered registers  /* optional */
    );
```

After the assembler code, additional and optional information is used. Take the inline product in the above code as an example (repeated here):

```
__asm__(
    ".intel_syntax noprefix;"
    "mov rbx,rdx;"
    "imul rbx,rcx;"
    "mov rax,rbx;"
    :"=a"(eproduct)
    :"d"(x), "c"(y)
    :"rbx"
    );
printf("The extended inline product is %d.\n", eproduct);
```

Each optional line starts with a colon (:), and you must respect the order of the instructions. The a, d, and c are called *register constraints*, and they map to the registers rax, rdx, and rcx, respectively. Here is how the register constraints map to the registers:

```
a -> rax, eax, ax, al
b -> rbx, ebx, bx, bl
c -> rcx, ecx, cx, cl
d -> rdx, edx, dx, dl
S -> rsi, esi, si
D -> rdi, edi, di
r -> any register
```

The :"=a"(eproduct) in the first optional line means that the output will be in rax, and rax will refer to the variable eproduct. Register rdx refers to x, and rcx refers to y, which are the input variables.

Finally, note that `rbx` is considered clobbered in the code and will be restored to its original value, because it was declared in the list of clobbered registers. In this case, leaving it clobbered does not crash the program; it is there just for illustrating the use. There is a lot more information to be found on the Internet about inline assembly, but as mentioned, you need to use inline assembly only in specific cases. Keep in mind that using inline assembly will make your C code less portable. See Figure 23-2.

```
jo@UbuntuDesktop:~/Desktop/linux64/gcc/29  inline 2$ make
gcc -o inline2 inline2.c -masm=intel
jo@UbuntuDesktop:~/Desktop/linux64/gcc/29  inline 2$ ./inline2
The global variables are 12 and 13
The extended inline asm sum of global variables is 25.

The local variables are 14 and 16
The extended inline asm sum is 30.
The extended inline product is 224.
The extended inline asm difference is -2.
jo@UbuntuDesktop:~/Desktop/linux64/gcc/29  inline 2$ █
```

Figure 23-2. *inline2.c output*

In later chapters, we will explain how to use assembly in Windows. It's good to know that inline assembly is not supported on x64 processors in Visual Studio; it is only supported on x86 processors. However, `gcc` does not have that limitation.

Summary

In this chapter, you learned about the following:

- Basic inline assembly
- Extended inline assembly

CHAPTER 24

Strings

When we think about strings, we humans normally assume that strings are a series of characters that form words or phrases that we can understand. But in assembly language, any list or array of contiguous memory places is considered a string, whether it's human-understandable or not. Assembly provides us with a number of powerful instructions for manipulating these blocks of data in an efficient way. In our examples, we will use readable characters, but keep in mind that in reality assembly does not care if the characters are readable. We will show how to move strings around, how to scan them, and how to compare strings.

As powerful as these instructions may be, we will propose even better functionality when we discuss SIMD instructions in later chapters. But let's start with the basic instructions here.

Moving Strings

Listing 24-1 shows the example code.

Listing 24-1. move_strings.asm

```
; move_strings.asm
%macro prnt 2
    mov     rax, 1      ; 1 = write
    mov     rdi, 1      ; 1 = to stdout
    mov     rsi, %1
    mov     rdx, %2
    syscall
      mov rax, 1
      mov rdi, 1
      mov rsi, NL
```

© Jo Van Hoey 2019
J. Van Hoey, *Beginning x64 Assembly Programming*, https://doi.org/10.1007/978-1-4842-5076-1_24

```
        mov rdx, 1
     syscall

%endmacro

section .data
      length        equ 95
      NL db 0xa
      string1 db "my_string of ASCII:"
      string2 db 10,"my_string of zeros:"
      string3 db 10,"my_string of ones:"
      string4 db 10,"again my_string of ASCII:"
      string5 db 10,"copy my_string to other_string:"
      string6 db 10,"reverse copy my_string to other_string:"
section .bss
      my_string   resb   length
      other_string resb length
section .text
      global main
main:
push rbp
mov  rbp, rsp
;--------------------------------------------------
;fill the string with printable ascii characters
            prnt string1,18
            mov rax,32
            mov rdi,my_string
            mov rcx, length
str_loop1: mov byte[rdi], al          ; the simple method
            inc rdi
            inc al
            loop str_loop1
            prnt my_string,length
;--------------------------------------------------
;fill the string with ascii 0's
            prnt string2,20
            mov rax,48
```

```
                mov rdi,my_string
                mov rcx, length
str_loop2: stosb                     ; no inc rdi needed anymore
                loop str_loop2
                prnt my_string,length
;----------------------------------------------------
;fill the string with ascii 1's
                prnt string3,19
                mov rax, 49
                mov rdi,my_string
                mov rcx, length
                rep stosb  ; no inc rdi and no loop needed anymore
                prnt my_string,length
;----------------------------------------------------
;fill the string again with printable ascii characters
                prnt string4,26
                mov rax,32
                mov rdi,my_string
                mov rcx, length
str_loop3:  mov byte[rdi], al          ; the simple method
                inc rdi
                inc al
                loop str_loop3
                prnt my_string,length
;----------------------------------------------------
;copy my_string to other_string
                prnt string5,32
                mov rsi,my_string          ;rsi source
                mov rdi,other_string       ;rdi destination
                mov rcx, length
                rep movsb
                prnt other_string,length
;----------------------------------------------------
;reverse copy my_string to other_string
                prnt string6,40
                mov rax, 48                    ;clear other_string
```

```
        mov rdi,other_string
        mov rcx, length
        rep stosb
        lea rsi,[my_string+length-4]
        lea rdi,[other_string+length]
        mov rcx, 27              ;copy only 27-1 characters
        std                      ;std sets DF, cld clears DF
        rep movsb
        prnt other_string,length
leave
ret
```

In this program, we use a macro (for more details on macros, see Chapter 18) to do the printing, but we could as well have used the C printf function, as we have done already so many times.

We start with creating a string with the 95 printable characters in the ASCII table, the first being 32 (the space) and the last being 126 (the tilde, or ~). There's nothing special here. We first print a title, and then we put the first ASCII code in rax, letting rdi point to the address of my_string in memory. Then we put the length of the string in rcx to use in a loop. In the loop, we copy one ASCII code from al to my_string, take the next code and write it to the next memory address in my_string, and so on. Finally, we print the string. Again, there's nothing new here.

In the next part, we modify the content of my_string to all 0s (ASCII 48). To do that, we put the string length again in rcx for building a loop. Then we use the instruction stosb to store the 1s (ASCII 49) to my_string. The instruction stosb only needs the start address of the string in rdi and the character to write in rax, and stosb steps to the next memory address in each repeat of the loop. We do not have to care about increasing rdi anymore.

In the next part of the program, we go one step further and get rid of the rcx loop. We use the instruction rep stosb for repeating the stosb a number of times. The number of repetitions is stored in rcx. This is a highly efficient method of initializing memory.

Next, we continue moving around memory content. Strictly speaking, we will be copying memory blocks, not moving copy content. First, we initialize our string again with the readable ASCII codes. We could optimize this code by using a macro or a function for that, instead of just repeating the code. Then we start the copying of the string/memory block: from my_string to other_string. The address of the source string goes into rsi, and the address of the destination string goes in rdi. This is easy to remember, because the *s* in rsi stands for source and the *d* in rdi stands for destination. Then use rep movsb, and we are done! The rep copying stops when rcx becomes 0.

In the last part of the program, we will *reverse move* memory content. The concept can be a little bit confusing; we go in some detail here. When using movsb, the content of DF (the direction flag) is taken into account. When DF=0, rsi and rdi are *increased* by 1, pointing to the next *higher* memory address. When DF=1, rsi and rdi are *decreased* by 1, pointing to the next *lower* memory address. This means that in our example with DF=1, rsi needs to point to the address of the highest memory address to be copied and decrease from there. In addition, rdi needs to point to the highest destination address and decrease from there. The intention is to "walk backward" when copying, that is, decreasing rsi and rdi with every loop. Be careful: rsi and rdi both are decreased; you cannot use the DF to increase one register and decrease another (reversing the string). In our example, we do not copy the whole string, but only the lowercase alphabet, and we put them at the higher memory places at the destination. The instruction lea rsi,[my_string+length-4] loads the effective address of my_string in rsi and skips four characters that are not part of the alphabet. The DF flag can be set to 1 with std and set to 0 with cld. Then we invoke the powerful rep movsb, and we are done.

Why do we put 27 in rcx when there are only 26 characters? It turns out that rep decreases rcx by 1 before anything else in the loop. You can verify that with a debugger such as SASM. Comment out all references to the prnt macro to avoid problems. You will see that SASM lets you step into the rep loop and verify the memory and registers. You can, of course, also look in the Intel manuals for information on rep; you will find something like the following under "Operation":

```
IF AddressSize = 16
    THEN
            Use CX for CountReg;
            Implicit Source/Dest operand for memory use of SI/DI;
    ELSE IF AddressSize = 64
            THEN Use RCX for CountReg;
            Implicit Source/Dest operand for memory use of RSI/RDI;
    ELSE
            Use ECX for CountReg;
            Implicit Source/Dest operand for memory use of ESI/EDI;
```

```
FI;
WHILE CountReg =/ 0
        DO
                Service pending interrupts (if any);
                Execute associated string instruction;
                CountReg ← (CountReg - 1);
                IF CountReg = 0
                    THEN exit WHILE loop; FI;
                IF (Repeat prefix is REPZ or REPE) and (ZF = 0)
                or (Repeat prefix is REPNZ or REPNE) and (ZF = 1)
                        THEN exit WHILE loop; FI;
        OD;
```

Here CountReg ← (CountReg - 1); tells us that the counter will be decreased first. Studying the operation of instructions can be useful for understanding the behavior of an instruction. As a final note, stosb and movsb work with bytes; there are also stosw, movsw, stosd, and movsd to work with words and double words, and rsi and rdi are accordingly incremented or decremented with 1 for bytes, 2 for words, and 4 for double words.

Figure 24-1 shows the output of our example program.

```
jo@UbuntuDesktop:~/Desktop/linux64/gcc/30 strings 1$ make
nasm -f elf64 -g -F dwarf move_strings.asm -l move_strings.lst
gcc -o move_strings move_strings.o
jo@UbuntuDesktop:~/Desktop/linux64/gcc/30 strings 1$ ./move_strings
my_string of ASCII
 !"#$%&'()*+,-./0123456789:;<=>?@ABCDEFGHIJKLMNOPQRSTUVWXYZ[\]^_`abcdefghijklmnopqrstuvwxyz{|}~

my_string of zeros:
0000000000000000000000000000000000000000000000000000000000000000000000000000000000000000000000

my_string of ones:
1111111111111111111111111111111111111111111111111111111111111111111111111111111111111111111111

again my_string of ASCII:
 !"#$%&'()*+,-./0123456789:;<=>?@ABCDEFGHIJKLMNOPQRSTUVWXYZ[\]^_`abcdefghijklmnopqrstuvwxyz{|}~

copy my_string to other_string:
 !"#$%&'()*+,-./0123456789:;<=>?@ABCDEFGHIJKLMNOPQRSTUVWXYZ[\]^_`abcdefghijklmnopqrstuvwxyz{|}~

reverse copy my_string to other_string:
00000000000000000000000000000000000000000000000000000000000000abcdefghijklmnopqrstuvwxyz
jo@UbuntuDesktop:~/Desktop/linux64/gcc/30 strings 1$ █
```

Figure 24-1. *move_strings.asm output*

Comparing and Scanning Strings

Moving and copying strings is important, but so is the ability to analyze strings. In the example code shown in Listing 24-2, we use the instruction cmpsb to compare two strings, and we use scasb to find a specific character in a string.

Listing 24-2. strings.asm

```
; strings.asm
extern printf
section .data
        string1     db "This is the 1st string.",10,0
        string2     db "This is the 2nd string.",10,0
        strlen2     equ $-string2-2
        string21    db "Comparing strings: The strings do not differ.",10,0
        string22    db "Comparing strings: The strings differ, "
                    db "starting at position: %d.",10,0
        string3     db "The quick brown fox jumps over the lazy dog.",0
        strlen3     equ $-string3-2
        string33    db "Now look at this string: %s",10,0
        string4     db "z",0
        string44    db "The character '%s' was found at position: %d.",10,0
        string45    db "The character '%s' was not found.",10,0
        string46    db "Scanning for the character '%s'.",10,0
section .bss
section .text
        global main
main:
        push    rbp
        mov     rbp,rsp
; print the 2 strings
        xor     rax,rax
        mov     rdi, string1
        call    printf
        mov     rdi, string2
        call    printf
```

```
; compare 2 strings -------------------------------------------------
      lea     rdi,[string1]
      lea     rsi,[string2]
      mov     rdx, strlen2
      call    compare1
      cmp     rax,0
      jnz     not_equal1
;strings are equal, print
      mov     rdi, string21
      call    printf
      jmp     otherversion
;strings are not equal, print
not_equal1:
      mov     rdi, string22
      mov     rsi, rax
      xor     rax,rax
      call    printf
; compare 2 strings, other verstion ------------------------------
otherversion:
      lea     rdi,[string1]
      lea     rsi,[string2]
      mov     rdx, strlen2
      call    compare2
      cmp     rax,0
      jnz     not_equal2
;strings are equal, print
      mov     rdi, string21
      call    printf
      jmp     scanning
;strings are not equal, print
not_equal2:
      mov     rdi, string22
      mov     rsi, rax
      xor     rax,rax
      call    printf
```

```
; scan for a character in a string -------------------------------
; first print the string
        mov     rdi,string33
        mov     rsi,string3
        xor     rax,rax
        call    printf
; then print the search argument, can only be 1 character
        mov     rdi,string46
        mov     rsi,string4
        xor     rax,rax
        call    printf
scanning:
        lea     rdi,[string3]     ;      string
        lea     rsi,[string4]     ;      search argument
        mov     rdx, strlen3
        call    cscan
        cmp     rax,0
        jz      char_not_found
;character found, print
        mov     rdi,string44
        mov     rsi,string4
        mov     rdx,rax
        xor     rax,rax
        call    printf
        jmp     exit
;character not found, print
char_not_found:
        mov     rdi,string45
        mov     rsi,string4
        xor     rax,rax
        call    printf
exit:
leave
ret
```

```
; FUNCTIONS ================================================================

; function compare 2 strings -----------------------------------------
compare1:     mov    rcx, rdx
              cld
cmpr:         cmpsb
              jne    notequal
              loop   cmpr
              xor    rax,rax
              ret
notequal:     mov    rax, strlen2
              dec    rcx             ;compute position
              sub    rax,rcx         ;compute position
              ret
              xor    rax,rax
              ret
;--------------------------------------------------------------------
; function compare 2 strings -----------------------------------------
compare2:     mov    rcx, rdx
              cld
              repe   cmpsb
              je     equal2
              mov    rax, strlen2
              sub    rax,rcx         ;compute position
              ret
equal2:       xor    rax,rax
              ret
;--------------------------------------------------------------------
;function scan a string for a character
cscan:        mov    rcx, rdx
              lodsb
              cld
              repne  scasb
              jne    char_notfound
              mov    rax, strlen3
```

```
            sub     rax,rcx         ;compute position
            ret
char_notfound:      xor rax,rax
            ret
```

For the comparison, we will discuss two versions. As before, we put the address of the first (source) string in rsi, the address of the second string (destination) in rdi, and the string length in rcx. Just to be sure, we clear the direction flag, DF, with cld. So, we walk forward in the strings.

The instruction cmpsb compares two bytes and sets the status flag ZF to 1 if the two compared bytes are equal or to 0 if the 2 bytes are not equal.

Using the ZF flag can be confusing. If ZF=1, this means the outcome of the instruction just executed was 0 (bytes equal). If ZF=0, this means the outcome of the instruction just executed was not 0 (bytes not equal). Thus, we have to find out whether and when ZF becomes 0. For testing ZF and continuing the execution based on the test result, we have a number of jump instructions, as shown here:

- jz: *Jump if zero* (ZF=1)

  - The equivalent je: *Jump if equal* (ZF=1) (bytes equal)

- jnz: *Jump if not zero* (ZF=0)

  - The equivalent jne: *Jump if not equal* (ZF=0) (bytes not equal)

The registers rsi and rdi are increased by cmpsb when DF is not set and decreased when DF is set. We create a loop that executes cmpsb, until ZF becomes 0. When ZF becomes 0, the execution jumps out of the loop and starts calculating the position of the differing character based on the value in rcx. However, rcx is adjusted only at the end of a loop, which was never completed, so we have to adjust rcx (decrease it with 1). The resulting position is returned to main in rax.

In the second version for comparing, we will use repe, a version of rep, meaning "repeat while equal." As before, cmpsb sets ZF according to the comparison, and ZF=1 means the bytes are equal. As soon as cmpsb sets ZF equal to 0, the repe loop is ended, and rcx can be used to compute the position where the differing character appeared. If the strings are completely the same, then rcx will be 0 and ZF will be 1. After repe, the instruction je tests if ZF equals 1. If ZF is 1, the strings are equal; if 0, the strings are not equal. We use rcx to calculate the differing position, so there's no need to adjust rcx, because repe decreases rcx first in every loop.

The scanning works similarly, but with `repne`, "repeat while not equal," instead of `repe`. We also use `lodsb` and load the byte at address `rsi` into `rax`. The instruction `scasb` compares the byte in `al` (the low byte in `rax`) with the byte pointed to by `rdi` and sets (1=equal) or resets (0=not equal) the ZF flag accordingly. The instruction `repne` looks at the status flag and continues if `ZF = 0`; that is, the 2 bytes are not equal. If the 2 bytes are equal, `scasb` sets ZF to 1, the `repne` loop stops, and `rcx` can be used to compute the position of the byte in the string.

The scanning works with only one character as a search argument; if you are wondering how to use a string as search argument, you will have to scan character by character. Or better yet, wait for the chapters on SIMD.

Figure 24-2 shows the output.

```
jo@UbuntuDesktop:~/Desktop/linux64/gcc/31 strings 2$ make
nasm -f elf64 -g -F dwarf strings.asm -l strings.lst
gcc -o strings strings.o
jo@UbuntuDesktop:~/Desktop/linux64/gcc/31 strings 2$ ./strings
This is the 1st string.
This is the 2nd string.
Comparing strings: The strings differ, starting at position: 13.
Now look at this string: The quick brown fox jumps over the lazy dog.
Scanning for the character 'z'.
The character 'z' was found at position: 38.
jo@UbuntuDesktop:~/Desktop/linux64/gcc/31 strings 2$ ▮
```

Figure 24-2. *strings.asm output*

Summary

In this chapter, you learned about the following:

- Moving and copying memory blocks in an extremely efficient way
- Using `movsb` and `rep`
- Comparing and scanning memory blocks
- Using `cmpsb`, `scasb`, `repe`, and `repne`

CHAPTER 25

Got Some ID?

Sometimes it is necessary to find out the functionality available in a processor. In your program, you can, for example, look for the presence or absence of a certain version of SSE. In the next chapter, we will use programs with SSE instructions, so we need to find out first which version of SSE is supported by our processor. There is an instruction for checking the CPU characteristics: cpuid.

Using cpuid

You first put a specific parameter in eax, then execute the instruction cpuid, and finally check the returned value in ecx and edx. Indeed, cpuid uses 32-bit registers.

The amount of information you can find out with cpuid is staggering. Go to the Intel manuals (https://software.intel.com/sites/default/files/managed/39/c5/325462-sdm-vol-1-2abcd-3abcd.pdf) and look up the cpuid instruction in Volume 2A. You will find several tables that show what is returned in ecx when you start cpuid with certain value in eax. This is only part of the information you can retrieve; another table shows the information returned in edx. Browse the Intel manual to see the possibilities.

Let's see an example of looking for SSE functionality that we will need in the next chapter. In the Intel manual, you find that you can use ecx bits 0, 19, and 20 and ecx bits 25 and 26 to find out which version of SSE is implemented in a processor.

Listing 25-1 shows the example program.

Listing 25-1. cpu.asm

```
; cpu.asm
extern printf
section .data
        fmt_no_sse db "This cpu does not support SSE",10,0
        fmt_sse42 db "This cpu supports SSE 4.2",10,0
```

© Jo Van Hoey 2019
J. Van Hoey, *Beginning x64 Assembly Programming*, https://doi.org/10.1007/978-1-4842-5076-1_25

```
        fmt_sse41 db "This cpu supports SSE 4.1",10,0
        fmt_ssse3 db "This cpu supports SSSE 3",10,0
        fmt_sse3 db "This cpu supports SSE 3",10,0
        fmt_sse2 db "This cpu supports SSE 2",10,0
        fmt_sse db "This cpu supports SSE",10,0
section .bss
section .text
    global main
main:
push rbp
mov   rbp,rsp
    call cpu_sse     ;returns 1 in rax if sse support, otherwise 0
leave
ret

cpu_sse:
    push rbp
    mov rbp,rsp
    xor r12,r12           ;flag SSE available
    mov eax,1             ;request CPU feature flags
    cpuid

;test for SSE
    test edx,2000000h             ;test bit 25 (SSE)
    jz sse2                       ;SSE available
    mov r12,1
    xor rax,rax
    mov rdi,fmt_sse
    push rcx                      ;modified by printf
    push rdx                      ;preserve result of cpuid
    call printf
    pop rdx
    pop rcx
sse2:
    test edx,4000000h             ;test bit 26 (SSE 2)
    jz sse3                       ;SSE 2 available
```

```
    mov r12,1
    xor rax,rax
    mov rdi,fmt_sse2
    push rcx                     ;modified by printf
    push rdx                     ;preserve result of cpuid
    call printf
    pop rdx
    pop rcx
sse3:
    test ecx,1                   ;test bit 0 (SSE 3)
    jz ssse3                     ;SSE 3 available
    mov r12,1
    xor rax,rax
    mov rdi,fmt_sse3
    push rcx                     ;modified by printf
    call printf
    pop rcx
ssse3:
    test ecx,9h                  ;test bit 0 (SSE 3)
    jz sse41                     ;SSE 3 available
    mov r12,1
    xor rax,rax
    mov rdi,fmt_ssse3
    push rcx                     ;modified by printf
    call printf
    pop rcx
sse41:
    test ecx,80000h              ;test bit 19 (SSE 4.1)
    jz sse42                     ;SSE 4.1 available
    mov r12,1
    xor rax,rax
    mov rdi,fmt_sse41
    push rcx                     ;modified by printf
    call printf
    pop rcx
```

```
sse42:
    test ecx,100000h              ;test bit 20 (SSE 4.2)
    jz wrapup                     ;SSE 4.2 available
    mov r12,1
    xor rax,rax
    mov rdi,fmt_sse42
    push rcx                      ;modified by printf
    call printf
    pop rcx
wrapup:
    cmp r12,1
    je sse_ok
    mov rdi,fmt_no_sse
    xor rax,rax
    call printf                   ;displays message if SSE not available
    jmp the_exit
sse_ok:
    mov rax,r12                   ;returns 1, sse supported
the_exit:
leave
ret
```

The main program calls only one function, cpu_sse, and if the return value is 1, the processor supports some version of SSE. If the return value is 0, you can forget about using SSE on that computer. In the function cpu_sse, we find out which SSE versions are supported. Put 1 in eax and execute the instruction cupid; as mentioned, the results will be returned in ecx and edx.

Using the test Instruction

The ecx and edx registers will be evaluated with a test instruction, which is a bit-wise logical and of the two operands. We could have used the cmp instruction, but test has a performance advantage. Of course, you can also use the instruction bt (see Chapter 17).

The `test` instruction sets the flags SF, ZF, and PF according to the test result. In the Intel manual, you will find the operation of the test instruction, as follows:

```
TEMP ← SRC1 AND SRC2;
SF ← MSB(TEMP);
IF TEMP = 0
    THEN ZF ← 1;
    ELSE ZF ← 0;
FI:
PF ← BitwiseXNOR(TEMP[0:7]);
CF ← 0;
OF ← 0;
(* AF is undefined *)
```

The important flag in our case is ZF. If ZF=0, then the result is nonzero; the SSE bit is 1, and the CPU supports that version of SSE. The instruction `jz` evaluates if ZF=1, and if so, the SSE version is not supported, and the execution jumps to the next part. Otherwise, the program prints a confirmation message.

In our example, after `cpuid` is executed, we test `edx`. The register `edx` has 32 bits, and we want to know if bit 25 is set, meaning that the CPU supports SSE (version 1). So, we need the second operand in the `test` instruction to have 1 in bit 25, with the other bits all 0. Remember that the lowest bit has index 0, and the highest has index 31. In binary, it looks like this:

```
0000 0010 0000 0000 0000 0000 0000 0000
```

In hexadecimal, it looks like this:

```
2000000
```

Remember, you can find plenty of binary to hexadecimal conversion tools on the Internet.

The execution "cascades" through the program, and if no SSE is supported, `r12` will remain 0. We did not use the return value, but you could check `rax`, the return value, to conclude whether any SSE is supported. Or you could modify the program to return the highest version of SSE.

Figure 25-1 shows the output.

```
jo@UbuntuDesktop:~/Desktop/linux64/gcc/32 cpu_sse$ make
nasm -f elf64 -g -F dwarf cpu_sse.asm -l cpu_sse.lst
gcc -o cpu_sse cpu_sse.o
jo@UbuntuDesktop:~/Desktop/linux64/gcc/32 cpu_sse$ ./cpu_sse
This cpu supports SSE.
This cpu supports SSE 2.
This cpu supports SSE 3.
This cpu supports SSSE 3.
This cpu supports SSE 4.1.
This cpu supports SSE 4.2.
jo@UbuntuDesktop:~/Desktop/linux64/gcc/32 cpu_sse$ █
```

Figure 25-1. *cpu_sse.asm output*

You could build a similar function to find out other CPU information and, depending on the returned result, choose to use certain functionality on this CPU and other functionality on another CPU.

In a later chapter, when we discuss AVX, we will again have to find out whether the CPU supports AVX.

Summary

In this chapter, you learned about the following:

- How to find out what functionality is supported by the CPU with `cpuid`

- How to use bits with the `test` instruction

CHAPTER 26

SIMD

SIMD is the abbreviation for **S**ingle **I**nstruction Stream, **M**ultiple **D**ata. SIMD is a term proposed by Michael J. Flynn and refers to the functionality that allows you to execute one instruction on multiple data "streams." SIMD can *potentially* improve the performance of your programs. SIMD is a form of parallel computing; however, in some cases, the execution on the different data streams can happen sequentially, depending on the hardware functionality and the instructions to be executed. You can find more about the Flynn taxonomy here:

```
https://ieeexplore.ieee.org/document/5009071/
```

and here:

```
https://en.wikipedia.org/wiki/Flynn%27s_taxonomy
```

The first implementation of SIMD was MMX, and nobody seems to know the exact meaning of MMX. It could mean Multi Media Extension or Multiple Math Extension or Matrix Math Extension. Anyway, MMX was superseded by Streaming SIMD Extension (SSE). Later SSE was extended by Advanced Vector Extension (AVX). Here we will give an introduction on SSE as a base to start, and in a later chapter we will give an introduction on AVX.

Scalar Data and Packed Data

A processor that supports SSE functionality has 16 additional 128-bit registers (xmm0 to xmm15) and a control register, mxcsr. We already used the xmm registers to do floating-point calculations, but we can do more with these advanced registers. The xmm registers can contain **scalar data** or **packed data**.

© Jo Van Hoey 2019
J. Van Hoey, *Beginning x64 Assembly Programming*, https://doi.org/10.1007/978-1-4842-5076-1_26

With scalar data, we mean just one value. When we put 3.141592654 in xmm0, then xmm0 contains a scalar value. We can also store multiple values in xmm0; these values are referred to as *packed data*. Here are the possibilities of storing values in an xmm register:

- Two 64-bit double-precision floating-point numbers

- Four 32-bit single-precision floating-point numbers

- Two 64-bit integers (quadwords)

- Four 32-bit integers (double words)

- Eight 16-bit short integers (words)

- Sixteen 8-bit bytes or characters

Schematically, it looks like Figure 26-1.

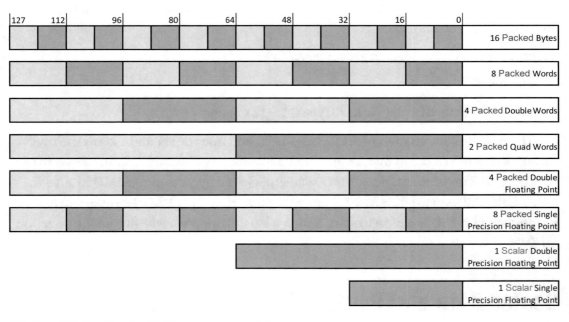

Figure 26-1. *Content of an xmm register*

There are distinct assembly instructions for scalar numbers and packed numbers. In the Intel manuals, you can see that there are a huge number of SSE instructions available. We will just use a couple of examples in this and the following chapters as an introduction to get you going.

In later chapters, we will use AVX functionality. AVX registers are double the size of xmm. The AVX registers are called **ymm** registers and have 256 bits. There is also AVX-512, which provides for AVX-512 registers that have 512 bits and are called **zmm** registers.

Because of the potential for parallel computing, SIMD can be used to speed up computations in a wide area of applications such as image processing, audio processing, signal processing, vector and matrix manipulations, and so on. In later chapters, we will use SIMD for doing matrix manipulations, but don't worry; we will limit the mathematics to basic matrix operations. The purpose is to learn SIMD, not linear algebra.

Unaligned and Aligned Data

Data in memory can be unaligned or aligned on certain addresses that are multiples of 16, 32, and so on. Aligning data in memory can drastically improve the performance of a program. Here is the reason why: aligned packed SSE instructions want to fetch memory chunks of 16 bytes at the time; see the left side of Figure 26-2. When data in memory is not aligned, the CPU has to do more than one fetch to get the needed 16-byte data, and that slows down the execution. We have two types of SSE instructions: aligned packed instructions and unaligned packed instructions. Unaligned packed instructions can deal with unaligned memory, but in general there is a performance disadvantage.

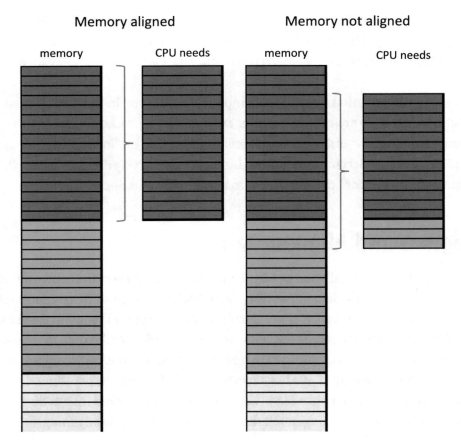

Figure 26-2. *Data alignment*

When using SSE, alignment means that data in section .data and in section .bss should be aligned on a 16-byte border. In NASM you can use the assembly directives align 16 and alignb 16 in front of the data to be aligned. In the upcoming chapters, you will see examples of this. For AVX, data should be aligned on a 32-byte border, and for AVX-512, data needs to be aligned on a 64-bit border.

Summary

In this chapter, you learned the following:

- SSE provides you with 16 additional 128-bit registers.

- You know the difference between scalar data and packed data.

- You know the importance of data alignment.

CHAPTER 27

Watch Your MXCSR

Before diving into SSE programming, you need to understand the SSE control and status register for floating-point operations, called mxcsr. It is a 32-bit register, of which only the lower 16 bits are used. Here is the layout:

Bit	Mnemonic	Meaning
0	IE	Invalid operation error
1	DE	Denormal error
2	ZE	Divide-by-zero error
3	OE	Overflow error
4	UE	Underflow error
5	PE	Precision error
6	DAZ	Denormals are zeros
7	IM	Invalid operation mask
8	DM	Denormal operation mask
9	ZM	Divide-by-zero mask
10	OM	Overflow mask
11	UM	Underflow mask
12	PM	Precision mask
13	RC	Rounding control
14	RC	Rounding control
15	FZ	Flush to zero

© Jo Van Hoey 2019
J. Van Hoey, *Beginning x64 Assembly Programming*, https://doi.org/10.1007/978-1-4842-5076-1_27

Bits 0 to 5 indicate when a floating-point exception has been detected, such as a divide by zero, or when because of a floating-point operation, a value loses some precision. Bits 7 to 12 are masks, controlling the behavior when a floating-point operation sets a flag in bits 0 to 5. If, for example, a divide-by-zero happens, normally a program would throw an error and possibly crash. When you set the divide-by-zero mask flag to 1, the program will not crash, and you can execute a certain instruction to mitigate the crash. The masks are by default set to 1 so that no SIMD floating-point exceptions will be raised. Two bits (bits 13 and 14) control the rounding, as shown here:

Bits	Meaning
00	Round to nearest
01	Round down
10	Round up
11	Truncate

We will not discuss all the status and mask details of the mxcsr register; refer to the Intel manuals for all details.

Manipulating the mxcsr Bits

The bits in the mxcsr register can be manipulated with the ldmxcsr and stmxcsr instructions. The default mxcsr state is 00001F80, or 0001 1111 1000 0000. All the mask bits are set, and rounding is set to nearest.

Listing 27-1 through Listing 27-4 show an example of what can be done with mxcsr.

Listing 27-1. mxcsr.asm

```
; mxcsr.asm
extern printf
extern print_mxcsr
extern print_hex
section .data
        eleven      dq      11.0
        two         dq      2.0
```

```
        three       dq    3.0
        ten         dq    10.0
        zero        dq    0.0
        hex         db    "0x",0
        fmt1        db    10,"Divide, default mxcsr:",10,0
        fmt2        db    10,"Divide by zero, default mxcsr:",10,0
        fmt4        db    10,"Divide, round up:",10,0
        fmt5        db    10,"Divide, round down:",10,0
        fmt6        db    10,"Divide, truncate:",10,0

        f_div       db    "%.1f divided by %.1f is %.16f, in hex: ",0
        f_before    db    10,"mxcsr before:",9,0
        f_after     db    "mxcsr after:",9,0
;mxcsr values
        default_mxcsr     dd 0001111110000000b
        round_nearest     dd 0001111110000000b
        round_down        dd 0011111110000000b
        round_up          dd 0101111110000000b
        truncate          dd 0111111110000000b

section .bss
        mxcsr_before    resd  1
        mxcsr_after     resd  1
        xmm             resq  1
section .text
        global main
main:
push rbp
mov  rbp,rsp

;division
;default mxcsr
        mov    rdi,fmt1
        mov    rsi,ten
        mov    rdx,two
```

```
        mov     ecx, [default_mxcsr]
        call    apply_mxcsr
;-----------------------------------------------
;division with precision error
;default mxcsr
        mov     rdi,fmt1
        mov     rsi,ten
        mov     rdx,three
        mov     ecx, [default_mxcsr]
        call    apply_mxcsr
;divide by zero
;default mxcsr
        mov     rdi,fmt2
        mov     rsi,ten
        mov     rdx,zero
        mov     ecx, [default_mxcsr]
        call    apply_mxcsr
;division with precision error
;round up
        mov     rdi,fmt4
        mov     rsi,ten
        mov     rdx,three
        mov     ecx, [round_up]
        call    apply_mxcsr
;division with precision error
;round up
        mov     rdi,fmt5
        mov     rsi,ten
        mov     rdx,three
        mov     ecx, [round_down]
        call    apply_mxcsr
;division with precision error
;truncate
        mov     rdi,fmt6
        mov     rsi,ten
        mov     rdx,three
```

```
      mov    ecx, [truncate]
      call   apply_mxcsr
;----------------------------------------------
;division with precision error
;default mxcsr
      mov    rdi,fmt1
      mov    rsi,eleven
      mov    rdx,three
      mov    ecx, [default_mxcsr]
      call   apply_mxcsr;division with precision error
;round up
      mov    rdi,fmt4
      mov    rsi,eleven
      mov    rdx,three
      mov    ecx, [round_up]
      call   apply_mxcsr
;division with precision error
;round up
      mov    rdi,fmt5
      mov    rsi,eleven
      mov    rdx,three
      mov    ecx, [round_down]
      call   apply_mxcsr
;division with precision error
;truncate
      mov    rdi,fmt6
      mov    rsi,eleven
      mov    rdx,three
      mov    ecx, [truncate]
      call   apply_mxcsr
leave
ret

;function ------------------------------------------
apply_mxcsr:
push  rbp
```

```
mov    rbp,rsp
       push rsi
       push rdx
       push rcx
       push rbp                ; one more for stack alignment
       call printf
       pop   rbp
       pop   rcx
       pop   rdx
       pop   rsi

       mov          [mxcsr_before],ecx
       ldmxcsr      [mxcsr_before]
       movsd        xmm2, [rsi] ; double precision float into xmm2
       divsd        xmm2, [rdx]    ; divide xmm2
       stmxcsr      [mxcsr_after]  ; save mxcsr to memory
       movsd        [xmm],xmm2     ; for use in print_xmm
       mov          rdi,f_div
       movsd        xmm0, [rsi]
       movsd        xmm1, [rdx]
       call         printf
       call         print_xmm
;print mxcsr
       mov          rdi,f_before
       call         printf
       mov          rdi, [mxcsr_before]
       call         print_mxcsr
       mov          rdi,f_after
       call         printf
       mov          rdi, [mxcsr_after]
       call         print_mxcsr
leave
ret
;function ----------------------------------------------
print_xmm:
push rbp
```

```
mov   rbp,rsp
      mov   rdi, hex     ;print 0x
      call  printf
      mov   rcx,8
.loop:
      xor   rdi,rdi
      mov   dil,[xmm+rcx-1]
      push  rcx
      call  print_hex
      pop   rcx
      loop  .loop
leave
ret
```

Listing 27-2. print_hex.c

```
// print_hex.c

#include <stdio.h>

void print_hex(unsigned char n){
        if (n < 16) printf("0");
        printf("%x",n);
}
```

Listing 27-3. print_mxcsr.c

```
// print_mxcsr.c

#include <stdio.h>

void print_mxcsr(long long n){
    long long s,c;
    for (c = 15; c >= 0; c--)
    {
        s = n >> c;
        // space after every 8th bit
        if ((c+1) % 4 == 0) printf(" ");
```

```
        if (s & 1)
                printf("1");
        else
                printf("0");
    }
    printf("\n");
}
```

Listing 27-4. makefile

```
mxcsr: mxcsr.o print_mxcsr.o print_hex.o
    gcc -o mxcsr mxcsr.o print_mxcsr.o print_hex.o -no-pie
mxcsr.o: mxcsr.asm
    nasm -f elf64 -g -F dwarf mxcsr.asm -l mxcsr.lst
print_mxcsr: print_mxcsr.c
    gcc -c print_mxcsr.c
print_hex: print_hex.c
    gcc -c print_hex.c
```

In this program, we show different rounding modes and a masked zero division. The default rounding is rounding to nearest. For example, in decimal, computing a positive number ending with a .5 or higher would be rounded to the higher number, and a negative number ending with a .5 or higher would be rounded to the lower (more negative) number. However, here we are rounding in hexadecimal, not decimal, and that does not always give the same result as rounding in decimal!

Figure 27-1 shows the output.

```
jo@UbuntuDesktop:~/Desktop/linux64/gcc/34   mxcsr$ ./mxcsr

Divide, default mxcsr:
10.0 divided by 2.0 is 5.0000000000000000, in hex: 0x4014000000000000
mxcsr before:     0001 1111 1000 0000
mxcsr after:      0001 1111 1000 0000

Divide, default mxcsr:
10.0 divided by 3.0 is 3.3333333333333335, in hex: 0x400aaaaaaaaaaaab
mxcsr before:     0001 1111 1000 0000
mxcsr after:      0001 1111 1010 0000

Divide by zero, default mxcsr:
10.0 divided by 0.0 is inf, in hex: 0x7ff0000000000000
mxcsr before:     0001 1111 1000 0000
mxcsr after:      0001 1111 1000 0100

Divide, round up:
10.0 divided by 3.0 is 3.3333333333333335, in hex: 0x400aaaaaaaaaaaab
mxcsr before:     0101 1111 1000 0000
mxcsr after:      0101 1111 1010 0000

Divide, round down:
10.0 divided by 3.0 is 3.3333333333333330, in hex: 0x400aaaaaaaaaaaaa
mxcsr before:     0011 1111 1000 0000
mxcsr after:      0011 1111 1010 0000

Divide, truncate:
10.0 divided by 3.0 is 3.3333333333333330, in hex: 0x400aaaaaaaaaaaaa
mxcsr before:     0111 1111 1000 0000
mxcsr after:      0111 1111 1010 0000

Divide, default mxcsr:
11.0 divided by 3.0 is 3.6666666666666665, in hex: 0x400d555555555555
mxcsr before:     0001 1111 1000 0000
mxcsr after:      0001 1111 1010 0000

Divide, round up:
11.0 divided by 3.0 is 3.6666666666666670, in hex: 0x400d555555555556
mxcsr before:     0101 1111 1000 0000
mxcsr after:      0101 1111 1010 0000

Divide, round down:
11.0 divided by 3.0 is 3.6666666666666665, in hex: 0x400d555555555555
mxcsr before:     0011 1111 1000 0000
mxcsr after:      0011 1111 1010 0000

Divide, truncate:
11.0 divided by 3.0 is 3.6666666666666665, in hex: 0x400d555555555555
mxcsr before:     0111 1111 1000 0000
mxcsr after:      0111 1111 1010 0000
jo@UbuntuDesktop:~/Desktop/linux64/gcc/34   mxcsr$ ▮
```

Figure 27-1. *mxcsr.asm output*

Analyzing the Program

Let's analyze the program. We have a number of divisions where we apply rounding. The divisions are done in the function apply_mxcsr. Before calling this function, we put the address of the print title in rdi, the dividend in rdi, and the divisor in rdx. Then we copy the desired mxcsr value from memory to ecx; for the first call, it's the default mxcsr value. Then we call apply_mxcsr. In this function, we print the title, without forgetting to first preserve the necessary registers and align the stack. We then store the value in ecx to mxcsr_before and load mxcsr with the value stored in mxcsr_before with the instruction ldmxcsr. The instruction ldmxcsr takes a 32-bit memory variable (double word) as the operand. The instruction divsd takes an xmm register as a first argument and an xmm register or 64-bit variable as a second operand. After the division is done, the content of the mxcsr register is stored in memory in the variable mxcsr_after with the instruction stmxcsr. We copy the quotient in xmm2 to memory in the variable xmm in order to print it.

We first print the quotient in decimal and then want to print it in hexadecimal on the same line. We cannot print a hexadecimal value with printf from within assembly (at least not in the version in use here); we have to create a function for doing that. So, we created the function print_xmm. This function takes the memory variable xmm and loads bytes into dil one by one in a loop. In the same loop, the custom-built C function print_hex is called for every byte. By using the decreasing loop counter rcx in the address, we also take care of little-endianness: the floating-point value is stored in memory in little-endian format!

Finally, mxcsr_before and mxcsr_after are displayed so that we can compare them. The function print_mxcsr is used to print the bits in mxcsr and is similar to the bit printing functions we used in previous chapters.

Some readers may find this complex; just step through the program with a debugger and observe the memory and registers.

Let's analyze the output: you can see that mxcsr does not change when we divide 10 by 2. When we divide 10 by 3, we have 3.333. Here mxcsr signals a precision error in bit 5. The default rounding, rounding to nearest, increases the last hexadecimal from a to b. In decimal, the rounding would be a rounding down; however, in hexadecimal, an a, which is higher than 8, will be rounded up to b.

We continue with a zero division: mxcsr signals a zero division in bit 2, but the program does not crash because the zero-division mask ZE is set. The result is inf or 0x7ff0000000000000.

The next division and round-up has the same result as rounding to nearest. The next two divisions with round-down and truncate result in a number with a last hexadecimal digit of a.

To show the difference in rounding, we do the same exercise with 11 divided by 3. This division results in a quotient with a low final hexadecimal digit. You can compare the rounding behavior.

As an exercise, clear the zero-division mask bit and rerun the program. You will see that the program will crash. The zero-division mask and the other masks allow you to catch errors and jump to some error procedure.

Summary

In this chapter, you learned about the following:

- The layout and purpose of the `mxcsr` register

- How to manipulate the `mxcsr` register

- How to round subtleties

CHAPTER 28

SSE Alignment

It's time to start the real SSE work! Although we have had a number of chapters on SSE, we only scratched the surface of the subject. There are hundreds of SIMD instructions (MMX, SSE, AVX), and investigating them in-depth would require another book or even a series of books. In this chapter, we will give a number of examples so that you know where to start. The purpose of these examples is to enable you to find your way in the multitude of SIMD instructions in the Intel manuals. In this chapter, we will discuss alignment, which we already covered briefly in Chapter 26.

Unaligned Example

Listing 28-1 shows how to add vectors using data that is unaligned in memory.

Listing 28-1. sse_unaligned.asm

```
; sse_unaligned.asm
extern printf
section .data
;single precision
    spvector1   dd      1.1
                dd      2.2
                dd      3.3
                dd      4.4
    spvector2   dd      1.1
                dd      2.2
                dd      3.3
                dd      4.4
```

© Jo Van Hoey 2019
J. Van Hoey, *Beginning x64 Assembly Programming*, https://doi.org/10.1007/978-1-4842-5076-1_28

```
;double precision
      dpvector1   dq    1.1
                  dq    2.2
      dpvector2   dq    3.3
                  dq    4.4

      fmt1 db "Single Precision Vector 1: %f, %f, %f, %f",10,0
      fmt2 db "Single Precision Vector 2: %f, %f, %f, %f",10,0
      fmt3 db "Sum of Single Precision Vector 1 and Vector 2:"
           db " %f, %f, %f, %f",10,0
      fmt4 db "Double Precision Vector 1: %f, %f",10,0
      fmt5 db "Double Precision Vector 2: %f, %f",10,0
      fmt6 db "Sum of Double Precision Vector 1 and Vector 2:"
           db " %f, %f",10,0

section .bss
      spvector_res resd 4
      dpvector_res resq 4
section .text
      global main
main:
push  rbp
mov   rbp,rsp

; add 2 single precision floating point vectors
      mov    rsi,spvector1
      mov    rdi,fmt1
      call   printspfp

      mov    rsi,spvector2
      mov    rdi,fmt2
      call   printspfp

      movups     xmm0, [spvector1]
      movups     xmm1, [spvector2]
      addps      xmm0,xmm1
      movups     [spvector_res], xmm0
      mov        rsi,spvector_res
```

```
        mov         rdi,fmt3
        call        printspfp

; add 2 double precision floating point vectors
        mov     rsi,dpvector1
        mov     rdi,fmt4
        call    printdpfp

        mov     rsi,dpvector2
        mov     rdi,fmt5
        call    printdpfp

        movupd      xmm0, [dpvector1]
        movupd      xmm1, [dpvector2]
        addpd       xmm0,xmm1
        movupd      [dpvector_res], xmm0
        mov         rsi,dpvector_res
        mov         rdi,fmt6
        call        printdpfp
leave
ret

printspfp:
push    rbp
mov     rbp,rsp
        movss       xmm0, [rsi]
        cvtss2sd    xmm0,xmm0
        movss       xmm1, [rsi+4]
        cvtss2sd    xmm1,xmm1
        movss       xmm2, [rsi+8]
        cvtss2sd    xmm2,xmm2
        movss       xmm3, [rsi+12]
        cvtss2sd    xmm3,xmm3
        mov         rax,4; four floats
        call        printf
leave
ret
```

```
printdpfp:
push    rbp
mov     rbp,rsp
        movsd       xmm0, [rsi]
        movsd       xmm1, [rsi+8]
        mov         rax,2; four floats
        call        printf
leave
ret
```

The first SSE instruction is movups (which means "move unaligned packed single precision"), which copies data from memory into xmm0 and xmm1. As a result, xmm0 contains one vector with four single-precision values, and xmm1 contains one vector with four single-precision values. Then we use addps (which means "add packed single precision") to add the two vectors; the resultant vector goes into xmm0 and is then transferred to memory. Then we print the result with the function printspfp. In the printspfp function, we copy every value from memory into xmm registers using movss (which means "move scalar single precision"). Because printf expects double-precision floating-point arguments, we convert the single-precision floating-point numbers to double precision with the instruction cvtss2sd (which means "convert scalar single to scalar double").

Next, we add two double-precision values. The process is similar to adding single-precision numbers, but we use movupd and addpd for double precision. The printdpfp function for printing double-precision is a bit simpler. We have only a two-element vector, and because we are already using double precision, we do not have to convert the vectors.

Figure 28-1 shows the output.

```
jo@UbuntuDesktop:~/Desktop/linux64/gcc/33 sse_unaligned$ make
nasm -f elf64 -g -F dwarf sse_unaligned.asm -l sse_unaligned.lst
gcc -o sse_unaligned sse_unaligned.o
jo@UbuntuDesktop:~/Desktop/linux64/gcc/33 sse_unaligned$ ./sse_unaligned
Single Precision Vector 1: 1.100000, 2.200000, 3.300000, 4.400000
Single Precision Vector 2: 1.100000, 2.200000, 3.300000, 4.400000
Sum of Single Precision Vector 1 and Vector 2: 2.200000, 4.400000, 6.600000, 8.800000
Double Precision Vector 1: 1.100000, 2.200000
Double Precision Vector 2: 3.300000, 4.400000
Sum of Double Precision Vector 1 and Vector 2: 4.400000, 6.600000
jo@UbuntuDesktop:~/Desktop/linux64/gcc/33 sse_unaligned$ ▇
```

Figure 28-1. *sse_unaligned.asm output*

Aligned Example

Listing 28-2 shows how to add two vectors.

Listing 28-2. sse_aligned.asm

```
; sse_aligned.asm
extern printf
section .data
        dummy     db        13
align 16
        spvector1 dd        1.1
                  dd        2.2
                  dd        3.3
                  dd        4.4
        spvector2 dd        1.1
                  dd        2.2
                  dd        3.3
                  dd        4.4

        dpvector1 dq        1.1
                  dq        2.2
        dpvector2 dq        3.3
                  dq        4.4

        fmt1 db "Single Precision Vector 1: %f, %f, %f, %f",10,0
        fmt2 db "Single Precision Vector 2: %f, %f, %f, %f",10,0
        fmt3 db "Sum of Single Precision Vector 1 and Vector 2:"
             db " %f, %f, %f, %f",10,0
```

```
      fmt4 db "Double Precision Vector 1: %f, %f",10,0
      fmt5 db "Double Precision Vector 2: %f, %f",10,0
      fmt6 db "Sum of Double Precision Vector 1 and Vector 2:"
           db " %f, %f",10,0

section .bss
alignb 16
        spvector_res resd 4
        dpvector_res resq 4
section .text
      global main
main:
push   rbp
mov    rbp,rsp

; add 2 single precision floating point vectors
      mov    rsi,spvector1
      mov    rdi,fmt1
      call   printspfp

      mov    rsi,spvector2
      mov    rdi,fmt2
      call   printspfp

      movaps      xmm0, [spvector1]
      addps       xmm0, [spvector2]

      movaps      [spvector_res], xmm0
      mov         rsi,spvector_res
      mov         rdi,fmt3
      call        printspfp

; add 2 double precision floating point vectors
      mov         rsi,dpvector1
      mov         rdi,fmt4
      call        printdpfp

      mov         rsi,dpvector2
      mov         rdi,fmt5
      call        printdpfp
```

```
        movapd      xmm0, [dpvector1]
        addpd       xmm0, [dpvector2]

        movapd      [dpvector_res], xmm0
        mov         rsi,dpvector_res
        mov         rdi,fmt6
        call        printdpfp
; exit
mov     rsp,rbp
pop     rbp         ; undo the push at the beginning
ret

printspfp:
push    rbp
mov     rbp,rsp
        movss       xmm0, [rsi]
        cvtss2sd    xmm0,xmm0   ;printf expects double precision argument
        movss       xmm1, [rsi+4]
        cvtss2sd    xmm1,xmm1
        movss       xmm2, [rsi+8]
        cvtss2sd    xmm2,xmm2
        movss       xmm3, [rsi+12]
        cvtss2sd    xmm3,xmm3
        mov         rax,4; four floats
        call printf
leave
ret

printdpfp:
push    rbp
mov     rbp,rsp
        movsd       xmm0, [rsi]
        movsd       xmm1, [rsi+8]
        mov         rax,2; two floats
        call printf
leave
ret
```

Here we create a dummy variable to make sure the memory is not 16-byte aligned. Then we use the NASM assembler directive align 16 in section .data and the directive alignb 16 in section .bss. You need to add these assembler directives before each data block that needs to be aligned.

The SSE instructions are slightly different from the unaligned version. We use movaps (which means "move aligned packed single precision") to copy data from memory into xmm0. Then we can immediately add the packed numbers from memory to the values in xmm0. This is different from the unaligned version, where we had to put the two values in an xmm register first. If we add the dummy variable to the unaligned example and try to use movaps instead of movups with a memory variable as a second operand, we risk having a runtime segmentation fault. Try it!

The register xmm0 contains the resulting sum vector with four single-precision values. Then we print the result with the function printspfp. In the printspfp function, we call every value from memory and put them into xmm registers. Because printf expects double-precision floating-point arguments, we convert the single-precision floating-point numbers to double precision with the instruction cvtss2sd ("convert scalar single to scalar double").

Next, we use double-precision values. The process is similar to using single precision, but we use movapd and addpd for double-precision values.

Figure 28-2 shows the output for the aligned example.

```
jo@UbuntuDesktop:~/Desktop/linux64/gcc/34 sse_aligned$ make
nasm -f elf64 -g -F dwarf sse_aligned.asm -l sse_aligned.lst
gcc -o sse_aligned sse_aligned.o
jo@UbuntuDesktop:~/Desktop/linux64/gcc/34 sse_aligned$ ./sse_aligned
Single Precision Vector 1: 1.100000, 2.200000, 3.300000, 4.400000
Single Precision Vector 2: 1.100000, 2.200000, 3.300000, 4.400000
Sum of Single Precision Vector 1 and Vector 2: 2.200000, 4.400000, 6.600000, 8.800000
Double Precision Vector 1: 1.100000, 2.200000
Double Precision Vector 2: 3.300000, 4.400000
Sum of Double Precision Vector 1 and Vector 2: 4.400000, 6.600000
jo@UbuntuDesktop:~/Desktop/linux64/gcc/34 sse_aligned$ ▊
```

Figure 28-2. *sse_aligned.asm output*

Figure 28-3 shows the unaligned example, with the dummy variable added as the second operand of movaps.

```
jo@UbuntuDesktop:~/Desktop/linux64/gcc/34 sse_unaligned$ make
nasm -f elf64 -g -F dwarf sse_unaligned.asm -l sse_unaligned.lst
gcc -o sse_unaligned sse_unaligned.o -no-pie
jo@UbuntuDesktop:~/Desktop/linux64/gcc/34 sse_unaligned$ ./sse_unaligned
Single Precision Vector 1: 1.100000, 2.200000, 3.300000, 4.400000
Single Precision Vector 2: 1.100000, 2.200000, 3.300000, 4.400000
Segmentation fault (core dumped)
jo@UbuntuDesktop:~/Desktop/linux64/gcc/34 sse_unaligned$ ▮
```

Figure 28-3. *sse_unaligned.asm segmentation fault*

Summary

In this chapter, you learned about the following:

- Scalar data and packed data

- Aligned and unaligned data

- How to align data

- Data movement and arithmetic instructions on packed data

- How to convert between single-precision and double-precision data

CHAPTER 29

SSE Packed Integers

In the previous chapter, we used floating-point values and instructions. SSE also provides a long list of instructions for manipulating integers, and just as in the previous chapter, we are going to show a couple of instructions to get you going.

SSE Instructions for Integers

Listing 29-1 shows an example program.

Listing 29-1. sse_integer.asm

```
; sse_integer.asm
extern printf

section .data

        dummy     db      13
align 16
        pdivector1 dd     1
                   dd     2
                   dd     3
                   dd     4
        pdivector2 dd     5
                   dd     6
                   dd     7
                   dd     8

        fmt1 db "Packed Integer Vector 1: %d, %d, %d, %d",10,0
        fmt2 db "Packed Integer Vector 2: %d, %d, %d, %d",10,0
        fmt3 db "Sum Vector: %d, %d, %d, %d",10,0
        fmt4 db "Reverse of Sum Vector: %d, %d, %d, %d",10,0
```

J. Van Hoey, *Beginning x64 Assembly Programming*, https://doi.org/10.1007/978-1-4842-5076-1_29

```
section .bss
alignb 16
      pdivector_res    resd 4
      pdivector_other resd 4

section .text
      global main
main:
push  rbp
mov   rbp,rsp

; print vector 1
      mov   rsi,pdivector1
      mov   rdi,fmt1
      call  printpdi
; print vector 2
      mov   rsi,pdivector2
      mov   rdi,fmt2
      call  printpdi

; add 2 aligned double int vectors
      movdqa      xmm0, [pdivector1]
      paddd       xmm0, [pdivector2]

; store the result in memory
      movdqa      [pdivector_res], xmm0
; print the vector in memory
      mov   rsi,pdivector_res
      mov   rdi,fmt3
      call  printpdi

; copy the memory vector to xmm3
      movdqa xmm3,[pdivector_res]
```

```
; extract the packed values from xmm3
      pextrd eax, xmm3, 0
      pextrd ebx, xmm3, 1
      pextrd ecx, xmm3, 2
      pextrd edx, xmm3, 3
; insert in xmm0 in reverse order
      pinsrd xmm0, eax, 3
      pinsrd xmm0, ebx, 2
      pinsrd xmm0, ecx, 1
      pinsrd xmm0, edx, 0

; print the reversed vector
      movdqa [pdivector_other], xmm0
      mov    rsi,pdivector_other
      mov    rdi,fmt4
      call   printpdi

; exit
mov    rsp,rbp
pop    rbp
ret

;print function-----------------------------------------
printpdi:
push   rbp
mov    rbp,rsp
      movdqa xmm0, [rsi]
      ; extract the packed values from xmm0
            pextrd esi, xmm0,0
            pextrd edx, xmm0,1
            pextrd ecx, xmm0,2
            pextrd r8d, xmm0,3
      mov    rax,0; no floats
      call   printf
leave
ret
```

Analyzing the Code

Here again we have two vectors, this time with integer values. We use the instruction movdqa to copy values into an xmm register. This instruction is for use with aligned data. Then paddd adds the values in the registers together and puts the result in xmm0. To use printf, we need to extract the integer values from the xmm registers and put them in the "regular" registers. Remember from the calling conventions that printf considers an xmm register to be a floating register. If we do not extract the integer values, printf will consider the values in an xmm register to be floating-point values and print the wrong values. For extracting and inserting packed integers, we use pinsrd and pextrd. We also reverse a vector to show how to insert values into a vector in an xmm register.

There are versions of movd, padd, pinsr, and pextr for bytes, words, double words, and quadwords, respectively.

Figure 29-1 shows the output.

```
jo@UbuntuDesktop:~/Desktop/linux64/gcc/35 sse_integer$ make
nasm -f elf64 -g -F dwarf sse_integer.asm -l sse_integer.lst
gcc -o sse_integer sse_integer.o
jo@UbuntuDesktop:~/Desktop/linux64/gcc/35 sse_integer$ ./sse_integer
Packed Integer Vector 1: 1, 2, 3, 4
Packed Integer Vector 2: 5, 6, 7, 8
Sum of Packed Integer Vector 1 and Vector 2: 6, 8, 10, 12
Reverse of Sum Vector: 12, 10, 8, 6
jo@UbuntuDesktop:~/Desktop/linux64/gcc/35 sse_integer$ █
```

Figure 29-1. *sse_integer.asm output*

Summary

In this chapter, you learned about the following:

- Integer packed data

- Instructions for inserting and extracting packed integers

- Instructions for copying and adding packed integers

CHAPTER 30

SSE String Manipulation

With SSE version 4.2, four compare-string instructions were introduced: two instructions for strings with implicit lengths and two instructions for strings with explicit lengths. Two of these four instructions use masks.

A string with an implicit length is a string with a terminating 0. For a string with an explicit length, the length has to be specified by some other means.

In this chapter, we will spend some time with SSE strings, because the compare instructions are a bit complicated and unusual, especially when using masks. Here are the instructions:

String	Instruction	arg1	arg2	arg3	Output
implicit	pcmpistri	xmm	xmm/m128	imm8	Index in ecx
implicit	pcmpistrm	xmm	xmm/m128	imm8	Mask in xmm0
explicit	pcmpestri	xmm	xmm/m128	imm8	Index in ecx
explicit	pcmpestrm	xmm	xmm/m128	imm8	Mask in xmm0

Here is what the instructions mean:

pcmpistri: **P**acked **comp**are **i**mplicit length **s**trings, **r**eturn **i**ndex

pcmpistrm: **P**acked **comp**are **i**mplicit length **s**trings, **r**eturn **m**ask

pcmpestri: **P**acked **comp**are **e**xplicit length **s**trings, **r**eturn **i**ndex

pcmpestrm: **P**acked **comp**are **e**xplicit length **s**trings, **r**eturn **m**ask

These compare instructions take three arguments. Argument 1 is always an xmm register, argument 2 can be an xmm register or a memory location, and argument 3 is an "immediate," which is a control byte (imm8 in the Intel manuals) that specifies how the instruction executes. The control byte has an important role, so we will spend some time explaining the details.

© Jo Van Hoey 2019
J. Van Hoey, *Beginning x64 Assembly Programming*, https://doi.org/10.1007/978-1-4842-5076-1_30

The imm8 Control Byte

Table 30-1 shows the layout of the control byte.

Table 30-1. *imm8 Control Byte*

Options	Bit Position	Bit Value	Operation	Meaning
	7	0	Reserved	Reserved
Output Format	6	0	Bit mask	xmm0 contains IntRes2 as a bit mask
		1	Byte mask	xmm0 contains IntRes2 as a byte mask
		0	Least significant index	Least significant index found in ecx
		1	Most significant index	Most significant index found in ecx
Polarity	5,4	00	+	IntRes2 = IntRes1
		01	-	IntRes2 = ~IntRes1
		10	Masked +	IntRes2 = IntRes1
		11	Masked -	IntRes2 = ~IntRes1
Aggregation and Comparison	3,2	00	Equal any	Match characters
		01	Equal range	Match characters in range
		10	Equal each	String compare
		11	Equal ordered	Substring search
Data Format	1,0	00	Packed unsigned bytes	
		01	Packed unsigned words	
		10	Packed signed bytes	
		11	Packed signed words	

The compare instructions take the input data (the format is specified in bits 1 and 0), execute aggregation and comparison actions (bits 2 and 3), which give an intermediate result (a match between arg1 and arg2). This result is called IntRes1 in the Intel manuals. The polarity is applied on IntRes1 to give IntRes2. IntRes2 is then used to output a result in the required format. Negative polarity (~IntRes1) means take the ones' complement of IntRes1 and put the result in IntRes2. That is, convert every 1 bit to a 0 bit and convert every 0 bit to a 1 bit. It's a logical NOT, in other words. The result in IntRes2 can be stored as a mask in xmm0 for the mask instructions pcmpistrm and pcmpestrm or as an index in ecx for pcmpistri and pcmpestri. Some examples will be helpful here.

Here are some control byte examples:

```
00001000 or 0x08:
    00 - packed unsigned bytes,
    10 - equal each,
    00 - positive polarity,
    00 - lowest significant index into ecx

01000100 or 0x44:
    00 - packed unsigned bytes,
    01 - equal range,
    00 - positive polarity,
    01 - xmm0 contains byte mask
```

Using the imm8 Control Byte

In this section we show how we can set the bits in the imm8 control byte in order to control the behavior of the packed string instructions. We added examples to illustrate the effect of the different settings.

Bits 0 and 1

Bits 0 and 1 indicate the data source format; the data source can be a packed byte or a packed word, unsigned or signed.

Bits 2 and 3

Bits 2 and 3 indicate the aggregation to be applied. The result is called IntRes1 (intermediate result 1). A block of 16 bytes is taken from the second operand and compared with the content in the first operand.

The aggregation can be as follows:

equal any (00) or find characters from a set: This means search operand 1 and look for any characters in operand 2. When you find a match, set the corresponding bit to 1 in IntRes1. Here's an example:

```
operand 1: "this is a joke!!"
operand 2: "i!"
IntRes1:    0010010000000011
```

equal range (01) or find characters from a range: This means search operand 1 and look for any characters in the range given in operand 2. When you find a match, set the corresponding bit to 1 in IntRes1. Here's an example:

```
operand 1: "this is a joke!!"
operand 2: "aj"
IntRes1:    0010010010100100
```

equal each (10) or string compare: This means compare any character in operand 1 to the corresponding character in operand 2. When you find a match, set the corresponding bit in IntRes1 to 1. Here's an example:

```
operand 1: "this is a joke!!"
operand 2: "this is no joke!"
IntRes1:    1111111100000000
```

equal ordered (11) or substring search: This means search operand 1 for the string in operand 2. When you find a match, set the corresponding bit in IntRes1 to 1. Here's an example:

```
operand 1: "this is a joke!!"
operand 2: "is"
IntRes1:    0010010000000000
```

Bits 4 and 5

Bits 4 and 5 apply the polarity and store the result in IntRes2.

Positive polarity (00) and (10): IntRes2 will be identical to IntRes1. Here's an example:

```
IntRes1:  0010010000000011
IntRes2:  0010010000000011
```

Negative polarity (01) and (11): IntRes2 will be the ones' complement, or the logical negation of IntRes1. Here's an example:

```
IntRes1:  0010010000000011
IntRes2:  1101101111111100
```

Bit 6

Bit 6 sets the output format, with two cases.

Not using a mask:

0: The index returned in ecx is the least significant bit set in IntRes2. Here's an example:

```
IntRes2:  0010010011000000
ecx = 6
In IntRes2, the first 1 bit is found at index 6 (counting
starts at 0 and from the right).
```

1: The index returned in ecx is the most significant bit set in IntRes2. Here's an example:

```
IntRes2:  0010010010100100
ecx = 13
In IntRes2, the last 1 bit is found at index 13 (counting
starts at 0 and from the right).
```

Using a mask:

0: IntRes2 is returned as a mask in the least significant bits of xmm0 (zero extension to 128 bits). Here's an example:

```
Search for all characters 'a' and 'e' in the
string = 'qdacdekkfijlmdoz'
then
xmm0: 024h
or in binary 0000000000100100
```

Note that the mask is reversed in xmm0.

1: IntRes2 is expanded into a byte/word mask into xmm0. Here's an example:

```
Search for all characters 'a' and 'e' in the
string = 'qdacdekkfijlmdoz'
then
xmm0:   00000000000000000000ff0000ff0000
```

Note that the mask is reversed in xmm0.

Bit 7 Reserved

Bit 7 is reserved.

The Flags

For the implicit length instructions, the flags are used in a way that is different from what you have seen in previous chapters (see the Intel manuals).

```
CF - Reset if IntRes2 is equal to zero, set otherwise
ZF - Set if any byte/word of xmm2/mem128 is null, reset otherwise
SF - Set if any byte/word of xmm1 is null, reset otherwise
OF - IntRes2[0]
AF - Reset
PF - Reset
```

For the explicit length instructions, the flags are also used in different ways, as follows (see the Intel manuals):

```
CF - Reset if IntRes2 is equal to zero, set otherwise
ZF - Set if absolute-value of EDX is < 16 (8), reset otherwise
SF - Set if absolute-value of EAX is < 16 (8), reset otherwise
OF - IntRes2[0]
AF - Reset
PF - Reset
```

In the examples in the following chapter, we will use the CF flag to see whether there was any result and ZF to detect the end of a string.

This theory might sound complicated; indeed, it's time for some practice.

Summary

In this chapter, you learned about the following:

- SSE string manipulation instructions

- The layout and use of the imm8 control byte

CHAPTER 31

Search for a Character

In this chapter, we will start using the control byte to help us find a specific character in a string.

Determining the Length of a String

In the first example, we will determine the length of a string by looking for a terminating 0.

Listing 31-1 shows the code.

Listing 31-1. sse_string_length.asm

```
; sse_string_length.asm
extern printf
section .data
;template          0123456789abcdef0123456789abcdef0123456789abcd  e
;template          123456789012345678901234567890123456789012345  7
     string1 db    "The quick brown fox jumps over the lazy river.",0
     fmt1 db       "This is our string: %s ",10,0
     fmt2 db       "Our string is %d characters long.",10,0
section .bss
section .text
     global main
main:
push   rbp
mov    rbp,rsp
     mov    rdi, fmt1
     mov    rsi, string1
     xor    rax,rax
     call   printf
```

© Jo Van Hoey 2019
J. Van Hoey, *Beginning x64 Assembly Programming*, https://doi.org/10.1007/978-1-4842-5076-1_31

```
        mov    rdi, string1
        call   pstrlen
        mov    rdi, fmt2
        mov    rsi, rax
        xor    rax,rax
        call   printf
leave
ret
;function to compute string length------------------------
pstrlen:
push  rbp
mov   rbp,rsp
        mov    rax,    -16         ; avoid changing later
        pxor   xmm0,  xmm0         ; 0 (end of string)
.not_found:
        add            rax, 16     ; avoid changing ZF later
                                   ; after pcmpistri
        pcmpistri   xmm0, [rdi + rax], 00001000b      ;'equal each'
        jnz            .not_found  ; 0 found?
        add            rax, rcx    ; rcx contains the index of the 0
        inc            rax         ; correct for index 0 at start
leave
ret
```

At the beginning of the program, we added two templates in comments to make the character counting easier for us. One template uses decimal numbering, starting at 1, and the other template uses hexadecimal numbering, starting at index 0.

```
;template     1234567890123456789012345678901234567890123456   7
;template     0123456789abcdef0123456789abcdef0123456789abcd   e
string1 db    "The quick brown fox jumps over the lazy river.",0
```

First, as usual, we print the strings. Then we call the custom-built search function pstrlen. Our function pstrlen scans for the first occurrence of a zero byte. The instruction pcmpistri analyzes blocks of 16 bytes at a time; we use rax as a block counter. If pcmpistri detects a zero byte in the current block, ZF will be set and used to decide whether to jump. We have to avoid that incrementing `rax` will impact the ZF flag just before the jump is evaluated, so we have to increment the ZF flag before `pcmpistri`. That is why we start with -16 in `rax`; now we can increase `rax` before using `pcmpistri`. Note the `pxor` instruction; it is the logical or instruction for xmm registers. SIMD has its own logical instructions!

The immediate control byte contains 00001000, which means the following:

00 Packed unsigned bytes

10 Equal each

00 Positive Polarity

0 Least significant index

0 Reserved

You might expect that we use "equal any" to find any 0. But instead, we are using "equal each"! Why is that?

You have to know that `pcmpistri` initializes `rcx` to contain the value 16, which is the number of bytes in a block. If a matching byte is found, `pcmpistri` will copy the index of the matching byte in `rcx`. If there is no match found, `rcx` will contain 16.

Look in the Intel manuals, specifically, in Volume 2B. Section 4.1.6, "Valid/Invalid Override of Comparisons," explains what happens when a block has "invalid" bytes, or bytes past the end of a string.

We can use this table to interpret our situation:

xmm0	Memory	Equal any	Equal each
Invalid	Invalid	Force false	Force true
Invalid	Valid	Force false	Force false

We have xmm0 invalid because we initialized it to contain 0 bytes. When we have a 16-byte block containing a 0 byte, in the case of "equal any," `pcmpistri` detects that one of the 16 bytes contains 0. At that moment, we have xmm0 invalid and memory invalid. However, `pcmpistri` is designed to "force false" in the case of "equal any." So, `pcmpistri` thinks there is no match and returns 16 in `rcx`, so the calculated string length will not be correct.

But when we use "equal each," xmm0 is invalid like before, and as soon as pcmpistri reads the terminating 0 byte in the block, it is designed to "force true." The index of the 0 byte is recorded in ecx. And that value in ecx can be used to correctly calculate the end of the string.

One caveat: the program reads in blocks of 16 bytes. That is okay as long as the place where the data is found is within a memory space allocated to the program. If it tries reading beyond the allowed memory border, the program will crash. You can avoid this by keeping track of where you are in the memory page (in most cases, pages are chunks of 4K bytes), and if you come close to the page border, start reading byte per byte. That way you will never accidentally try to cross over from an allowed memory page to a memory page of another process. We did not implement this feature to complicate the explanation and the example program. But be warned that such a situation can happen.

Figure 31-1 shows the output. As you can see, the string length includes the terminating null.

```
jo@UbuntuDesktop:~/Desktop/linux64/gcc/36 sse_string_length$ make
nasm -f elf64 -g -F dwarf sse_string_length.asm -l sse_string_length.lst
gcc -o sse_string_length sse_string_length.o -no-pie
jo@UbuntuDesktop:~/Desktop/linux64/gcc/36 sse_string_length$ ./sse_string_length
This is our string: The quick brown fox jumps over the lazy river.
Our string is 47 characters long.
jo@UbuntuDesktop:~/Desktop/linux64/gcc/36 sse_string_length$ 
```

Figure 31-1. *sse_string_length.asm output*

Searching in Strings

Now that we know how to determine the length of a string, let's do some searching in strings (see Listing 31-2).

Listing 31-2. sse_string_search.asm

```
; sse_string_search.asm
extern printf
section .data
;template       12345678901234567890123456789012345678901234567890012345   6
;template       0123456789abcdef0123456789abcdef0123456789abc   d
string1 db      "the quick brown fox jumps over the lazy river",0
```

```
string2        db      "e",0
fmt1           db      "This is our string: %s ",10,0
fmt2           db      "The first '%s' is at position %d.",10,0
fmt3           db      "The last '%s' is at position %d.",10,0
fmt4           db      "The character '%s' didn't show up!.",10,0

section .bss
section .text
      global main
main:
push    rbp
mov     rbp,rsp
        mov     rdi, fmt1
        mov     rsi, string1
        xor     rax,rax
        call    printf

; find the first occurrence
        mov     rdi, string1
        mov     rsi, string2
        call    pstrscan_f
        cmp     rax,0
        je      no_show
        mov     rdi, fmt2
        mov     rsi, string2
        mov     rdx, rax
        xor     rax,rax
        call    printf

; find the last occurrence
        mov     rdi, string1
        mov     rsi, string2
        call    pstrscan_l
        mov     rdi, fmt3
        mov     rsi, string2
        mov     rdx, rax
        xor     rax,rax
```

```
        call    printf
        jmp     exit
no_show:
        mov     rdi, fmt4
        mov     rsi, string2
        xor     rax, rax
        call    printf
exit:
leave
ret
;------ find the first occurrence ---------------------
pstrscan_f:
push    rbp
mov     rbp,rsp
        xor     rax, rax
        pxor    xmm0, xmm0
        pinsrb  xmm0, [rsi],0
.block_loop:
        pcmpistri  xmm0, [rdi + rax], 00000000b
        jc      .found
        jz      .none
        add     rax, 16
        jmp     .block_loop
.found:
        add     rax, rcx            ; rcx contains the position of the char
        inc     rax                 ; start counting from 1 instead of 0
leave
ret
.none:
        xor     rax,rax             ; nothing found, return 0
leave
ret
;------ find the last occurrence ---------------------
pstrscan_l:
push    rbp
```

```
mov    rbp,rsp
push   rbx                   ; callee saved
push   r12                   ; callee saved
       xor    rax, rax
       pxor   xmm0, xmm0
       pinsrb xmm0, [rsi],0
       xor    r12,r12
.block_loop:
       pcmpistri  xmm0, [rdi + rax], 01000000b
       setz   bl
       jc     .found
       jz     .done
       add    rax, 16
       jmp    .block_loop
.found:
       mov    r12, rax
       add    r12, rcx    ; rcx contains the position of the char
       inc    r12
       cmp    bl,1
       je     .done
       add    rax,16
       jmp    .block_loop
pop r12                      ; callee saved
pop rbx                      ; callee saved
leave
ret
.done:
       mov    rax,r12
pop r12                      ; callee saved
pop rbx                      ; callee saved
leave
ret
```

At the beginning of the program, we added two templates in comments to make the character counting easier for us.

Here, `string1` contains the string, and `string2` contains the search argument. We will be searching for the first and last occurrences of the search argument. First, we print the strings; then we call the custom-built functions. We have separate functions for finding the first occurrence of the character and the last occurrence. The function `pstrscan_f` scans for the first occurrence of the search argument. The instruction `pcmpistri` treats blocks of 16 bytes at a time; we use `rax` as a block counter. We clear `xmm0` with the `pxor` instruction. With `pinsrb`, we put the search argument in the low byte of `xmm0` (byte 0). We use "equal any" to find the occurrences, and as soon as an occurrence is found, `rcx` indicates the index of the matching byte in the current 16-byte block. If no occurrence is found in the current block, the value 16 is put into `rcx`. With `jc`, we check if `CF=1`. If so, we find a match; `rcx` is added to `rax`, which contains the number of bytes already screened in previous blocks, and then `rax` is returned, corrected for the counting to start at 1 instead of 0.

If `CF=0`, we check with `jz` to see if we have reached the last block. `pcmpistri` sets `ZF=1` when a null byte is detected, and `rax` is cleared, because no match was found. And the function returns with 0.

Of course, we did not do any error checking; if the string is not null terminated, you may get erroneous results. Try to delete the 0 at the end of the string and watch the result.

The function `pstrscan_l` scans for the last match of the search argument. This is more complicated than just looking for the first match and exiting. We have to read all 16-byte blocks and keep track of the last occurrence in a block. So even when we find an occurrence, we have to continue the loop until we find a terminating zero. To keep an eye on the terminating zero, we set register `bl` to 1 as soon as we detect the zero. The register `r12` is used to record the index of the most recent match. See Figure 31-2.

```
jo@UbuntuDesktop:~/Desktop/linux64/gcc/36 sse_string_search$ make
nasm -f elf64 -g -F dwarf sse_string_search.asm -l sse_string_search.lst
gcc -o sse_string_search sse_string_search.o -no-pie
jo@UbuntuDesktop:~/Desktop/linux64/gcc/36 sse_string_search$ ./sse_string_search
This is our string: the quick brown fox jumps over the lazy river
The first 'e' is at position 3.
The last 'e' is at position 44.
jo@UbuntuDesktop:~/Desktop/linux64/gcc/36 sse_string_search$ ▮
```

Figure 31-2. *sse_string_search.asm output*

Summary

In this chapter, you learned about the following:

- Using `pcmpistri` to scan for characters and string length

- Interpreting the outcome of `pcmpistri` with different control bytes

CHAPTER 32

Compare Strings

In the previous chapter, we used strings with implicit lengths, which means that these strings are terminated by a null byte. In this chapter, we will compare strings with implicit lengths and strings with explicit lengths.

Implicit Length

Instead of matching characters, we will look for characters that differ. Listing 32-1 shows the example code we will discuss.

Listing 32-1. sse_string2_imp.asm

```
; sse_string2_imp.asm
; compare strings implicit length
extern printf
section .data
        string1     db      "the quick brown fox jumps over the lazy"
                    db      " river",10,0
        string2     db      "the quick brown fox jumps over the lazy"
                    db      " river",10,0
        string3     db      "the quick brown fox jumps over the lazy
                            " dog",10,0
    fmt1    db "Strings 1 and 2 are equal.",10,0
    fmt11   db "Strings 1 and 2 differ at position %i.",10,0
    fmt2    db "Strings 2 and 3 are equal.",10,0
    fmt22   db "Strings 2 and 3 differ at position %i.",10,0
section .bss
section .text
        global main
```

© Jo Van Hoey 2019

J. Van Hoey, *Beginning x64 Assembly Programming*, https://doi.org/10.1007/978-1-4842-5076-1_32

```
main:
push   rbp
mov    rbp,rsp
;first print the strings
       mov    rdi, string1
       xor    rax,rax
       call   printf
       mov    rdi, string2
       xor    rax,rax
       call   printf
       mov    rdi, string3
       xor    rax,rax
       call   printf
; compare string 1 and 2
       mov    rdi, string1
       mov    rsi, string2
       call   pstrcmp
       mov    rdi,fmt1
       cmp    rax,0
       je     eql1          ;the strings are equal
       mov    rdi,fmt11     ;the strings are unequal
  eql1:
       mov    rsi, rax
       xor    rax,rax
       call   printf
; compare string 2 and 3
       mov    rdi, string2
       mov    rsi, string3
       call   pstrcmp
       mov    rdi,fmt2
       cmp    rax,0
       je     eql2          ;the strings are equal
       mov    rdi,fmt22     ;the strings are unequal
```

```
eql2:
      mov    rsi, rax
      xor    rax,rax
      call   printf
; exit
leave
ret
;string compare------------------------------------------------
pstrcmp:
push  rbp
mov   rbp,rsp
      xor    rax, rax           ;
      xor    rbx, rbx           ;
.loop: movdqu    xmm1, [rdi + rbx]
      pcmpistri  xmm1, [rsi + rbx], 0x18 ; equal each | neg polarity
      jc         .differ
      jz         .equal
      add        rbx, 16
      jmp        .loop

.differ:
      mov rax,rbx
      add rax,rcx     ;the position of the differing character
      inc rax         ;because the index starts at 0
.equal:
leave
ret
```

As usual, we first print the strings; we then call a function, pstrcmp, to compare the strings. The essential information is in the function pstrcmp. The control byte is 0x18 or 00011000, that is, from right to left: packed integer bytes, equal each, negative polarity, and ecx, which contains the index to the first occurrence. The instruction pcmpistri makes use of the flags; you can find the following in the Intel manuals:

> CFlag: Reset if IntRes2 is equal to zero; set otherwise.

> ZFlag: Set if any byte/word of xmm2/mem128 is null; reset otherwise.

SFlag: Set if any byte/word of xmm1 is null; reset otherwise.

OFlag: IntRes2[0].

AFlag: Reset.

PFlag: Reset.

In the example, pcmpistri puts a 1 for every match into the corresponding position in IntRes1. When a differing byte is found, a zero is written in the corresponding position in IntRes1. Then IntRes2 is formed and applies negative polarity to IntRes1. IntRes2 will contain a 1 at the differing index (negative polarity), so IntRes2 will not be zero, and CF will be set to 1. The loop will then be interrupted, and pstrcmp will return with the position of the differing character in rax. If CF is not set but pcmpistri detects the terminating zero, the function will return with 0 in rax.

Figure 32-1 shows the output.

```
jo@ubuntu18:~/Desktop/Book/37 sse_string2_imp$ ./sse_string2
the quick brown fox jumps over the lazy river
the quick brown fox jumps over the lazy river
the quick brown fox jumps over the lazy dog
Strings 1 and 2 are equal.
Strings 2 and 3 differ at position 41.
jo@ubuntu18:~/Desktop/Book/37 sse_string2_imp$ ▉
```

Figure 32-1. *sse_string2_imp.asm output*

Explicit Length

Most of the time we use strings with implicit lengths, but Listing 32-2 shows an example of strings with explicit lengths.

Listing 32-2. sse_string3_exp.asm.

```
; sse_string3_exp.asm
; compare strings explicit length
extern printf
section .data
    string1      db      "the quick brown fox jumps over the "
                 db      "lazy river"
    string1Len equ $ - string1
```

```
        string2       db        "the quick brown fox jumps over the "
                      db        "lazy river"
        string2Len equ $ - string2
        dummy  db "confuse the world"
        string3       db        "the quick brown fox jumps over the "
                      db        "lazy dog"
        string3Len equ $ - string3

        fmt1  db "Strings 1 and 2 are equal.",10,0
        fmt11 db "Strings 1 and 2 differ at position %i.",10,0
        fmt2  db "Strings 2 and 3 are equal.",10,0
        fmt22 db "Strings 2 and 3 differ at position %i.",10,0

section .bss
        buffer resb 64
section .text
        global main
main:
push   rbp
mov    rbp,rsp
; compare string 1 and 2
        mov        rdi, string1
        mov        rsi, string2
        mov        rdx, string1Len
        mov        rcx, string2Len
        call       pstrcmp
        push       rax     ;push result on stack for later use

; print the string1 and 2 and the result
;-------------------------------------------------------------
; first build the string with newline and terminating 0
; string1
        mov        rsi,string1
        mov        rdi,buffer
        mov        rcx,string1Len
        rep        movsb
        mov        byte[rdi],10 ; add NL to buffer
```

271

```
    inc       rdi           ; add terminating 0 to buffer
    mov       byte[rdi],0
;print
    mov       rdi, buffer
    xor       rax,rax
    call      printf
; string2
    mov       rsi,string2
    mov       rdi,buffer
    mov       rcx,string2Len
    rep       movsb
    mov       byte[rdi],10 ; add NL to buffer
    inc       rdi           ; add terminating 0 to buffer
    mov       byte[rdi],0
;print
    mov       rdi, buffer
    xor       rax,rax
    call      printf
;-------------------------------------------------------------
; now print the result of the comparison
    pop       rax       ;recall the return value
    mov       rdi,fmt1
    cmp       rax,0
    je        eql1
    mov       rdi,fmt11
 eql1:
    mov       rsi, rax
    xor       rax,rax
    call      printf
;-------------------------------------------------------------
;-------------------------------------------------------------
; compare string 2 and 3
    mov       rdi, string2
    mov       rsi, string3
    mov       rdx, string2Len
```

```
    mov       rcx, string3Len
    call      pstrcmp
    push      rax

; print the string3 and the result
;----------------------------------------------------------------
; first build the string with newline and terminating 0
; string3
    mov       rsi,string3
    mov       rdi,buffer
    mov       rcx,string3Len
    rep       movsb
    mov       byte[rdi],10 ; add NL to buffer
    inc       rdi          ; add terminating 0 to buffer
    mov       byte[rdi],0
;print
    mov       rdi, buffer
    xor       rax,rax
    call      printf
;----------------------------------------------------------------
; now print the result of the comparison
    pop       rax                   ; recall the return value
    mov       rdi,fmt2
    cmp       rax,0
    je        eql2
    mov       rdi,fmt22
eql2:
    mov       rsi, rax
    xor       rax,rax
    call      printf

; exit
leave
ret
;----------------------------------------------------------------
pstrcmp:
push    rbp
```

```
mov     rbp,rsp
        xor     rbx, rbx
        mov     rax,rdx         ;rax contains length of 1st string
        mov     rdx,rcx         ;rdx contains length of 2nd string
        xor     rcx,rcx         ;rcx as index
.loop:
        movdqu      xmm1, [rdi + rbx]
        pcmpestri xmm1, [rsi + rbx], 0x18 ; equal each|neg. polarity
        jc      .differ
        jz      .equal
        add     rbx, 16
        sub     rax,16
        sub     rdx,16
        jmp     .loop
.differ:
        mov     rax,rbx
        add     rax,rcx     ; rcx contains the differing position
        inc     rax         ; because the counter starts at 0
        jmp     exit
.equal:
        xor     rax,rax
exit:
leave
ret
```

As you can see, using explicit length can sometimes complicate things. Then why use it? Many communication protocols use it, or your application may require that you use 0s in your data. One way or another we have to provide the length of the strings. In our case, we computed the length of the strings from the memory locations in section. data. However, printf expects zero-terminated strings. So, after we demonstrate how to compare strings with explicit lengths, we rebuild the strings in a buffer, add a newline and a terminating null in the buffer, and hand over the buffer to printf.

Now take a look at pstrcmp, the compare function. The length of the first string goes into rax, and the length of the second string goes into rdx. Then we start a loop: we load the address of the 16-byte block into an xmm1 register and call pcmpestri, with control byte 0x18 as before. Next, let's at the flags; you can find the following in the Intel manuals:

CFlag: Reset if IntRes2 is equal to zero; set otherwise.

ZFlag: Set if absolute value of EDX is less than 16 (8); reset otherwise.

SFlag: Set if absolute value of EAX is less than 16 (8); reset otherwise.

OFlag: IntRes2[0].

AFlag: Reset.

PFlag: Reset.

Note that pcmpestri and pcmpistri use ZF and SF differently. Instead of ZF signaling a terminating null, at every loop we decrease rax and rdx, and when one of them goes below 16, the loop is terminated.

Figure 32-2 shows the output.

```
jo@ubuntu18:~/Desktop/Book/38_0 sse_string3_exp$ ./sse_string3
the quick brown fox jumps over the lazy river
the quick brown fox jumps over the lazy river
Strings 1 and 2 are equal.
the quick brown fox jumps over the lazy dog
Strings 2 and 3 differ at position 41.
jo@ubuntu18:~/Desktop/Book/38_0 sse_string3_exp$ ▉
```

Figure 32-2. *sse_string3_exp.asm output*

Summary

In this chapter, you learned about the following:

- Implicit and explicit string lengths
- Negative polarity
- Using flags

CHAPTER 33

Do the Shuffle!

With the unmasked string instructions, we have a few options. We can find a first or last occurrence of a character, but finding all occurrences is more challenging. We can compare strings and find a difference, but finding all differences is more complicated. Luckily, we also have string instructions that use masks, which makes them much more powerful. But before diving into mask instructions, we need to look at shuffling.

A First Look at Shuffling

Shuffling means moving around packed values. The moving can be within the same xmm register or from one xmm register to another xmm register, or it can be from a 128-bit memory location to an xmm register.

Listing 33-1 shows the example code.

Listing 33-1. shuffle.asm

```
; shuffle.asm
extern printf
section .data
        fmt0  db "These are the numbers in memory: ",10,0
        fmt00 db "This is xmm0: ",10,0
        fmt1  db "%d ",0
        fmt2  db "Shuffle-broadcast double word %i:",10,0
        fmt3  db "%d %d %d %d",10,0
        fmt4  db "Shuffle-reverse double words:",10,0
        fmt5  db "Shuffle-reverse packed bytes in xmm0:",10,0
        fmt6  db "Shuffle-rotate left:",10,0
        fmt7  db "Shuffle-rotate right:",10,0
```

© Jo Van Hoey 2019
J. Van Hoey, *Beginning x64 Assembly Programming*, https://doi.org/10.1007/978-1-4842-5076-1_33

```
        fmt8    db  "%c%c%c%c%c%c%c%c%c%c%c%c%c%c%c%c",10,0
        fmt9    db  "Packed bytes in xmm0:",10,0
        NL      db  10,0

        number1     dd 1
        number2     dd 2
        number3     dd 3
        number4     dd 4

        char  db "abcdefghijklmnop"
        bytereverse db 15,14,13,12,11,10,9,8,7,6,5,4,3,2,1,0
section .bss
section .text
        global main
main:
push  rbp
mov   rbp,rsp
        sub  rsp,32      ;stackspace for the original xmm0
                         ;and for the modified xmm0
; SHUFFLING DOUBLE WORDS
; first print the numbers in reverse
        mov   rdi, fmt0
        call  printf
        mov   rdi, fmt1
        mov   rsi, [number4]
        xor   rax,rax
        call  printf
        mov   rdi, fmt1
        mov   rsi, [number3]
        xor   rax,rax
        call  printf
        mov   rdi, fmt1
        mov   rsi, [number2]
        xor   rax,rax
        call  printf
        mov   rdi, fmt1
```

```
        mov    rsi, [number1]
        xor    rax,rax
        call   printf
        mov    rdi, NL
        call   printf

; build xmm0 with the numbers
        pxor        xmm0,xmm0
        pinsrd      xmm0, dword[number1],0
        pinsrd      xmm0, dword[number2],1
        pinsrd      xmm0, dword[number3],2
        pinsrd      xmm0, dword[number4],3
        movdqu      [rbp-16],xmm0    ;save xmm0 for later use
        mov         rdi, fmt00
        call        printf           ;print title
        movdqu      xmm0,[rbp-16]    ;restore xmm0 after printf
        call        print_xmm0d      ;print xmm0
        movdqu      xmm0,[rbp-16]    ;restore xmm0 after printf

; SHUFFLE-BROADCAST
; shuffle: broadcast least significant dword (index 0)
        movdqu      xmm0,[rbp-16]        ;restore xmm0
        pshufd      xmm0,xmm0,00000000b  ;shuffle
        mov         rdi,fmt2
        mov         rsi, 0               ;print title
        movdqu      [rbp-32],xmm0        ;printf destroys xmm0
        call        printf
        movdqu      xmm0,[rbp-32]    ;restore xmm0 after printf
        call        print_xmm0d      ;print the content of xmm0

; shuffle: broadcast dword index 1
        movdqu      xmm0,[rbp-16]        ;restore xmm0
        pshufd      xmm0,xmm0,01010101b  ;shuffle
        mov         rdi,fmt2
        mov         rsi, 1               ;print title
        movdqu      [rbp-32],xmm0        ;printf destroys xmm0
        call        printf
```

```
        movdqu    xmm0,[rbp-32]    ;restore xmm0 after printf
        call      print_xmm0d      ;print the content of xmm0

; shuffle: broadcast dword index 2
        movdqu    xmm0,[rbp-16]         ;restore xmm0
        pshufd    xmm0,xmm0,10101010b   ;shuffle
        mov       rdi,fmt2
        mov       rsi, 2                ;print title
        movdqu    [rbp-32],xmm0         ;printf destroys xmm0
        call      printf
        movdqu    xmm0,[rbp-32]    ;restore xmm0 after printf
        call      print_xmm0d      ;print the content of xmm0

; shuffle: broadcast dword index 3
        movdqu    xmm0,[rbp-16]         ;restore xmm0
        pshufd    xmm0,xmm0,11111111b   ;shuffle
        mov       rdi,fmt2
        mov       rsi, 3                ;print title
        movdqu    [rbp-32],xmm0         ;printf destroys xmm0
        call      printf
        movdqu    xmm0,[rbp-32]    ;restore xmm0 after printf
        call      print_xmm0d      ;print the content of xmm0

; SHUFFLE-REVERSE
; reverse double words
        movdqu    xmm0,[rbp-16]         ;restore xmm0
        pshufd    xmm0,xmm0,00011011b   ;shuffle
        mov       rdi,fmt4              ;print title
        movdqu    [rbp-32],xmm0         ;printf destroys xmm0
        call      printf
        movdqu    xmm0,[rbp-32]    ;restore xmm0 after printf
        call      print_xmm0d      ;print the content of xmm0

; SHUFFLE-ROTATE
; rotate left
        movdqu    xmm0,[rbp-16]         ;restore xmm0
        pshufd    xmm0,xmm0,10010011b   ;shuffle
```

```
        mov       rdi,fmt6                ;print title
        movdqu    [rbp-32],xmm0           ;printf destroys xmm0
        call      printf
        movdqu    xmm0,[rbp-32]     ;restore xmm0 after printf
        call      print_xmm0d       ;print the content of xmm0

; rotate right
        movdqu    xmm0,[rbp-16]           ;restore xmm0
        pshufd    xmm0,xmm0,00111001b     ;shuffle
        mov       rdi,fmt7                ;print title
        movdqu    [rbp-32],xmm0           ;printf destroys xmm0
        call      printf
        movdqu    xmm0,[rbp-32]     ;restore xmm0 after printf
        call      print_xmm0d       ;print the content of xmm0

;SHUFFLING BYTES
        mov       rdi, fmt9
        call      printf            ;print title
        movdqu    xmm0,[char]       ;load the character in xmm0
        movdqu    [rbp-32],xmm0     ;printf destroys xmm0
        call      print_xmm0b       ;print the bytes in xmm0
        movdqu    xmm0,[rbp-32]     ;restore xmm0 after printf
        movdqu    xmm1,[bytereverse]      ;load the mask
        pshufb    xmm0,xmm1               ;shuffle bytes
        mov       rdi,fmt5                ;print title
        movdqu    [rbp-32],xmm0           ;printf destroys xmm0
        call      printf
        movdqu    xmm0,[rbp-32]     ;restore xmm0 after printf
        call      print_xmm0b       ;print the content of xmm0
leave
ret
;function to print double words--------------------
print_xmm0d:
push  rbp
mov   rbp,rsp
```

```
        mov         rdi, fmt3
        xor         rax,rax
        pextrd      esi, xmm0,3     ;extract the double words
        pextrd      edx, xmm0,2     ;in reverse, little endian
        pextrd      ecx, xmm0,1
        pextrd      r8d, xmm0,0
        call        printf
leave
ret
;function to print bytes---------------------------
print_xmm0b:
push  rbp
mov   rbp,rsp
        mov         rdi, fmt8
        xor         rax,rax
        pextrb      esi, xmm0,0     ;in reverse, little endian
        pextrb      edx, xmm0,1     ;use registers first and
        pextrb      ecx, xmm0,2     ;then the stack
        pextrb      r8d, xmm0,3
        pextrb      r9d, xmm0,4
        pextrb      eax, xmm0,15
        push  rax
        pextrb      eax, xmm0,14
        push  rax
        pextrb      eax, xmm0,13
        push  rax
        pextrb      eax, xmm0,12
        push  rax
        pextrb      eax, xmm0,11
        push  rax
        pextrb      eax, xmm0,10
        push  rax
        pextrb      eax, xmm0,9
        push  rax
        pextrb      eax, xmm0,8
```

```
        push    rax
        pextrb      eax, xmm0,7
        push    rax
        pextrb      eax, xmm0,6
        push    rax
        pextrb      eax, xmm0,5
        push    rax
        xor         rax,rax
        call    printf
leave
ret
```

First, we reserve space on the stack for variables of 128 bytes. We need this space for "pushing" xmm registers on the stack. We cannot use the standard push/pop instructions with xmm registers; we must use memory addressing to copy them to and from the stack. We use rbp, the base pointer, as a point of reference.

We print the numbers we will use as packed values. Then we load the numbers as double words into xmm0 with the instruction pinsrd (which means "packed insert double"). We save (push) xmm0 as a local stack variable with the instruction movdqu [rbp-16],xmm0. (We reserved space for this local variable at the start of the program.) Every time we execute printf, xmm0 will be modified, intentionally or not. So, we have to preserve and restore the original value of xmm0 if needed. The instruction movdqu is used to move unaligned packed integer values. To help visualize the results of the shuffling, we take into account little-endian formatting when printing. Doing so will show you xmm0, as you can see in a debugger such as SASM.

To shuffle, we need a destination operand, a source operand, and a shuffle mask. The mask is an 8-bit immediate. We will discuss some useful examples of shuffling and the respective masks in the following sections.

- Shuffle broadcast

- Shuffle reverse

- Shuffle rotate

Shuffle Broadcast

A picture can make everything more understandable. Figure 33-1 shows four examples of shuffle broadcast.

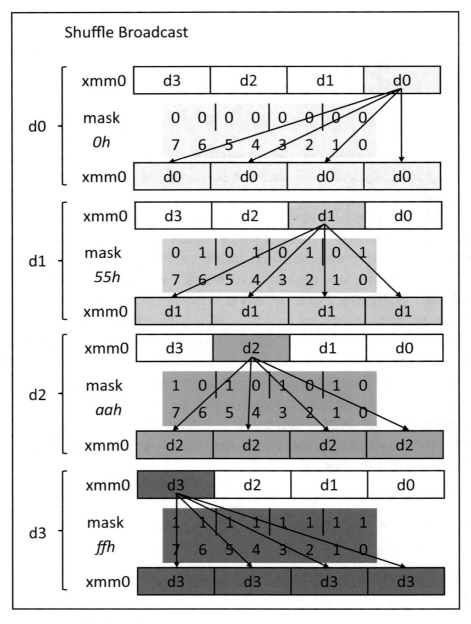

Figure 33-1. *Shuffle broadcast*

In the figure, the source and target are both xmm0. The lowest significant double word, d0, is specified in the mask as 00b. The second lowest, d1, is specified as 01b. The third, d2, is specified as 10b. The fourth, d3, is specified as 11b. The binary mask 10101010b, or aah in hexadecimal, works as follows: put d2 (10b) in the four target packed double-word positions. Similarly, the mask 11111111b would place d3 (11b) in the four target packed double word positions.

When you study the code, you will see the following simple shuffle instruction:

```
pshufd xmm0,xmm0,10101010b
```

We accomplish a broadcast of the third-lowest element in xmm0. Because the function printf modifies xmm0, we need to save the content of xmm0 by storing it to memory before calling printf. In fact, we need to do more work to protect the content of xmm0 than to do the shuffling itself.

Of course, you are not limited to the four masks we presented here; you can create any 8-bit mask and mix and shuffle as you like.

Shuffle Reverse

Figure 33-2 shows the schematic overview of a shuffle reverse.

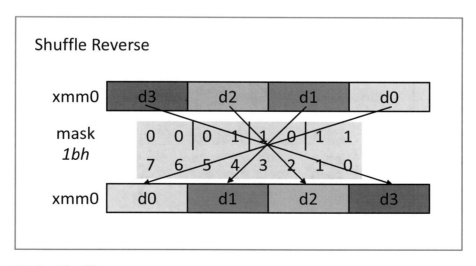

Figure 33-2. *Shuffle reverse*

The mask is 00011011b or 1bh, and that translates to the following:

11 (value in d3) goes into position 0

01 (value in d2) goes into position 1

10 (value in d1) goes into position 2

00 (value in d0) goes into position 3

As you can see in the example code, this is simple to code in assembly language, as shown here:

```
pshufd xmm0,xmm0,1bh
```

Shuffle Rotate

There are two versions of shuffle rotate: rotate left and rotate right. It just a matter of providing the correct mask as the last argument of the shuffle instruction. Figure 33-3 shows the schematic overview.

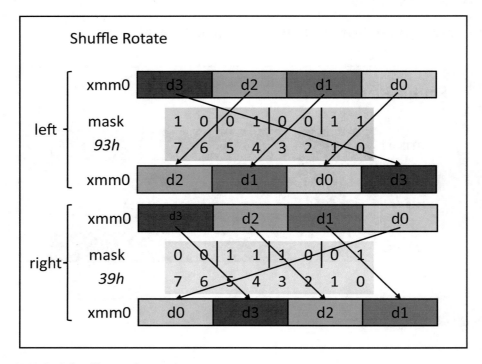

Figure 33-3. *Shuffle rotate*

Here it is in assembly language:

```
pshufd xmm0,xmm0,93h
pshufd xmm0,xmm0,39h
```

Shuffle Bytes

You can shuffle double words with pshufd and words with pshufw. You can also shuffle high words and low words with pshufhw and pshuflw, respectively. You can find all the details in the Intel manuals. All these instructions use a source operand, a target operand, and a mask specified with an immediate. Providing an immediate as a mask has its limitations: it is inflexible, and you have to provide the mask at assembly time, not at runtime.

But there is a solution: shuffle bytes.

You can shuffle bytes with pshufb. This instruction takes only two operands: a target xmm register operand and a mask stored in an xmm register or 128-bit memory location. In the previous code, we reversed the string 'char' with pshufb. We provide a mask at memory location bytereverse in section .data; the mask demands that we put byte 15 in position 0, byte 14 in position 1, and so on. We copy the string to be shuffled in xmm0 and the mask in xmm1, so the shuffle instruction is then as follows:

```
pshufb xmm0, xmm1
```

Then the magic happens. Remember, the mask goes in the second operand; the source is the same as the destination and goes in the first operand.

The nice thing here is that we do not have to provide the mask at assemble time as an immediate. The mask can be built in xmm1 as a result of a computation at runtime.

Finally, Figure 33-4 shows the output of the example code.

```
jo@UbuntuDesktop:~/Desktop/linux64/gcc/38_1 shuffle$ make
nasm -f elf64 -g -F dwarf shuffle.asm -l shuffle.lst
gcc -o shuffle shuffle.o -no-pie
jo@UbuntuDesktop:~/Desktop/linux64/gcc/38_1 shuffle$ ./shuffle
These are the numbers in memory:
4 3 2 1
This is xmm0:
4 3 2 1
Shuffle-broadcast double word 0:
1 1 1 1
Shuffle-broadcast double word 1:
2 2 2 2
Shuffle-broadcast double word 2:
3 3 3 3
Shuffle-broadcast double word 3:
4 4 4 4
Shuffle-reverse double words:
1 2 3 4
Shuffle-rotate left:
3 2 1 4
Shuffle-rotate right:
1 4 3 2
Packed bytes in xmm0:
abcdefghijklmnop
Shuffle-reverse packed bytes in xmm0:
ponmlkjihgfedcba
jo@UbuntuDesktop:~/Desktop/linux64/gcc/38_1 shuffle$ █
```

Figure 33-4. shuffle.asm output

Summary

In this chapter, you learned about the following:

- Shuffle instructions

- Shuffle masks

- Runtime masks

- How to use the stack with xmm registers

CHAPTER 34

SSE String Masks

Now that we know how to shuffle, we can discuss string masks.

Remember that SSE provides two string manipulation instructions that use a mask: `pcmpistrm` and `pcmpestrm`. We will be using implicit length instructions. At first, using masks looks complicated, but once you get the hang of it, you will see how powerful masking can be.

Searching for Characters

Listing 34-1, Listing 34-4, and Listing 34-3 show the example.

Listing 34-1. string4.asm

```
; sse_string4.asm
; find a character
extern print16b
extern printf
section .data
     string1      db      "qdacdekkfijlmdoza"
                  db      "becdfgdklkmdddaf"
                  db      "fffffffdedeee",10,0
     string2      db      "e",0
     string3      db      "a",0
     fmt          db      "Find all the characters '%s' "
                  db      "and '%s' in:",10,0
     fmt_oc       db      "I found %ld characters '%s'"
                  db      "and '%s'",10,0
     NL           db      10,0
section .bss
```

© Jo Van Hoey 2019
J. Van Hoey, *Beginning x64 Assembly Programming*, https://doi.org/10.1007/978-1-4842-5076-1_34

```
section .text
      global main
main:
push  rbp
mov   rbp,rsp

;print the search characters
      mov    rdi, fmt
      mov    rsi, string2
      mov    rdx, string3
      xor    rax,rax
      call   printf
;print the target string
      mov    rdi, string1
      xor    rax,rax
      call   printf
; search the string and print mask
      mov    rdi, string1
      mov    rsi, string2
      mov    rdx, string3
      call   pcharsrch
;print the number of occurences of string2
      mov    rdi, fmt_oc
      mov    rsi, rax
      mov    rdx, string2
      mov    rcx, string3
      call   printf
; exit
leave
ret
;----------------------------------------------------------------
;function searching for and printing the mask
pcharsrch:               ;packed character search
push  rbp
mov   rbp,rsp
```

```
        sub     rsp,16       ;provide stack space for pushing xmm1
        xor     r12,r12      ;for the running total of occurrences
        xor     rcx,rcx      ;for signaling the end
        xor     rbx,rbx      ;for address calculation
        mov     rax,-16      ;for counting bytes, avoid flag setting
;build xmm1, load the search character
        pxor    xmm1,xmm1    ; clear xmm1
        pinsrb      xmm1,byte[rsi],0    ; first char at index 0
        pinsrb      xmm1,byte[rdx],1    ;second char at index 1
.loop:
        add         rax,16       ;avoid ZF flag setting
        mov         rsi,16       ;if no terminating 0, print 16 bytes
        movdqu      xmm2,[rdi+rbx]     ;load 16 bytes of the string in xmm2
        pcmpistrm xmm1,xmm2,40h    ;'equal each' and 'byte mask in xmm0'
        setz    cl               ;if terminating 0 detected
;if terminating 0 found, determine position
        cmp     cl,0
        je      .gotoprint    ;no terminating 0 found
        ;terminating null found
        ;less than 16 bytes left
        ;rdi contains address of string
        ;rbx contains #bytes in blocks handled so far
        add     rdi,rbx          ;address of remaining part of string
        push    rcx              ;caller saved (cl in use)
        call    pstrlen          ;rax returns the length
        pop     rcx              ;caller saved
        dec     rax              ;length without 0
        mov     rsi,rax          ;length of remaining mask bytes
;print the mask
.gotoprint:
        call print_mask
;keep running total of matches
        popcnt      r13d,r13d    ;count the number of 1 bits
        add         r12d,r13d    ;keep the number of occurences in r12d
        or          cl,cl        ; terminating 0 detected?
```

```
        jnz             .exit
        add             rbx,16      ;preprare for the next 16 bytes
        jmp             .loop
.exit:
        mov     rdi, NL         ;add a newline
        call    printf
        mov     rax,r12         ;number of occurences
leave
ret
;-------------------------------------------------------------
;function for finding the terminating 0
pstrlen:
push   rbp
mov    rbp,rsp
        sub             rsp,16      ;for saving xmm0
        movdqu          [rbp-16],xmm0 ;push xmm0
        mov             rax, -16    ;avoid flag setting later
        pxor            xmm0, xmm0  ;search for 0 (end of string)
.loop:  add   rax, 16                ;avoid setting ZF
        pcmpistri       xmm0, [rdi + rax], 0x08 ;'equal each'
        jnz             .loop       ;0 found?
        add             rax, rcx    ;rax = bytes already handled
                                    ;rcx = bytes handled in terminating loop
        movdqu          xmm0,[rbp-16] ;pop xmm0
leave
ret
;-------------------------------------------------------------
;function for printing the mask
;xmm0 contains the mask
;rsi contains the number of bits to print (16 or less)
print_mask:
push   rbp
mov    rbp,rsp
        sub     rsp,16                  ;for saving xmm0
        call    reverse_xmm0 ;little endian
```

```asm
        pmovmskb        r13d,xmm0       ;mov byte mask to r13d
        movdqu          [rbp-16],xmm1 ;push xmm1 because of printf
        push    rdi             ;rdi contains string1
        mov     edi,r13d        ;contains mask to be printed
        push    rdx             ;contains the mask
        push    rcx             ;contains end of string flag
        call    print16b
        pop     rcx
        pop     rdx
        pop     rdi
        movdqu xmm1,[rbp-16] ;pop xmm1
leave
ret
;-------------------------------------------------------------
;function for reversing, shuffling xmm0
reverse_xmm0:
section .data
;mask for reversing
        .bytereverse db 15,14,13,12,11,10,9,8,7,6,5,4,3,2,1,0
section .text
push    rbp
mov     rbp,rsp
        sub     rsp,16
        movdqu [rbp-16],xmm2
        movdqu xmm2,[.bytereverse]          ;load the mask in xmm2
        pshufb xmm0,xmm2                     ;do the shuffle
        movdqu xmm2,[rbp-16]                 ;pop xmm2
leave                               ;returns the shuffled xmm0
ret
```

Listing 34-2. print16b.c

```c
// print16b.c
#include <stdio.h>
#include <string.h>
void print16b(long long n, int length){
```

```
    long long s,c;
    int i=0;
    for (c = 15; c >= 16-length; c--)
    {
        s = n >> c;
        if (s & 1)
            printf("1");
        else
            printf("0");
    }
}
```

Listing 34-3. makefile

```
sse_string4: sse_string4.o print16b.o
    gcc -o sse_string4 sse_string4.o print16b.o -no-pie
sse_string4.o: sse_string4.asm
    nasm -f elf64 -g -F dwarf sse_string4.asm -l sse_string4.lst
printb: print16b.c
    gcc -c print16b.c
```

The main part of the program is quite simple, but as with the previous examples, the program is complicated by the fact that we want to print some result on the screen. We could have avoided the printing parts and used a debugger to study the results in the registers and memory. But coping with the challenges of printing is fun, right?

Figure 34-1 shows the output.

```
jo@ubuntu18:~/Desktop/Book/39 sse_string4$ ./sse_string4
Find all the characters 'e' and 'a' in:
qdacdekkfijlmdozabecdfgdklkmdddaffffffffffdedeee
001001000000000010100000000000100000000010111
I found 9 characters 'e'and 'a'
jo@ubuntu18:~/Desktop/Book/39 sse_string4$ █
```

Figure 34-1. *sse_string4.asm output*

In our example program, we are going to search for two characters in a string. We provide a string, aptly called string1, and we look for the character 'e', which we stored in string2, and the character 'a', stored in string3.

We use a number of functions. Let's first discuss the function reverse_xmm0. This function takes xmm0 as an argument and reverses the order of the bytes using a shuffle. By doing so, we will be able to print xmm0 starting with the least significant bytes first and thus print in little-endian format. That is why we presented shuffling in the previous chapter.

We also have a function to measure the length of a string: pstrln. We need this because we will be reading 16-byte blocks. The last block will probably not contain 16-bytes, so for the last block, we need to determine the position of the terminating 0. This will help us to print a mask that has the same length as the string.

Our custom function pcharsrch, which takes the three strings as arguments, is where the action takes place. In the function we first do some housekeeping such as initializing registers. Register xmm1 will be used as a mask; we store the characters to search for in xmm1 with the instruction pinsrb (packed insert bytes). Then we start looping, copying each time 16 bytes of string1 in xmm2, in search of our character, or the terminating null. We use the masking instruction pcmpistrm (**p**acked **comp**are **i**mplicit length **str**ing with a **m**ask). The pcmpistrm instruction takes as a third operand an immediate control byte specifying what to do, in this case "equal any" and a "byte mask in xmm0." So, we will be looking for "any" character that "equals" our search strings. For every matching character in xmm2, the bit in xmm0 that corresponds to the position of the matching character in xmm2 will be set to 1. The pcmpistrm instruction does not have xmm0 as an operand, but it is used implicitly. The return mask will always be kept in xmm0.

The difference with pcmistri is that pcmistri would return an index of 1, matching the position in ecx. But pcmpistrm will return all matching positions in xmm0 for the 16-byte block. That allows you to drastically cut down on the number of steps to execute in order to find all matches.

You can use a bit mask or a byte mask for xmm0 (set or clear bit 6 in the control byte). We used a byte mask so that you can read the xmm0 register more easily with a debugger, two ffs in xmm0 indicate a byte with all the bits set to 1.

After the first 16-byte block is investigated, we verify whether we have found a terminating 0 and store the result of the verification in cl for later use. We want to print the mask stored in xmm0 with the function print_mask. In the debugger, notice that the byte mask is reversed in xmm0, because of the little-endian format. So, before printing, we have to reverse it; that is what we do in our function reverse_xmm0. Then we call our C function print16b to print the reversed mask. However, we cannot provide xmm0 as an argument to print16b, because under the covers print16b is using printf, and printf will interpret xmm0 as a floating-point value, not a byte mask. So, before calling print16b, we transfer the bit mask in xmm0 to r13d, with the instruction pmovmksb (which means "move byte mask"). We will use r13d later for counting; for printing we copy it to edi. We store xmm1 on the stack for later use.

We call the C function print16b to print the mask. This function takes edi (the mask) and rsi (length, passed from the caller) as arguments.

Upon returning to pcharsrch, we count the number of 1s in r13d with the instruction popcnt and update the counter in r12d. We also determine whether we have to exit the loop because a terminating null was detected in the block of bytes.

Before calling print_mask, when a terminating 0 is found, the relevant length of the last block is determined with the function pstrlen. The start address of that block is determined by adding rbx, containing the already screened bytes from previous blocks, to rdi, the address of string1. The string length, returned in rax, is used to compute the number of remaining mask bytes in xmm0 that are passed in rsi to print.

Isn't printing a lot of fun?

Don't be overwhelmed by the printing stuff. Concentrate first on how masks work, which is the main purpose of this chapter.

What can we do with a mask returned by pcmpistrm? Well, the resulting mask can be used, for example, to count all the occurrences of a search argument or to find all occurrences and replace them with something else, creating your own find-and-replace functionality.

Now let's look at another search.

Searching for a Range of Characters

A range can be any number of characters to search for, e.g., all uppercase characters, all characters between *a* and *k*, all characters that represent digits, and so on.

Listing 34-4 shows how to search a string for uppercase characters.

Listing 34-4. string5.asm

```
; sse_string5.asm
; find a range of characters
extern print16b
extern printf
section .data
     string1       db      "eeAecdkkFijlmeoZa"
                   db      "bcefgeKlkmeDad"
                   db      "fdsafadfaseeE",10,0
     startrange    db      "A",10,0        ;look for uppercase
     stoprange     db      "Z",10,0
     NL            db      10,0
     fmt           db      "Find the uppercase letters in:",10,0
     fmt_oc        db      "I found %ld uppercase letters",10,0
section .bss
section .text
     global main
main:
push   rbp
mov    rbp,rsp
;first print the  string
     mov    rdi, fmt        ;title
     xor    rax,rax
     call   printf
     mov    rdi, string1    ;string
     xor    rax,rax
     call   printf
; search the string
     mov    rdi, string1
     mov    rsi, startrange
     mov    rdx, stoprange
     call   prangesrch
; print the number of occurences
     mov    rdi, fmt_oc
```

```
        mov     rsi, rax
        xor     rax,    rax
        call    printf
leave
ret
;-------------------------------------------------------------
;function searching for and printing the mask
prangesrch:             ;packed range search
push    rbp
mov     rbp,rsp
        sub     rsp,16      ;room for pushing xmm1
        xor     r12,r12     ;for the number of occurences
        xor     rcx,rcx     ;for signaling the end
        xor     rbx,rbx     ;for address calculation
        mov     rax,-16     ;avoid ZF flag setting
;build xmm1
        pxor        xmm1,xmm1   ; make sure everything is cleared
        pinsrb      xmm1,byte[rsi],0 ;startrange at index 0
        pinsrb      xmm1,byte[rdx],1 ;stoprange at index 1
.loop:
        add         rax,16
        mov         rsi,16 ;if no terminating 0, print 16 bytes
        movdqu      xmm2,[rdi+rbx]
        pcmpistrm   xmm1,xmm2,01000100b ; equal each|byte mask in xmm0
        setz        cl          ;terminating 0 detected
;if terminating 0 found, determine position
        cmp     cl,0
        je      .gotoprint      ;no terminating 0 found
        ;terminating null found
        ;less than 16 bytes left
        ;rdi contains address of string
        ;rbx contains #bytes in blocks handled so far
        add     rdi,rbx             ;take only the tail of the string
        push    rcx                 ;caller saved (cl in use)
        call    pstrlen             ;determine the position of the 0
```

```
        pop     rcx                 ;caller saved
        dec     rax                 ;length without 0
        mov     rsi,rax             ;bytes in tail
;print the mask
.gotoprint:
        call print_mask
;keep running total of matches
        popcnt r13d, r13d       ;count the number of 1 bits
        add     r12d, r13d      ;keep the number of occurences in r12
        or      cl,cl           ;terminating 0 detected?
        jnz     .exit
        add     rbx,16          ;prepare for next block
        jmp     .loop
.exit:
        mov     rdi, NL
        call    printf
        mov     rax, r12 ;return the number of occurences
leave
ret
;-------------------------------------------------------------
pstrlen:
push   rbp
mov    rbp,rsp
        sub             rsp,16          ;for pushing xmm0
        movdqu          [rbp-16],xmm0 ;push xmm0
        mov     rax, -16            ;avoid ZF flag setting later
        pxor    xmm0, xmm0          ;search for 0 (end of string)
.loop:
        add     rax, 16     ; avoid setting ZF when rax = 0 after pcmpistri
        pcmpistri    xmm0, [rdi + rax], 0x08 ;'equal each'
        jnz             .loop       ;0 found?
        add             rax, rcx    ;rax = bytes already handled
                                    ;rcx = bytes handled in terminating loop
```

```asm
        movdqu          xmm0,[rbp-16]       ;pop xmm0
leave
ret
;---------------------------------------------------------------
;function for printing the mask
;xmm0 contains the mask
;rsi contains the number of bits to print (16 or less)
print_mask:
push   rbp
mov    rbp,rsp
        sub             rsp,16              ;for saving xmm0
        call            reverse_xmm0        ;little endian
        pmovmskb        r13d,xmm0           ;mov byte mask to r13d
        movdqu          [rbp-16],xmm1       ;push xmm1 because of printf
        push            rdi                 ;rdi contains string1
        mov             edi, r13d           ;contains mask to be printed
        push            rdx                 ;contains the mask
        push            rcx                 ;contains end of string flag
        call            print16b
        pop             rcx
        pop             rdx
        pop             rdi
        movdqu          xmm1,[rbp-16] ;pop xmm1
leave
ret
;---------------------------------------------------------------
;function for reversing, shuffling xmm0
reverse_xmm0:
section .data
;mask for reversing
        .bytereverse db 15,14,13,12,11,10,9,8,7,6,5,4,3,2,1,0
section .text
push   rbp
mov    rbp,rsp
        sub        rsp,16
```

```
        movdqu [rbp-16],xmm2
        movdqu xmm2,[.bytereverse]         ;load the mask in xmm2
        pshufb xmm0,xmm2                    ;do the shuffle
        movdqu xmm2,[rbp-16]               ;pop xmm2
leave                              ;returns the shuffled xmm0
ret
```

This program is almost entirely the same as the previous one; we just gave `string2` and `string3` more meaningful names. Most important, we changed the control byte that is handed to `pcmpistrm` to 01000100b, which means "equal range" and "mask byte in xmm0."

The print handling is the same as in the previous section.

Figure 34-2 shows the output.

```
jo@ubuntu18:~/Desktop/Book/40 sse_string5$ ./sse_string5
Find the uppercase letters in:
eeAecdkkFijlmeoZabcefgeKlkmeDadfdsafadfaseeE
00100000100000010000000100001000000000000001
I found 6 uppercase letters
jo@ubuntu18:~/Desktop/Book/40 sse_string5$
```

Figure 34-2. *sse_string5.asm output*

Let's see one more example.

Searching for a Substring

Listing 34-5 shows the code.

Listing 34-5. string6.asm

```
; sse_string6.asm
; find a substring
extern print16b
extern printf
section .data
        string1     db      "a quick pink dinosour jumps over the "
                    db      "lazy river and the lazy dinosour "
                    db      "doesn't mind",10,0
```

```
        string2        db      "dinosour",0
        NL             db      10,0
        fmt            db      "Find the substring '%s' in:",10,0
        fmt_oc         db      "I found %ld %ss",10,0

section .bss
section .text
        global main
main:
push   rbp
mov    rbp,rsp

;first print the strings
        mov     rdi, fmt
        mov     rsi, string2
        xor     rax,rax
        call    printf
        mov     rdi, string1
        xor     rax,rax
        call    printf
; search the string
        mov     rdi, string1
        mov     rsi, string2
        call    psubstringsrch
;print the number of occurences of the substring
        mov     rdi, fmt_oc
        mov     rsi, rax
        mov     rdx, string2
        call    printf
leave
ret
;----------------------------------------------------------------
;function searching substringand printing the mask

psubstringsrch:          ;packed substring search
push   rbp
mov    rbp,rsp
```

```
        sub     rsp,16      ;room for saving xmm1
        xor     r12,r12     ;running total of occurences
        xor     rcx,rcx     ;for signaling the end
        xor     rbx,rbx     ;for address calculation
        mov     rax,-16     ;avoid ZF flag setting
;build xmm1, load substring
        pxor    xmm1,xmm1
        movdqu  xmm1,[rsi]
.loop:
        add     rax,16      ; avoid ZF flag setting
        mov     rsi,16      ;if no 0, print 16 bytes
        movdqu  xmm2,[rdi+rbx]
        pcmpistrm xmm1,xmm2,01001100b ;'equal ordered'|'byte mask in xmm0'
        setz    cl    ; terminating 0 detected

;if terminating 0 found, determine position
        cmp     cl,0
        je      .gotoprint    ; no terminating 0 found
        ;terminating null found
        ;less than 16 bytes left
        ;rdi contains address of string
        ;rbx contains #bytes in blocks handled so far
        add     rdi,rbx             ;take only the tail of the string
        push    rcx                 ;caller saved (cl in use)
        call    pstrlen             ;rax returns the position of the 0
        push    rcx                 ;caller saved (cl in use)
        dec     rax                 ;length without 0
        mov     rsi,rax             ;length of remaining bytes

;print the mask
.gotoprint:
        call print_mask
;keep running total of matches
        popcnt  r13d,r13d    ;count the number of 1 bits
        add     r12d,r13d    ;keep the number of occurences in r12
        or      cl,cl        ;terminating 0 detected?
```

```
        jnz     .exit
        add     rbx,16          ;prepare for next block
        jmp     .loop
.exit:
        mov     rdi, NL
        call    printf
        mov     rax, r12 ;return the number of occurences
leave
ret
;--------------------------------------------------------------
pstrlen:
push  rbp
mov   rbp,rsp
        sub     rsp,16          ;for pushing xmm0
        movdqu  [rbp-16],xmm0 ;push xmm0
        mov     rax, -16            ;avoid ZF flag setting later
        pxor    xmm0, xmm0      ;search for 0 (end of string)
.loop:
        add     rax, 16         ; avoid setting ZF when rax = 0 after pcmpistri
        pcmpistri    xmm0, [rdi + rax], 0x08 ;'equal each'
        jnz     .loop           ;0 found?
        add     rax, rcx        ;rax = bytes already handled
                                ;rcx = bytes handled in terminating loop
        movdqu  xmm0,[rbp-16] ;pop xmm0
leave
ret
;--------------------------------------------------------------
;function for printing the mask
;xmm0 contains the mask
;rsi contains the number of bits to print (16 or less)
print_mask:
push  rbp
mov   rbp,rsp
        sub             rsp,16          ;for saving xmm0
        call            reverse_xmm0  ;little endian
```

```
        pmovmskb        r13d,xmm0       ;mov byte mask to edx
        movdqu          [rbp-16],xmm1 ;push xmm1 because of printf
        push            rdi             ;rdi contains string1
        mov             edi,r13d        ;contains mask to be printed
        push            rdx             ;contains the mask
        push            rcx             ;contains end of string flag
        call            print16b
        pop             rcx
        pop             rdx
        pop             rdi
        movdqu          xmm1,[rbp-16] ;pop xmm1
leave
ret
;-------------------------------------------------------------
;function for reversing, shuffling xmm0
reverse_xmm0:
section .data
;mask for reversing
        .bytereverse db 15,14,13,12,11,10,9,8,7,6,5,4,3,2,1,0
section .text
push    rbp
mov     rbp,rsp
        sub       rsp,16
        movdqu [rbp-16],xmm2
        movdqu xmm2,[.bytereverse] ;load the mask in xmm2
        pshufb xmm0,xmm2            ;do the shuffle
        movdqu xmm2,[rbp-16]        ;pop xmm2
leave                              ;returns the shuffled xmm0
ret
```

We used almost the same code as before; we only changed the strings, and the control byte contains "equal ordered" and "byte mask in xmm0." Pretty easy, isn't it?

Figure 34-3 shows the output.

```
jo@ubuntu18:~/Desktop/Book/41 sse_string6$ ./sse_string6
Find the substring 'dinosour' in:
a quick pink dinosour jumps over the lazy river and the lazy dinosour doesn't mind
0000000000000100000000000000000000000000000000000000000000000100000000000000000000
I found 2 dinosours
jo@ubuntu18:~/Desktop/Book/41 sse_string6$ █
```

Figure 34-3. sse_string6.asm output

Summary

In this chapter, you learned about the following:

- Using string masks

- Searching for characters, ranges, and substrings

- Printing masks from xmm registers

CHAPTER 35

AVX

Advanced Vector Extensions (AVX) is an extension of SSE. Whereas SSE provides 16 xmm registers, each 128 bits wide, AVX offers 16 ymm registers, each 256 bits wide. The lower half of each ymm register is in fact the corresponding xmm register. The xmm registers are aliases of the ymm registers. AVX-512 is a further extension offering 32 zmm registers, each 512 bits wide.

In addition to these registers, AVX extends the SSE instructions and provides a whole range of additional new instructions. After you work your way through the SSE chapters in this book, you will not find it too difficult to navigate the large number of SSE and AVX instructions.

In this chapter, we will first explain which AVX version is supported by the processor, and then we will show an example program.

Test for AVX Support

Listing 35-1 shows a program to find out whether your CPU supports AVX.

Listing 35-1. cpu_avx.asm

```
; cpu_avx.asm
extern printf
section .data
    fmt_noavx      db        "This cpu does not support AVX.",10,0
    fmt_avx        db        "This cpu supports AVX.",10,0
    fmt_noavx2     db        "This cpu does not support AVX2.",10,0
    fmt_avx2       db        "This cpu supports AVX2.",10,0
    fmt_noavx512   db        "This cpu does not support AVX-512.",10,0
    fmt_avx512     db        "This cpu supports AVX-512.",10,0
```

© Jo Van Hoey 2019
J. Van Hoey, *Beginning x64 Assembly Programming*, https://doi.org/10.1007/978-1-4842-5076-1_35

```
section .bss
section .text
      global main
main:
push  rbp
mov   rbp,rsp
      call   cpu_sse       ; returns 1 in rax if AVX supported, otherwise 0
leave
ret

cpu_sse:
push  rbp
mov   rbp,rsp
;test for avx
      mov    eax,1         ; request CPU feature flags
      cpuid
      mov    eax,28        ; test bit 28 in ecx
      bt     ecx,eax
      jnc    no_avx
      xor    rax,rax
      mov    rdi,fmt_avx
      call   printf
;test for avx2
      mov    eax,7         ; request CPU feature flags
      mov    ecx,0
      cpuid
      mov    eax,5         ; test bit 5 in ebx
      bt     ebx,eax
      jnc    the_exit
      xor    rax,rax
      mov    rdi,fmt_avx2
      call   printf
;test for avx512 foundation
      mov    eax,7         ; request CPU feature flags
      mov    ecx,0
      cpuid
```

```
        mov     eax,16          ; test bit 16 in ebx
        bt      ebx,eax
        jnc     no_avx512
        xor     rax,rax
        mov     rdi,fmt_avx512
        call    printf
        jmp     the_exit
no_avx:
        mov     rdi,fmt_noavx
        xor     rax,rax
        call    printf          ; displays message if AVX not available
        xor     rax,rax         ; returns 0, no AVX
        jmp     the_exit        ; and exits

no_avx2:
        mov     rdi,fmt_noavx2
        xor     rax,rax
        call    printf          ; displays message if AVX not available
        xor     rax,rax         ; returns 0, no AVX
        jmp     the_exit        ; and exits

no_avx512:
        mov     rdi,fmt_noavx512
        xor     rax,rax
        call    printf          ; displays message if AVX not available
        xor     rax,rax         ; returns 0, no AVX
        jmp     the_exit              ; and exits
the_exit:
leave
ret
```

This program is similar to the program we used to test for SSE support, but we have to look for AVX flags now. So, there is nothing special here; you can find more details of which registers to use and what information can be retrieved in the Intel manual, Volume 2, in the section on cpuid.

Figure 35-1 shows the output.

```
jo@ubuntu18:~/Desktop/Book/42 cpu_avx$ ./cpu_avx
This cpu supports AVX.
This cpu supports AVX2.
This cpu does not support AVX-512.
jo@ubuntu18:~/Desktop/Book/42 cpu_avx$ █
```

Figure 35-1. *cpu_avx.asm output*

Example AVX Program

Listing 35-2 is adapted from the SSE unaligned example in Chapter 28.

Listing 35-2. avx_unaligned.asm

```
; avx_unaligned.asm
extern printf
section .data
        spvector1       dd      1.1
                        dd      2.1
                        dd      3.1
                        dd      4.1
                        dd      5.1
                        dd      6.1
                        dd      7.1
                        dd      8.1

        spvector2       dd      1.2
                        dd      1.2
                        dd      3.2
                        dd      4.2
                        dd      5.2
                        dd      6.2
                        dd      7.2
                        dd      8.2

        dpvector1       dq      1.1
                        dq      2.2
                        dq      3.3
                        dq      4.4
```

```
    dpvector2       dq      5.5
                    dq      6.6
                    dq      7.7
                    dq      8.8

    fmt1    db      "Single Precision Vector 1:",10,0
    fmt2    db      10,"Single Precision Vector 2:",10,0
    fmt3    db      10,"Sum of Single Precision Vector 1 and Vector 2:",10,0
    fmt4    db      10,"Double Precision Vector 1:",10,0
    fmt5    db      10,"Double Precision Vector 2:",10,0
    fmt6    db      10,"Sum of Double Precision Vector 1 and Vector 2:",10,0

section .bss
    spvector_res    resd    8
    dpvector_res    resq    4
section .text
    global main
main:
push    rbp
mov     rbp,rsp
;SINGLE PRECISION FLOATING POINT VECTORS
;load vector1 in the register ymm0
    vmovups         ymm0, [spvector1]
;extract ymm0
    vextractf128    xmm2,ymm0,0     ;first part of ymm0
    vextractf128    xmm2,ymm0,1     ;second part of ymm0
;load vector2 in the register ymm1
    vmovups         ymm1, [spvector2]
;extract ymm1
    vextractf128    xmm2,ymm1,0
    vextractf128    xmm2,ymm1,1
;add 2 single precision floating point vectors
    vaddps          ymm2,ymm0,ymm1
    vmovups [spvector_res],ymm2
;print the vectors
    mov     rdi,fmt1
```

311

```
        call    printf
        mov     rsi,spvector1
        call    printspfpv
        mov     rdi,fmt2
        call    printf
        mov     rsi,spvector2
        call    printspfpv
        mov     rdi,fmt3
        call    printf
        mov     rsi,spvector_res
        call    printspfpv
;DOUBLE PRECISION FLOATING POINT VECTORS
;load vector1 in the register ymm0
        vmovups         ymm0, [dpvector1]
;extract ymm0
        vextractf128    xmm2,ymm0,0     ;first part of ymm0
        vextractf128    xmm2,ymm0,1     ;second part of ymm0
;load vector2 in the register ymm1
        vmovups         ymm1, [dpvector2]
;extract ymm1
        vextractf128    xmm2,ymm1,0
        vextractf128    xmm2,ymm1,1
; add 2 double precision floating point vectors
        vaddpd          ymm2,ymm0,ymm1
        vmovupd         [dpvector_res],ymm2
;print the vectors
        mov     rdi,fmt4
        call    printf
        mov     rsi,dpvector1
        call    printdpfpv
        mov     rdi,fmt5
        call    printf
        mov     rsi,dpvector2
        call    printdpfpv
        mov     rdi,fmt6
```

```
        call    printf
        mov     rsi,dpvector_res
        call    printdpfpv
leave
ret

printspfpv:
section .data
        .NL     db      10,0
        .fmt1           db      "%.1f,  ",0
section .text
push    rbp
mov     rbp,rsp
        push            rcx
        push            rbx
        mov             rcx,8
        mov             rbx,0
        mov             rax,1
.loop:
        movss           xmm0,[rsi+rbx]
        cvtss2sd        xmm0,xmm0
        mov             rdi,.fmt1
        push            rsi
        push            rcx
        call            printf
        pop             rcx
        pop             rsi
        add             rbx,4
        loop            .loop
        xor             rax,rax
        mov             rdi,.NL
        call            printf
        pop             rbx
        pop             rcx
leave
ret
```

```
printdpfpv:
section .data
        .NL  db    10,0
        .fmt db    "%.1f,  %.1f,  %.1f,  %.1f",0
section .text
push    rbp
mov     rbp,rsp
        mov    rdi,.fmt
        mov    rax,4  ; four floats
        call   printf
        mov    rdi,.NL
        call   printf
leave
ret
```

In this program, we use the 256-bit ymm registers and some new instructions. For example, we use vmovups to put unaligned data in a ymm register. We use SASM to view the registers. After the vmovups instructions, ymm0 contains the following:

{0x4083333340466666400666663f8ccccd,0x4101999a40e3333340c3333340a33333}

Here is what it looks like converted to decimal:

{4.1 3.1 2.1 1.1 ,   8.1 7.1 6.1 5.1}

Look at where the values are stored, which can be confusing.

Just for the sake of the demo, we extract data from a ymm register, and we use vextractf128 to put packed floating-point values from ymm0 to xmm2, 128 bits at a time. You could use extractps to further extract floating-point values and store them in general-purpose registers.

New are instructions with three operands, as shown here:

```
    vaddps ymm2,ymm0,ymm1
```

Add ymm1 to ymm0 and store the result in ymm2.

The print functions simply load the values from memory into an xmm register, convert single precision to double precision where needed, and then call printf.

Figure 35-2 shows the output.

```
jo@ubuntu18:~/Desktop/Book/43 avx_unaligned$ ./avx_unaligned
Single Precision Vector 1:
1.1,   2.1,   3.1,   4.1,   5.1,   6.1,   7.1,   8.1,

Single Precision Vector 2:
1.2,   1.2,   3.2,   4.2,   5.2,   6.2,   7.2,   8.2,

Sum of Single Precision Vector 1 and Vector 2:
2.3,   3.3,   6.3,   8.3,   10.3,   12.3,   14.3,   16.3,

Double Precision Vector 1:
1.1,   2.2,   3.3,   4.4

Double Precision Vector 2:
5.5,   6.6,   7.7,   8.8

Sum of Double Precision Vector 1 and Vector 2:
6.6,   8.8,   11.0,   13.2
jo@ubuntu18:~/Desktop/Book/43 avx_unaligned$ █
```

Figure 35-2. *avx_unaligned.asm output*

Summary

In this chapter, you learned about the following:

- How to determine CPU support for AVX

- That AVX uses 16 256-bit ymm registers

- That the 128-bit xmm registers are aliased ymm registers

- How to extract values from ymm registers

CHAPTER 36

AVX Matrix Operations

Instead of summing up a number of possibly interesting AVX instructions, let's look at some matrix operations using AVX. This is a long chapter with several pages of code; a lot will be familiar, but we will introduce several new instructions here.

We will show matrix multiplication and matrix inversion. In the next chapter, we will show how to transpose a matrix.

Example Matrix Code

Listing 36-1 shows the example code.

Listing 36-1. matrix4x4.asm

```
; matrix4x4.asm
extern printf

section .data
        fmt0    db      10,"4x4 DOUBLE PRECISION FLOATING POINT MATRICES",10,0
        fmt1    db      10,"This is matrixA:",10,0
        fmt2    db      10,"This is matrixB:",10,0
        fmt3    db      10,"This is matrixA x matrixB:",10,0
        fmt4    db      10,"This is matrixC:",10,0
        fmt5    db      10,"This is the inverse of matrixC:",10,0
        fmt6    db      10,"Proof: matrixC x inverse =",10,0
        fmt7    db      10,"This is matrixS:",10,0
        fmt8    db      10,"This is the inverse of matrixS:",10,0
        fmt9    db      10,"Proof: matrixS x inverse =",10,0
        fmt10   db      10,"This matrix is singular!",10,10,0
```

© Jo Van Hoey 2019
J. Van Hoey, *Beginning x64 Assembly Programming*, https://doi.org/10.1007/978-1-4842-5076-1_36

```
        align 32
          matrixA      dq      1.,   3.,   5.,   7.
                       dq      9.,  11.,  13.,  15.
                       dq     17.,  19.,  21.,  23.
                       dq     25.,  27.,  29.,  31.

          matrixB      dq      2.,   4.,   6.,   8.
                       dq     10.,  12.,  14.,  16.
                       dq     18.,  20.,  22.,  24.
                       dq     26.,  28.,  30.,  32.

          matrixC      dq      2.,          11.,        21.,       37.
                       dq      3.,          13.,        23.,       41.
                       dq      5.,          17.,        29.,       43.
                       dq      7.,          19.,        31.,       47.

          matrixS      dq      1.,    2.,    3.,       4.
                       dq      5.,    6.,    7.,       8.
                       dq      9.,   10.,   11.,      12.
                       dq     13.,   14.,   15.,      16.

section .bss
      alignb 32
      product resq 16
      inverse resq 16
section .text
      global main
main:
push  rbp
mov   rbp,rsp
; print title
      mov     rdi, fmt0
      call    printf
; print matrixA
      mov     rdi,fmt1
      call    printf
      mov     rsi,matrixA
      call    printm4x4
```

```
; print matrixB
        mov     rdi,fmt2
        call    printf
        mov     rsi,matrixB
        call    printm4x4
; compute the product matrixA x matrixB
        mov     rdi,matrixA
        mov     rsi,matrixB
        mov     rdx,product
        call    multi4x4
; print the product
        mov     rdi,fmt3
        call    printf
        mov     rsi,product
        call    printm4x4

; print matrixC
        mov     rdi,fmt4
        call    printf
        mov     rsi,matrixC
        call    printm4x4
; compute the inverse of matrixC
        mov     rdi,matrixC
        mov     rsi,inverse
        call    inverse4x4
        cmp     rax,1
        je      singular
; print the inverse
        mov     rdi,fmt5
        call    printf
        mov     rsi,inverse
        call    printm4x4
; proof multiply matrixC and inverse
        mov     rsi,matrixC
        mov     rdi,inverse
```

```
        mov     rdx,product
        call    multi4x4
; print the proof
        mov     rdi,fmt6
        call    printf
        mov     rsi,product
        call    printm4x4

; Singular matrix
; print matrixS
        mov     rdi,fmt7
        call    printf
        mov     rsi,matrixS
        call    printm4x4
; compute the inverse of matrixS
        mov     rdi,matrixS
        mov     rsi,inverse
        call    inverse4x4
        cmp     rax,1
        je      singular
; print the inverse
        mov     rdi,fmt8
        call    printf
        mov     rsi,inverse
        call    printm4x4
; proof multiply matrixS and inverse
        mov     rsi,matrixS
        mov     rdi,inverse
        mov     rdx,product
        call    multi4x4
; print the proof
        mov     rdi,fmt9
        call    printf
        mov     rsi,product
        call    printm4x4
        jmp     exit
```

```
singular:
; print error
      mov     rdi,fmt10
      call printf
exit:
leave
ret

inverse4x4:
section .data
      align 32
      .identity    dq        1., 0., 0., 0.
                   dq        0., 1., 0., 0.
                   dq        0., 0., 1., 0.
                   dq        0., 0., 0., 1.

      .minus_mask  dq        8000000000000000h
      .size        dq        4                  ;4 x 4 matrices
      .one         dq        1.0
      .two         dq        2.0
      .three       dq        3.0
      .four        dq        4.0

section .bss
      alignb 32
      .matrix1 resq 16          ;intermediate matrix
      .matrix2 resq 16          ;intermediate matrix
      .matrix3 resq 16          ;intermediate matrix
      .matrix4 resq 16          ;intermediate matrix
      .matrixI resq 16

      .mxcsr resd 1      ;used for checking zero division

section .text
push   rbp
mov    rbp,rsp
      push    rsi        ;save address of inverse matrix
      vzeroall            ;clear all ymm registers
```

```
; compute the intermediate matrices
; compute the intermediate matrix2
; rdi contains address of the original matrix
      mov     rsi,rdi
      mov     rdx,.matrix2
      push    rdi
      call    multi4x4
      pop     rdi

; compute the intermediate matrix3
      mov     rsi,.matrix2
      mov     rdx,.matrix3
      push    rdi
      call    multi4x4
      pop     rdi

; compute the intermediate matrix4
      mov     rsi,.matrix3
      mov     rdx,.matrix4
      push    rdi
      call    multi4x4
      pop     rdi

;compute the traces
;compute trace1
      mov     rsi,[.size]
      call    vtrace
      movsd   xmm8,xmm0     ;trace 1 in xmm8
;compute trace2
      push    rdi                 ; save address of the original matrix
      mov     rdi,.matrix2
      mov     rsi,[.size]
      call    vtrace
      movsd   xmm9,xmm0    ;trace 2 in xmm9
;compute trace3
      mov     rdi,.matrix3
      mov     rsi,[.size]
```

```
        call    vtrace
        movsd   xmm10,xmm0    ;trace 3 in xmm10
;compute trace4
        mov     rdi,.matrix4
        mov     rsi,[.size]
        call    vtrace
        movsd   xmm11,xmm0    ;trace 4 in xmm11

; compute the coefficients
; compute coefficient p1
; p1 = -s1
        vxorpd          xmm12,xmm8,[.minus_mask] ;p1 in xmm12
; compute coefficient p2
; p2 = -1/2 * (p1 * s1 + s2)
        movsd           xmm13,xmm12    ;copy p1 to xmm13
        vfmadd213sd     xmm13,xmm8,xmm9 ;xmm13=xmm13*xmm8+xmm9
        vxorpd          xmm13,xmm13,[.minus_mask]
        divsd           xmm13,[.two] ;divide by 2 and p2 in xmm13
; compute coefficient p3
; p3 = -1/3 * (p2 * s1 + p1 * s2 + s3)
        movsd           xmm14,xmm12                 ;copy p1 to xmm14
        vfmadd213sd     xmm14,xmm9,xmm10 ;p1*s2+s3;xmm14=xmm14*xmm9+xmm10
        vfmadd231sd     xmm14,xmm13,xmm8  ;xmm14+p2*s1;xmm14=xmm14+xmm13*xmm8
        vxorpd          xmm14,xmm14,[.minus_mask]
        divsd           xmm14,[.three]              ;p3 in xmm14
; compute coefficient p4
; p4 = -1/4 * (p3 * s1 + p2 * s2 + p1 * s3 + s4)
        movsd           xmm15,xmm12    ;copy p1 to xmm15
        vfmadd213sd     xmm15,xmm10,xmm11 ;p1*s3+s4;xmm15=xmm15*xmm10+xmm11
        vfmadd231sd     xmm15,xmm13,xmm9  ;xmm15+p2*s2;xmm15=xmm15+xmm13*xmm9
        vfmadd231sd     xmm15,xmm14,xmm8  ;xmm15+p3*s1;xmm15=xmm15+xmm14*xmm8
        vxorpd          xmm15,xmm15,[.minus_mask]
        divsd           xmm15,[.four]     ;p4 in xmm15

;multiply matrices with proper coefficient
```

323

```
        mov             rcx,[.size]
        xor             rax,rax

        vbroadcastsd        ymm1,xmm12 ; p1
        vbroadcastsd        ymm2,xmm13 ; p2
        vbroadcastsd        ymm3,xmm14 ; p3

        pop rdi     ; restore the address of the original matrix

.loop1:
        vmovapd             ymm0,[rdi+rax]
        vmulpd              ymm0,ymm0,ymm2
        vmovapd             [.matrix1+rax],ymm0

        vmovapd             ymm0,[.matrix2+rax]
        vmulpd              ymm0,ymm0,ymm1
        vmovapd             [.matrix2+rax],ymm0

        vmovapd             ymm0,[.identity+rax]
        vmulpd              ymm0,ymm0,ymm3
        vmovapd             [.matrixI+rax],ymm0

        add             rax,32
        loop            .loop1

;add the four matrices and multiply by -1/p4
        mov             rcx,[.size]
        xor             rax,rax
 ;compute -1/p4
        movsd           xmm0, [.one]
        vdivsd          xmm0,xmm0,xmm15     ;1/p4
 ;check for zero division
        stmxcsr         [.mxcsr]
        and             dword[.mxcsr],4
        jnz             .singular

; no zero division
        pop             rsi             ;recall address of inverse matrix
        vxorpd          xmm0,xmm0,[.minus_mask]   ;-1/p4
        vbroadcastsd ymm2,xmm0
```

324

```
        ;loop through the rows
.loop2:
            ;add the rows
            vmovapd         ymm0,[.matrix1+rax]
            vaddpd          ymm0, ymm0, [.matrix2+rax]
            vaddpd          ymm0, ymm0, [.matrix3+rax]
            vaddpd          ymm0, ymm0, [.matrixI+rax]
            vmulpd          ymm0,ymm0,ymm2          ;multiply the row with -1/p4
            vmovapd         [rsi+rax],ymm0
            add             rax,32
            loop            .loop2

            xor             rax,rax     ;return 0, no error
leave
ret

.singular:
            mov             rax,1       ;return 1, singular matrix
leave
ret
;-------------------------------------------------------
; trace computation
vtrace:
push    rbp
mov     rbp,rsp
;build the matrix in memory
            vmovapd         ymm0, [rdi]
            vmovapd         ymm1, [rdi+32]
            vmovapd         ymm2, [rdi+64]
            vmovapd         ymm3, [rdi+96]
            vblendpd        ymm0,ymm0,ymm1,0010b
            vblendpd        ymm0,ymm0,ymm2,0100b
            vblendpd        ymm0,ymm0,ymm3,1000b
            vhaddpd         ymm0,ymm0,ymm0
            vpermpd         ymm0,ymm0,00100111b
            haddpd          xmm0,xmm0
```

```
leave
ret
;-------------------------------------------------------
printm4x4:
section .data
      .fmt db        "%f",9,"%f",9, "%f",9,"%f",10,0
section .text
push  rbp
mov   rbp,rsp
push rbx              ;callee saved
push r15              ;callee saved
      mov rdi,.fmt
      mov rcx,4
      xor rbx,rbx           ;row counter
.loop:
      movsd  xmm0, [rsi+rbx]
      movsd  xmm1, [rsi+rbx+8]
      movsd  xmm2, [rsi+rbx+16]
      movsd  xmm3, [rsi+rbx+24]
      mov    rax,4         ;four floats
      push   rcx                 ;caller saved
      push   rsi                 ;caller saved
      push   rdi                 ;caller saved
            ;align stack if needed
            xor r15,r15
            test rsp,0xf       ;last byte is 8 (not aligned)?
            setnz r15b         ;set if not aligned
            shl r15,3          ;multiply by 8
            sub rsp,r15        ;substract 0 or 8
      call   printf
            add rsp,r15        ;add 0 or 8 to restore rsp
      pop    rdi
      pop    rsi
      pop    rcx
      add    rbx,32       ;next row
      loop   .loop
```

```
pop r15
pop rbx
leave
ret
;--------------------------------------------------------
multi4x4:
push   rbp
mov    rbp,rsp

       xor rax,rax
       mov rcx,4
       vzeroall               ;zero all ymm
.loop:
       vmovapd        ymm0, [rsi]

       vbroadcastsd ymm1,[rdi+rax]
       vfmadd231pd    ymm12,ymm1,ymm0

       vbroadcastsd ymm1,[rdi+32+rax]
       vfmadd231pd    ymm13,ymm1,ymm0

       vbroadcastsd ymm1,[rdi+64+rax]
       vfmadd231pd    ymm14,ymm1,ymm0

       vbroadcastsdymm1,[rdi+96+rax]
       vfmadd231pd    ymm15,ymm1,ymm0

       add rax,8     ;one element has 8 bytes, 64 bits
       add rsi,32    ;every row has 32 bytes, 256 bits

       loop .loop

;move the result to memory, row per row
       vmovapd        [rdx], ymm12
       vmovapd        [rdx+32], ymm13
       vmovapd        [rdx+64], ymm14
       vmovapd        [rdx+96], ymm15
       xor            rax,rax   ;return value
leave
ret
```

The interesting parts of this code are in the functions. The main function is for initializing the program, calling functions, and printing. The matrices we use in this example are 4×4 double-precision floating-point matrices. Note the 32-byte alignment of the matrices; in AVX we use ymm registers, with a size of 32 bytes. We will analyze the program function by function.

Matrix Print: printm4x4

We read the matrix one row at a time into four xmm registers, and then we push a number of registers onto the stack. These registers will be modified by printf, so we have to preserve them. Then we align the stack on a 16-byte boundary. Because of normal operation, rsp will be aligned on an 8-byte boundary. To align the stack on a 16-byte boundary, we cannot use the trick with the and instruction from Chapter 16. This is because with the and instruction, we do not know whether rsp will be changed or not. And we need the correct stack pointer because we pop the pushed registers after printf. If rsp was changed, we need to return it to its previous value before popping; otherwise, the wrong values will be popped from the stack. If rsp was not changed, we do not need to adjust it.

We will use the test instruction and 0xf to verify the alignment of the stack. If the last hexadecimal digit of rsp is a 0, then rsp is 16-byte aligned. If the last digit contains anything other than 0, then the last half-byte will have at least one of its bits set to 1. The test instruction is similar to an and instruction. If the last half-byte of rsp has one or more bits set to 1, the result of the comparison will be nonzero, and the zero-flag ZF will be cleared. The setnz (set-if-non-zero) instruction reads the zero flag (ZF), and if the ZF is not set, setnz will put 0000 0001 into r15b. If that happens, it means that rsp is not 16-byte aligned, and we will subtract 8 to put it on a 16-byte boundary. We left-shift r15b three times to obtain the decimal value 8 and do the subtraction. After the execution of printf, we restore the correct stack address by adding r15 back to rsp, that is, adding 8 if we had to align or adding 0 if we did not have to align. The stack is then where it was before our alignment, and we can pop the registers.

Matrix Multiplication: multi4x4

In the sample code and in the following explanation, we use the following two matrices:

$$A = \begin{bmatrix} 1 & 3 & 5 & 7 \\ 9 & 11 & 13 & 15 \\ 17 & 19 & 21 & 23 \\ 25 & 27 & 29 & 31 \end{bmatrix} \qquad B = \begin{bmatrix} 2 & 4 & 6 & 8 \\ 10 & 12 & 14 & 16 \\ 18 & 20 & 22 & 24 \\ 26 & 28 & 30 & 32 \end{bmatrix}$$

If you studied some linear algebra, you probably learned to multiply matrices as follows: to obtain element c_{11} of matrix C = AB, you compute the following:

$$a_{11}b_{11} + a_{12}b_{21} + a_{13}b_{31} + a_{14}b_{41}$$

With our example, it looks like this:

```
1x2 + 3x10 + 5x18 + 7x26 = 304
```

As another example, element c_{32} would be computed as follows:

$$a_{31}b_{12} + a_{32}b_{22} + a_{33}b_{32} + a_{34}b_{42}$$

With our example, it looks like this:

```
17x4 + 19x12 + 21x20 + 23x28 = 1360
```

This is efficient for manual computation; however, we are going to use a method that is more appropriate for a computer. We will use the ymm registers for keeping running totals and for updating the totals in subsequent loops. Here we make use of the power of AVX instructions.

First, we clear all the ymm registers with vzeroall. Then we go into a loop four times, once for every row in matrixB. A row of four double-precision values from matrixB is loaded in ymm0. Then a value from a sequentially selected column of matrixA is broadcasted into ymm1. The register rax serves as a column counter, and the column values are at offset 0, 32, 64, and 96. Broadcasting means that all four quadwords (8 bytes each) will contain that value. Then the values in ymm1 are multiplied with the values in ymm0 and added to ymm12. The multiplying and adding are done with one instruction called vfmadd231pd, which means "vector fused multiply add packed double."

The 231 indicates how the registers are used. There are multiple variants of vfmadd (132, 213, 231), and there are variants for double precision and single precision. We used 231, which means multiply the second operand with the third operand, add to the first operand, and put the result in the first operand. This is done for every column value of the matrixA column, and then the iteration continues; the next row of matrixB is loaded, and the computation restarts.

Walk through the program with your favorite debugger. Look at how the registers ymm12, ymm13, ymm14, and ymm15 keep the running totals, and finally give the product. Your debugger probably will give the values in the ymm registers in hexadecimal and little-endian format. To make it easy, here are the details of what is happening at every step:

rdi					rsi				
	32 bytes						32 bytes		
	8 bytes	8 bytes	8 bytes	8 bytes		8 bytes	8 bytes	8 bytes	8 bytes
0–31	1	3	5	7	0–31	2	4	6	8
32–63	9	11	13	15	32–63	10	12	14	16
64–95	17	19	21	23	64–95	18	20	22	24
96–127	25	27	29	31	96–127	26	28	30	32

Here is the first loop:

vmovapd ymm0, [rsi]	ymm0	2	4	6	8
vbroadcastsd ymm1,[rdi+0]	ymm1	1	1	1	1
vfmadd231pd ymm12,ymm1,ymm0	ymm12	2	4	6	8
vbroadcastsd ymm1,[rdi+32+0]	ymm1	9	9	9	9
vfmadd231pd ymm13,ymm1,ymm0	ymm13	18	36	54	72
vbroadcastsd ymm1,[rdi+64+0]	ymm1	17	17	17	17
vfmadd231pd ymm14,ymm1,ymm0	ymm14	34	68	102	136
vbroadcastsd ymm1,[rdi+96+0]	ymm1	25	25	25	25
vfmadd231pd ymm15,ymm1,ymm0	ymm15	50	100	150	200

Here is the second loop:

vmovapd ymm0, [rsi+32]	ymm0	10	12	14	16
vbroadcastsd ymm1,[rdi+8]	ymm1	3	3	3	3
vfmadd231pd ymm12,ymm1,ymm0	ymm12	32	40	48	56
vbroadcastsd ymm1,[rdi+32+8]	ymm1	11	11	11	11
vfmadd231pd ymm13,ymm1,ymm0	ymm13	128	168	208	248
vbroadcastsd ymm1,[rdi+64+8]	ymm1	19	19	19	19
vfmadd231pd ymm14,ymm1,ymm0	ymm14	224	296	368	440
vbroadcastsd ymm1,[rdi+96+8]	ymm1	27	27	27	27
vfmadd231pd ymm15,ymm1,ymm0	ymm15	320	424	528	632

Here is the third loop:

vmovapd ymm0, [rsi+32+32]	ymm0	18	20	22	24
vbroadcastsd ymm1,[rdi+8+8]	ymm1	5	5	5	5
vfmadd231pd ymm12,ymm1,ymm0	ymm12	122	140	158	176
vbroadcastsd ymm1,[rdi+32+8+8]	ymm1	13	13	13	13
vfmadd231pd ymm13,ymm1,ymm0	ymm13	362	428	494	560
vbroadcastsd ymm1,[rdi+64+8+8]	ymm1	21	21	21	21
vfmadd231pd ymm14,ymm1,ymm0	ymm14	602	716	830	944
vbroadcastsd ymm1,[rdi+96+8+8]	ymm1	29	29	29	29
vfmadd231pd ymm15,ymm1,ymm0	ymm15	842	1004	1166	1328

Here is the fourth and last loop:

vmovapd ymm0, [rsi+32+32+32]	ymm0	26	28	30	32
vbroadcastsd ymm1,[rdi+8+8+8]	ymm1	7	7	7	7
vfmadd231pd ymm12,ymm1,ymm0	ymm12	304	336	368	400
vbroadcastsd ymm1,[rdi+32+8+8+8]	ymm1	15	15	15	15
vfmadd231pd ymm13,ymm1,ymm0	ymm13	752	848	944	1040

(*continued*)

vbroadcastsd ymm1,[rdi+64+8+8+8]	ymm1	23	23	23	23
vfmadd231pd ymm14,ymm1,ymm0	ymm14	1200	1360	1520	1680
vbroadcastsd ymm1,[rdi+96+8+8+8]	ymm1	31	31	31	31
vfmadd231pd ymm15,ymm1,ymm0	ymm15	1648	1872	2096	2320

Matrix Inversion: Inverse4x4

Mathematicians have developed a range of algorithms to efficiently compute the inverse of a matrix. It is not our intent to provide you with an inversion program with all the bells and whistles; we just want to show how to use AVX.

We will use a method based on the *Cayley-Hamilton theorem* about characteristic polynomials. Here is an interesting site with more information on characteristic polynomials: http://www.mcs.csueastbay.edu/~malek/Class/Characteristic.pdf.

Caley-Hamilton Theorem

From the Cayley-Hamilton theorem, we have the following for matrix A:

$$A^n + p_1 A^{n-1} + \cdots + p_{n-1}A + p_n I = 0$$

where A^n is A to the power of n. For example, A^3 is AAA, the matrix A three times multiplied with itself. The p's are coefficients to be determined, I is the identity matrix, and 0 is the zero matrix.

Multiply the previous equation by A^{-1}, divide by $-p_n$, rearrange the terms, and you obtain a formula for the inverse, as shown here:

$$\frac{1}{-p_n}\left[A^{n-1} + p_1 A^{n-2} + \cdots + p_{n-2}A + p_{n-1}I \right] = A^{-1}$$

So, to find the inverse of matrix A, we need to do a number of matrix multiplications, and we need a method to find the p's.

For a 4×4 matrix A, we have the following:

$$\frac{1}{-p_4}\left[A^3 + p_1 A^2 + p_2 A + p_3 I \right] = A^{-1}$$

Leverrier Algorithm

To compute the p coefficients, we use the Leverrier algorithm, also covered at `http://www.mcs.csueastbay.edu/~malek/Class/Characteristic.pdf`. First, we find the traces of the matrices, that is, the sum of the elements on the diagonal from the upper left to the lower right. Let's call s_n the trace of the matrix A^n.

For a 4×4 matrix A, we compute the traces of the power matrices of A, as shown here:

s_1 for A

s_2 for AA

s_3 for AAA

s_4 for $AAAA$

Leverrier gives us the following then:

$$p_1 = -s_1$$

$$p_2 = -\frac{1}{2}\left(p_1 s_1 + s_2\right)$$

$$p_3 = -\frac{1}{3}\left(p_2 s_1 + p_1 s_2 + s_3\right)$$

$$p_4 = -\frac{1}{4}\left(p_3 s_1 + p_2 s_2 + p_1 s_3 + s_4\right)$$

Pretty simple, right? Apart from some elaborate matrix multiplications to obtain the traces, of course.

The Code

In our function `inverse4x4`, we have a separate `section .data`, where we put our identity matrix and some variables we will use later. First, we compute the power matrices and store them in `matrix2`, `matrix3`, and `matrix4`. We will not use `matrix1` yet. Then we call the function `vtrace` for every matrix to compute the traces. In the `vtrace` function, we first build our matrix in the ymm registers (`ymm0`, `ymm1`, `ymm2`, `ymm3`), each containing a row. Then we use the instruction `vblendpd`, which has four operands: two source operands, one destination operand, and a control mask. We want to extract the diagonal elements in rows 2, 3, and 4 and put them as packed values in ymm0, at locations index 1, 2, and 3. At location 0, we keep the trace element of ymm0.

The mask determines which packed values are selected from the source operands. A 1 in the mask means at this location, select the value from the second source operand. A 0 in the mask means at this location, select the value from the first source operand. See Figure 36-1 for a schematic overview, but note that in the figure we display the values in the registers in such a way that they correspond with the bit mask indexes. In your debugger, you will see that the positions in ymm0 are a1, a0, a3, a2.

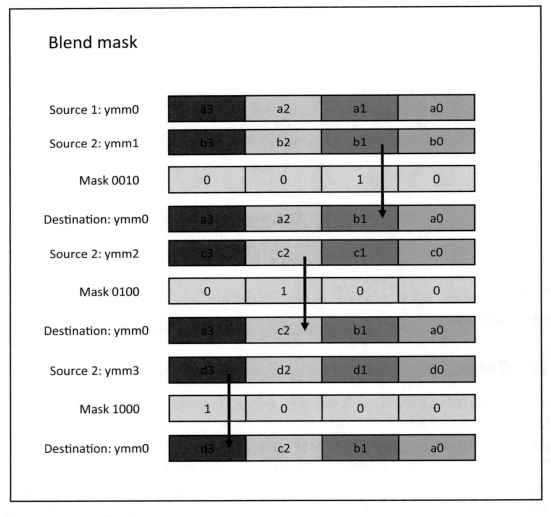

Figure 36-1. *Blend mask*

In the first trace computation, after the blending, the ymm0 register contains the trace elements 2, 13, 29, 47. You can check this with SASM. Don't be fooled by the order of the values of ymm0 as represented: 13, 2, 47, 29. We now have to sum these values. This can easily be done by extracting and simply adding, but for the sake of the demo, we will use AVX instructions. We apply the horizontal add instruction vhaddpd. ymm0 then contains 15, 15, 76, 76, which are the sum of the two lower values and the sum of the two higher values. Then we execute a permutation vpermpd with mask 00100111. Each two-bit value selects a value in the source operand; see Figure 36-2 for an explanation. Now the lower half of ymm0, which is xmm0, contains two values, so we have to add these to obtain the trace. We execute a horizontal add on xmm0 with haddpd. We store the traces in xmm8, xmm9, xmm10, and xmm11 for later use.

It's a bit overkill to obtain the trace, don't you think? We did it this way just to show a couple of AVX instructions and how to use masks.

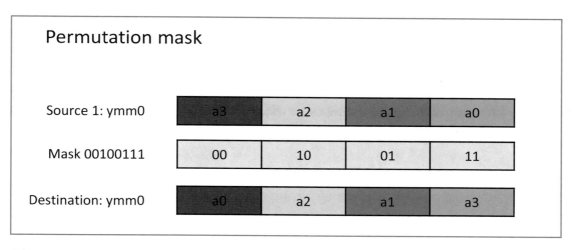

Figure 36-2. *Permutation mask*

When we have all the traces, we can compute the p-coefficients. See how we change the sign of a value by applying a minus mask and the instruction vxorpd. We use the vfmadd213sd and vfmadd231sd to do additions and multiplications in one instruction. The instruction vfmadd213sd means multiply the first and second operands, add a third operand, and put the result in the first operand. The instruction vfmadd231sd means multiply the second and third operands, add the first operand, and put the result in the first operand. There is a list of similar instructions in the Intel manual. Study them carefully.

When we have all the coefficients, we scalar-multiply `matrix`, `matrix2`, `matrix3`, and `matrixI` with the coefficients, according to the previous formulae. The result of multiplication with `matrix` is put into `matrix1`. We do not need `matrix4` anymore, so to save memory, we could have used the space for `inverse` as temporary memory instead of `matrix4`.

We have to divide by coefficient p_4, so we have to check that p_4 is nonzero. In this case, we could have done this simple operation after computing p_4 earlier, but we wanted to show how to use the `mxcsr` register. We set the zero-division mask bit in `mxcsr` and do the division with the instruction `vdivsd`. If after division the third bit (index 2) in the `mxcsr` register is set, then we had a zero division, and the matrix is singular and cannot be inversed. In the `and` instruction, we used decimal 4, which is 0000 0100 in binary, so we are checking the third bit indeed. If we had a zero division, we head for the exit with 1 in `rax` to signal the error to the caller.

When a matrix is singular, the program will not crash because zero division is masked by default in the `mxcsr` register. After you finish the analysis of this code, comment out the part that checks for zero division and see what happens.

If p_4 is nonzero, we add the four matrices and scalar-multiply the result with $-1/p_4$. We do the addition and multiplication in the same loop. When everything goes fine, we have the inverse, and we return to the caller with 0 in `rax`.

Figure 36-3 shows the output.

```
jo@UbuntuDesktop:~/Desktop/linux64/gcc/44 avx_matrix$ make
nasm -f elf64 -g -F dwarf matrix4x4.asm -l matrix4x4.lst
gcc -o matrix4x4 matrix4x4.o -no-pie
jo@UbuntuDesktop:~/Desktop/linux64/gcc/44 avx_matrix$ ./matrix4x4

4x4 DOUBLE PRECISION FLOATING POINT MATRICES

This is matrixA:
1.000000        3.000000        5.000000        7.000000
9.000000        11.000000       13.000000       15.000000
17.000000       19.000000       21.000000       23.000000
25.000000       27.000000       29.000000       31.000000

This is matrixB:
2.000000        4.000000        6.000000        8.000000
10.000000       12.000000       14.000000       16.000000
18.000000       20.000000       22.000000       24.000000
26.000000       28.000000       30.000000       32.000000

This is matrixA x matrixB:
304.000000      336.000000      368.000000      400.000000
752.000000      848.000000      944.000000      1040.000000
1200.000000     1360.000000     1520.000000     1680.000000
1648.000000     1872.000000     2096.000000     2320.000000

This is matrixC:
2.000000        11.000000       21.000000       37.000000
3.000000        13.000000       23.000000       41.000000
5.000000        17.000000       29.000000       43.000000
7.000000        19.000000       31.000000       47.000000

This is the inverse of matrixC:
1.000000        -1.000000       -1.000000       1.000000
-2.000000       1.833333        0.944444        -0.888889
1.000000        -1.100000       -0.066667       0.233333
0.000000        0.133333        -0.188889       0.077778

Proof: matrixC x inverse =
1.000000        0.000000        0.000000        0.000000
0.000000        1.000000        0.000000        0.000000
-0.000000       -0.000000       1.000000        -0.000000
0.000000        0.000000        -0.000000       1.000000

This is matrixS:
1.000000        2.000000        3.000000        4.000000
5.000000        6.000000        7.000000        8.000000
9.000000        10.000000       11.000000       12.000000
13.000000       14.000000       15.000000       16.000000

This matrix is singular!
```

Figure 36-3. matrix4x4.asm output

Summary

In this chapter, you learned about the following:

- AVX matrix operations

- AVX instruction with three operands

- AVX fuse operations

- Use of masks for blending and permutations

CHAPTER 37

Matrix Transpose

Let's do one last matrix operation that is useful: transposing. We have coded two versions, one using *unpacking* and one using *shuffling*.

Example Transposing Code

Listing 37-1 shows the code.

Listing 37-1. transpose4x4.asm

```
; transpose4x4.asm
extern printf

section .data
    fmt0    db      "4x4 DOUBLE PRECISION FLOATING POINT MATRIX
                    TRANSPOSE",10,0
    fmt1    db      10,"This is the matrix:",10,0
    fmt2    db      10,"This is the transpose (unpack):",10,0
    fmt3    db      10,"This is the transpose (shuffle):",10,0

    align   32
    matrix dq       1.,     2.,     3.,     4.
           dq       5.,     6.,     7.,     8.
           dq       9.,     10.,    11.,    12.
           dq       13.,    14.,    15.,    16.
section .bss
    alignb          32
    transpose       resd    16
```

© Jo Van Hoey 2019
J. Van Hoey, *Beginning x64 Assembly Programming*, https://doi.org/10.1007/978-1-4842-5076-1_37

```
section .text
      global main
main:
push  rbp
mov   rbp,rsp

; print title
      mov     rdi, fmt1
      call    printf

; print matrix
      mov     rdi,fmt1
      call    printf
      mov     rsi,matrix
      call    printm4x4

; compute transpose unpack
      mov     rdi, matrix
      mov     rsi, transpose
      call    transpose_unpack_4x4

;print the result
      mov     rdi, fmt2
      xor     rax,rax
      call    printf
      mov     rsi, transpose
      call    printm4x4

; compute transpose shuffle
      mov     rdi, matrix
      mov     rsi, transpose
      call    transpose_shuffle_4x4
```

```
;print the result
      mov     rdi, fmt3
      xor     rax,rax
      call    printf
      mov     rsi, transpose
      call    printm4x4
leave
ret
;------------------------------------------------------------
transpose_unpack_4x4:
push  rbp
mov   rbp,rsp
;load matrix into the registers
      vmovapd        ymm0,[rdi]    ;  1    2    3    4
      vmovapd        ymm1,[rdi+32] ;  5    6    7    8
      vmovapd        ymm2,[rdi+64] ;  9   10   11   12
      vmovapd        ymm3,[rdi+96] ; 13   14   15   16
;unpack
      vunpcklpd ymm12,ymm0,ymm1            ;  1    5    3    7
      vunpckhpd ymm13,ymm0,ymm1            ;  2    6    4    8
      vunpcklpd ymm14,ymm2,ymm3            ;  9   13   11   15
      vunpckhpd ymm15,ymm2,ymm3            ; 10   14   12   16
;permutate
      vperm2f128 ymm0,ymm12,ymm14, 00100000b   ; 1    5    9   13
      vperm2f128 ymm1,ymm13,ymm15, 00100000b   ; 2    6   10   14
      vperm2f128 ymm2,ymm12,ymm14, 00110001b   ; 3    7   11   15
      vperm2f128 ymm3,ymm13,ymm15, 00110001b   ; 4    8   12   16
;write to memory
      vmovapd        [rsi],    ymm0
      vmovapd        [rsi+32],ymm1
      vmovapd        [rsi+64],ymm2
      vmovapd        [rsi+96],ymm3
leave
ret
;------------------------------------------------------------
```

341

```
transpose_shuffle_4x4:
push   rbp
mov    rbp,rsp
;load matrix into the registers
       vmovapd      ymm0,[rdi]    ;  1   2   3   4
       vmovapd      ymm1,[rdi+32] ;  5   6   7   8
       vmovapd      ymm2,[rdi+64] ;  9  10  11  12
       vmovapd      ymm3,[rdi+96] ; 13  14  15  16
;shuffle
       vshufpd      ymm12,ymm0,ymm1, 0000b    ;  1   5   3   7
       vshufpd      ymm13,ymm0,ymm1, 1111b    ;  2   6   4   8
       vshufpd      ymm14,ymm2,ymm3, 0000b    ;  9  13  11  15
       vshufpd      ymm15,ymm2,ymm3, 1111b    ; 10  14  12  16
;permutate
       vperm2f128 ymm0,ymm12,ymm14, 00100000b  ;  1   5   9  13
       vperm2f128 ymm1,ymm13,ymm15, 00100000b  ;  2   6  10  14
       vperm2f128 ymm2,ymm12,ymm14, 00110001b  ;  3   7  11  15
       vperm2f128 ymm3,ymm13,ymm15, 00110001b  ;  4   8  12  16
;write to memory
       vmovapd      [rsi],    ymm0
       vmovapd      [rsi+32],ymm1
       vmovapd      [rsi+64],ymm2
       vmovapd      [rsi+96],ymm3
leave
ret
;------------------------------------------------------------
printm4x4:
section .data
       .fmt   db     "%.f",9,"%.f",9, "%.f",9,"%.f",10,0
```

```
section .text
push   rbp
mov    rbp,rsp
push   rbx                 ;callee saved
push   r15                 ;callee saved
       mov    rdi,.fmt
       mov    rcx,4
       xor    rbx,rbx      ;row counter
.loop:
       movsd  xmm0, [rsi+rbx]
       movsd  xmm1, [rsi+rbx+8]
       movsd  xmm2, [rsi+rbx+16]
       movsd  xmm3, [rsi+rbx+24]
       mov            rax,4  ;four floats
         push rcx           ;caller saved
         push rsi           ;caller saved
         push rdi           ;caller saved
         ;align stack if needed
         xor  r15,r15
         test rsp,0fh       ;last byte is 8 (not aligned)?
         setnz        r15b          ;set if not aligned
         shl  r15,3         ;multiply by 8
         sub  rsp,r15       ;substract 0 or 8
       call   printf
         add  rsp,r15       ;add 0 or 8
         pop  rdi
         pop  rsi
         pop  rcx
         add  rbx,32        ;next row
         loop .loop
pop r15
pop rbx
leave
ret
```

Figure 37-1 shows the output.

```
jo@ubuntu18:~/Desktop/Book/45 avx_transpose$ ./transpose4x4

This is the matrix:

This is the matrix:
1        2        3        4
5        6        7        8
9        10       11       12
13       14       15       16

This is the transpose (unpack):
1        5        9        13
2        6        10       14
3        7        11       15
4        8        12       16

This is the transpose (shuffle):
1        5        9        13
2        6        10       14
3        7        11       15
4        8        12       16
jo@ubuntu18:~/Desktop/Book/45 avx_transpose$ █
```

Figure 37-1.   transpose4x4.asm

The Unpack Version

First a remark about little-endian and packed ymm values. When in the example we have the rows 1, 2, 3, 4, then the little-endian format would be 4, 3, 2, 1. However, because ymm stores packed values in our example, ymm in SASM would look like this: 2, 1, 4, 3. You can verify this with your debugger. This can be confusing when debugging your program. In what follows we will use the little-endian format of 4, 3, 2, 1, and we will not use the 2, 1, 4, 3, format.

With the previous remarks in mind, when the matrix is loaded in the ymm registers, these registers have the following layout (the example values in parentheses):

ymm0	high qword2 (4)	low qword2 (3)	high qword1 (2)	low qword1 (1)
ymm1	high qword4 (8)	low qword4 (7)	high qword3 (6)	low qword3 (5)

...

The vunpcklpd instruction in the following:

```
vunpcklpd ymm12,ymm0,ymm1
```

takes the first low quadword from operands 2 and 3 and stores them in operand 1 and then takes the second-lowest quadwords in a similar way to produce the following:

ymm12	low qword4 (7)	low qword2 (3)	low qword3 (5)	low qword1 (1)

Similarly, the instruction vunpckhpd takes the high quadwords from operands 2 and 3 and stores them in operand 1 in a similar fashion.

```
vunpckhpd ymm13,ymm0,ymm1
```

ymm13	high qword4 (8)	high qword2 (4)	high qword3 (6)	high qword1 (2)

The purpose of this method of unpacking is to change column pairs to row pairs. For example, $\begin{bmatrix} 1 \\ 5 \end{bmatrix}$ becomes $[1\ 5]$.

After the unpacking, the ymm registers look as follows in little-endian format:

ymm12	7	3	5	1
ymm13	8	4	6	2
ymm14	15	11	13	9
ymm15	16	12	14	10

In human-readable format, instead of little-endian format, we have the following:

1	5	3	7
2	6	4	8
9	13	11	15
10	14	12	16

Now we have to permutate values between the rows to get the values in the correct order. In little-endian format, we need to obtain the following:

13	9	5	1
14	10	6	2
15	11	7	3
16	12	8	4

You may notice that the two lower values of ymm12 and ymm13 are in the correct place. Similarly, the two upper values of ymm14 and ymm15 are in the correct position.

We have to move the two lower values of ymm14 to the upper values of ymm12 and the two lower values of ymm15 to the upper values of ymm13.

The two upper values from ymm12 have to go to the lower values of ymm14, and we want the two upper values of ymm13 to go into the lower positions of ymm15.

The operation for doing that is called *permutation*. With vperm2f128, we can permutate pairs of two values (128 bits). We use a mask to control the permutation: for example, mask 00110001 means starts at the low bits. Remember in the following explanation that indexing starts at 0.

- **01**: Take the 128-byte high field from source 1 and put it at destination position 0.

- **00**: This has a special meaning; see the following explanation.

- **11**: Take the 128-byte high field from source 2 and put it at destination position 128.

- **00**: This has a special meaning; see the following explanation.

Here again we use little-endian format (4, 3, 2, 1) and do not consider the order in which these values are stored in the ymm registers.

So, in fact, the two 128-bit fields of the two sources are numbered sequentially.

- Source 1 low field = 00

- Source 1 high field = 01

- Source 2 low field = 10

- Source 2 high field = 11

Special meaning means if you set the third bit (index 3) in the mask, the destination low field will be zeroed, and if you set the seventh bit (index 7) in the mask, the destination high field will be zeroed.

The second, third, sixth, and seventh bits are not used here. In most cases, you can read a mask such as 00110001 as follows: 00**110001**.

This is what happens in the program:

```
vperm2f128      ymm0, ymm12, ymm14, 00100000b
```

We have 00**1**00000 here.

- The lower 00 means take the ymm12 low field (5, 1) and put it in the low field of ymm0.

- The higher 10 means take the ymm14 low field (13, 9) and put it in the high field of ymm0.

ymm12	7	3	5	1
ymm14	15	11	13	9
ymm0	13	9	5	1

Now ymm0 contains a row that is finished. Next comes the next row.

```
vperm2f128      ymm1, ymm13, ymm15, 00100000b
```

We have 00**1**00000 here.

- The lower 00 means take the ymm13 low field (6, 2) and put it in the low field of ymm1.

- The higher 10 means take the ymm15 low field (14, 10) and put it in the high field of ymm1.

ymm13	8	4	6	2
ymm15	16	12	14	10
ymm1	14	10	6	2

Now ymm1 contains a row that is finished. Here's the next one:

```
vperm2f128      ymm2, ymm12, ymm14, 00110001b
```

We have **0011**00**01** here:

- The lower 01 means take the ymm13 high field (7, 3) and put it in the low field of ymm2.

- The higher 11 means take the ymm15 high field (15, 11) and put it in the high field of ymm2.

ymm12	7	3	5	1
ymm14	15	11	13	9
ymm2	15	11	7	3

Now ymm2 contains a row that is finished. Last one!

```
vperm2f128    ymm3, ymm13, ymm15, 00110001b
```

We have **0011**00**01** here.

- The lower 01 means take the ymm13 high field (8,4) and put it in the low field of ymm3.

- The higher 11 means take the ymm15 high field (16,12) and put it in the high field of ymm3.

ymm13	8	4	6	2
ymm15	16	12	14	10
ymm3	16	12	8	4

And we are done permutating. All that's left is to copy the rows from the ymm registers into the correct order in memory.

The Shuffle Version

We already used a shuffle instruction called pshufd in Chapter 33. Here we use the instruction vshufpd, which also uses a mask to control the shuffle. Don't get confused; the instruction pshufd uses an 8-bit mask. The masks we will be using here count as only 4 bits.

Again, we are using little-endian format (remember 4, 3, 2, 1) and do not care how the packed values are stored in the ymm registers. That is the processor's business.

Refer to the following table and the examples that follow this explanation. The two lower bits in the mask control which packed values go into the destination's two lower positions; the two upper bits in the mask control which packed values go into the destination's two upper positions. Bits 0 and 2 specify which value to take from source 1, and bits 1 and 3 specify which value to take from source 2.

Select from upper two values in source 2.	Select from upper two values in source 1.	Select from lower two values in source 2.	Select from lower two values in source 1.
0 = lower value of source 2	0 = lower value of source 1	0 = lower value of source 2	0 = lower value of source 1
1 = higher value of source 2	1 = higher value of source 1	1 = higher value of source 2	1 = higher value of source 1

The two lower values in each of the sources can never end up in the higher positions at the destinations, and the two higher values in each of the source can never end up in the lower positions of the destination. See Figure 37-2 for a schematic overview of a few example masks.

Shuffle mask

Source 1: ymm0	a3	a2	a1	a0
Source 2: ymm1	b3	b2	b1	b0
Mask 0000	0	0	0	0
Destination: ymm3	b2	a2	b0	a0

Source 1: ymm0	a3	a2	a1	a0
Source 2: ymm1	b3	b2	b1	b0
Mask 1111	1	1	1	1
Destination: ymm3	b3	a3	b1	a1

Source 1: ymm0	a3	a2	a1	a0
Source 2: ymm1	b3	b2	b1	b0
Mask 0110	0	1	1	0
	b2	a3	b1	a0

Source 1: ymm0	a3	a2	a1	a0
Source 2: ymm1	b3	b2	b1	b0
Mask 0011	0	0	1	1
	b2	a2	b1	a1

Figure 37-2. *Shuffle mask examples*

Here is how it works in our program:

```
vshufpd      ymm12,ymm0,ymm1, 0000b
```

ymm0	4	3	2	1
ymm1	8	7	6	5
ymm12	Low upper ymm1	Low upper ymm0	Low lower ymm1	Low lower ymm0
	7	3	5	1

```
vshufpd      ymm13,ymm0,ymm1, 1111b
```

ymm0	4	3	2	1
ymm1	8	7	6	5
ymm13	High upper ymm1	High upper ymm0	High lower ymm1	High lower ymm0
	8	4	6	2

```
vshufpd      ymm14,ymm2,ymm3, 0000b
```

ymm2	12	11	10	9
ymm3	16	15	14	13
ymm14	Low upper ymm3	Low upper ymm2	Low lower ymm3	Low lower ymm2
	15	11	13	9

Finally, here's the last example:

```
vshufpd      ymm15,ymm2,ymm3, 1111b
```

ymm2	12	11	10	9
ymm3	16	15	14	13
ymm15	High upper ymm3	High upper ymm2	High lower ymm3	High lower ymm2
	16	12	14	10

After applying the shuffle mask, we have eight pairs of values in the ymm registers. We chose the registers so that we obtained the same intermediate result as in the unpacked version. Now the pairs need to be rearranged in the right places to form the transpose. We do that in exactly the same way as in the unpack section by permutating fields (blocks) of 128 bits with `vperm2f128`.

Summary

In this chapter, you learned about the following:

- That there are two ways to transpose a matrix

- How to use shuffle, unpack, and permutate instructions

- That there are different masks for shuffle, unpack, and permutate

CHAPTER 38

Performance Optimization

You will agree that a lot of the AVX instructions are far from intuitive, especially the different mask layouts that make the code difficult to read and understand. Moreover, the bit masks are sometimes written in hexadecimal notation, so you have to convert them first to binary notation to see what they do.

In this chapter, we will demonstrate that using AVX instructions can dramatically improve performance, and the effort of using AVX pays off in a number of cases. You can find an interesting white paper on benchmarking code at `https://www.intel.com/content/dam/www/public/us/en/documents/white-papers/ia-32-ia-64-benchmark-code-execution-paper.pdf`.

In our examples, we will use the measuring method presented in this white paper.

Transpose Computation Performance

In the example code shown in Listing 38-1, we have two methods of computing the transpose matrix, one using "classic" assembler instructions and another using AVX instructions. We added code to measure the execution times of both algorithms.

Listing 38-1. transpose.asm

```
; transpose.asm
extern printf

section .data
    fmt0    db    "4x4 DOUBLE PRECISION FLOATING POINT MATRIX
                  TRANSPOSE",10,0
    fmt1    db    10,"This is the matrix:",10,0
    fmt2    db    10,"This is the transpose (sequential version): ",10,0
    fmt3    db    10,"This is the transpose (AVX version): ",10,0
    fmt4    db    10,"Number of loops: %d",10,0
```

© Jo Van Hoey 2019
J. Van Hoey, *Beginning x64 Assembly Programming*, https://doi.org/10.1007/978-1-4842-5076-1_38

```
        fmt5    db      "Sequential version elapsed cycles: %d",10,0
        fmt6    db      "AVX Shuffle version elapsed cycles: %d",10,0

        align   32
        matrix          dq      1.,     2.,     3.,     4.
                        dq      5.,     6.,     7.,     8.
                        dq      9.,     10.,    11.,    12.
                        dq      13.,    14.,    15.,    16.

        loops   dq      10000

section .bss
        alignb          32
        transpose       resq            16

        bahi_cy         resq    1   ;timers for avx version
        balo_cy         resq    1
        eahi_cy         resq    1
        ealo_cy         resq    1

        bshi_cy         resq    1   ;timers for sequential version
        bslo_cy         resq    1
        eshi_cy         resq    1
        eslo_cy         resq    1

section .text
        global main
main:
push    rbp
mov     rbp,rsp
; print title
        mov     rdi, fmt0
        call    printf
; print matrix
        mov     rdi,fmt1
        call    printf
        mov     rsi,matrix
        call    printm4x4
```

```
; SEQUENTIAL VERSION
; compute transpose
        mov    rdi, matrix
        mov    rsi, transpose
        mov    rdx, [loops]

;start measuring the cycles
        cpuid
        rdtsc
        mov    [bshi_cy],edx
        mov    [bslo_cy],eax

        call seq_transpose

;stop measuring the cycles
        rdtscp
        mov    [eshi_cy],edx
        mov    [eslo_cy],eax
        cpuid

;print the result
        mov    rdi,fmt2
        call   printf
        mov    rsi,transpose
        call   printm4x4

; AVX VERSION
; compute transpose
        mov    rdi, matrix
        mov    rsi, transpose
        mov    rdx, [loops]
;start measuring the cycles
        cpuid
        rdtsc
        mov    [bahi_cy],edx
        mov    [balo_cy],eax

        call AVX_transpose
```

```
;stop measuring the cycles
     rdtscp
     mov    [eahi_cy],edx
     mov    [ealo_cy],eax
     cpuid

;print the result
     mov    rdi,fmt3
     call   printf
     mov    rsi,transpose
     call   printm4x4

;print the loops
     mov    rdi,fmt4
     mov    rsi,[loops]
     call   printf
;print the cycles
;cycles sequential version
     mov    rdx,[eslo_cy]
     mov    rsi,[eshi_cy]
     shl    rsi,32
     or     rsi,rdx          ;rsi contains end time

     mov    r8,[bslo_cy]
     mov    r9,[bshi_cy]
     shl    r9,32
     or     r9,r8            ;r9 contains start time

     sub    rsi,r9           ;rsi contains elapsed
   ;print the timing result
     mov    rdi,fmt5
     call   printf

;cycles AVX blend version
     mov    rdx,[ealo_cy]
     mov    rsi,[eahi_cy]
     shl    rsi,32
     or     rsi,rdx            ;rsi contains end time
```

```asm
        mov    r8,[balo_cy]
        mov    r9,[bahi_cy]
        shl    r9,32
        or     r9,r8              ;r9 contains start time

        sub    rsi,r9             ;rsi contains elapsed
    ;print the timing result
        mov   rdi,fmt6
        call  printf
leave
ret
;-------------------------------------------------------
seq_transpose:
push  rbp
mov   rbp,rsp
.loopx:                          ; the number of loops
        pxor      xmm0,xmm0
        xor       r10,r10
        xor       rax,rax
        mov       r12,4
        .loopo:
                push   rcx
                mov    r13,4
                .loopi:
                        movsd   xmm0, [rdi+r10]
                movsd  [rsi+rax], xmm0
                add           r10,8
                add           rax,32
                dec           r13
                jnz    .loopi
                add    rax,8
                xor    rax,10000000b     ;rax - 128
                inc    rbx
                dec    r12
        jnz    .loopo
        dec rdx
```

```
jnz .loopx
leave
ret
;-------------------------------------------------------------
AVX_transpose:
push   rbp
mov    rbp,rsp
.loopx:                      ; the number of loops
;load matrix into the registers
      vmovapd        ymm0,[rdi]     ;  1   2   3    4
      vmovapd        ymm1,[rdi+32] ;  5   6   7    8
      vmovapd        ymm2,[rdi+64] ;  9  10  11   12
      vmovapd        ymm3,[rdi+96] ; 13  14  15   16
;shuffle
      vshufpd        ymm12,ymm0,ymm1,  0000b      ;  1   5   3   7
      vshufpd        ymm13,ymm0,ymm1,  1111b      ;  2   6   4   8
      vshufpd        ymm14,ymm2,ymm3,  0000b      ;  9  13  11  15
      vshufpd        ymm15,ymm2,ymm3,  1111b      ; 10  14  12  16
;permutate
      vperm2f128     ymm0,ymm12,ymm14,     00100000b    ;  1   5   9  13
      vperm2f128     ymm1,ymm13,ymm15,     00100000b    ;  2   6  10  14
      vperm2f128     ymm2,ymm12,ymm14,     00110001b    ;  3   7  11  15
      vperm2f128     ymm3,ymm13,ymm15,     00110001b    ;  4   8  12  16
;write to memory
      vmovapd        [rsi],    ymm0
      vmovapd        [rsi+32],ymm1
      vmovapd        [rsi+64],ymm2
      vmovapd        [rsi+96],ymm3
      dec rdx
      jnz .loopx
leave
ret
;-------------------------------------------------------------
printm4x4:
section .data
      .fmt    db       "%f",9,"%f",9, "%f",9,"%f",10,0
```

358

```
section .text
push   rbp
mov    rbp,rsp
       push    rbx              ;callee saved
       push    r15         ;callee saved
       mov             rdi,.fmt
       mov             rcx,4
       xor             rbx,rbx      ;row counter
.loop:
       movsd  xmm0, [rsi+rbx]
       movsd  xmm1, [rsi+rbx+8]
       movsd  xmm2, [rsi+rbx+16]
       movsd  xmm3, [rsi+rbx+24]
       mov             rax,4          ; four floats
         push          rcx     ;caller saved
         push          rsi     ;caller saved
         push          rdi     ;caller saved
         ;align stack if needed
         xor  r15,r15
         test rsp,0fh        ;last byte is 8 (not aligned)?
         setnz        r15b              ;set if not aligned
         shl  r15,3               ;multiply by 8
         sub  rsp,r15       ;substract 0 or 8
              call    printf
         add  rsp,r15         ;add 0 or 8
         pop  rdi
         pop  rsi
         pop  rcx
         add  rbx,32      ;next row
         loop .loop
pop r15
pop rbx
leave
ret
```

Before we call the transpose function, we start the timing process. Modern processors support out-of-order execution code, which could result in instructions being executed at the wrong moment, before we start the timing or after we stop the timing. To avoid that, we need to use "serializing" instructions, which are instructions that guarantee that our timing instructions measure only what we want to measure. See the previous white paper for a more detailed explanation. One such instruction that can be used for serializing is cpuid. Before starting the timer with rdtsc, we execute cpuid. We use rdtsc to write the beginning timestamp counter "low cycles" in register eax and "high cycles" in edx; these values are stored in memory. The instruction rdtsc uses these two registers for historical reasons: in 32-bit processors, one register would be too small to hold the timer counts. One 32-bit register is used for the lower part of the timer counter value, and another register is used for the higher part. After recording the beginning timer counter values, we execute the code we want to measure and use the rdtscp instruction to stop the measurement. The ending "high cycles" and "low cycles" counters are stored again in memory, and cpuid is executed once again to make sure that no execution of instructions is postponed by the processor.

We use a 64-bit processor environment, so we shift left 32 the higher timestamp values and then xor the higher timestamp value with the lower timestamp value to obtain the complete timestamps in a 64-bit register. The difference between the beginning counter values and the ending counter values gives the number of cycles used.

The function seq_transpose uses "classic" instructions, and the function AVX_transpose is the transpose_shuffle4x4 function from the previous chapter. The functions are executed a large number of times as specified in the variable loops.

Figure 38-1 shows the output.

```
jo@UbuntuDesktop:~/Desktop/linux64/gcc/46 performance1$ make
nasm -f elf64 -g -F dwarf transpose.asm -l transpose.lst
gcc -o transpose transpose.o -no-pie
jo@UbuntuDesktop:~/Desktop/linux64/gcc/46 performance1$ ./transpose
4x4 DOUBLE PRECISION FLOATING POINT MATRIX TRANSPOSE

This is the matrix:
1.000000        2.000000        3.000000        4.000000
5.000000        6.000000        7.000000        8.000000
9.000000        10.000000       11.000000       12.000000
13.000000       14.000000       15.000000       16.000000

This is the transpose (sequential version):
1.000000        5.000000        9.000000        13.000000
2.000000        6.000000        10.000000       14.000000
3.000000        7.000000        11.000000       15.000000
4.000000        8.000000        12.000000       16.000000

This is the transpose (AVX version):
1.000000        5.000000        9.000000        13.000000
2.000000        6.000000        10.000000       14.000000
3.000000        7.000000        11.000000       15.000000
4.000000        8.000000        12.000000       16.000000

Number of loops: 10000
Sequential version elapsed cycles: 132687
AVX Shuffle version elapsed cycles: 12466
jo@UbuntuDesktop:~/Desktop/linux64/gcc/46 performance1$ █
```

Figure 38-1. *transpose.asm output*

You can see that using AVX instructions spectacularly speeds up the processing.

Intel has a volume dedicated to code optimization: https://software.intel.com/sites/default/files/managed/9e/bc/64-ia-32-architectures-optimization-manual.pdf.

This manual has a lot of interesting information on improving the performance of assembly code. Search for *handling port 5 pressure* (currently covered in Chapter 14). In that section, you will find several versions of a transpose algorithm for 8×8 matrices as well as the performance impact of different instructions. In the previous chapter, we demonstrated two ways of transposing a matrix, using unpacking and using shuffle. The Intel manuals go much deeper into the details of this subject; if performance is important to you, there are treasures to be found there.

Trace Computation Performance

Here is an example showing that AVX instructions are not always faster than "classic" assembly instructions. This example computes the trace of an 8×8 matrix:

```
; trace.asm
extern printf
section .data
        fmt0    db      "8x8 SINGLE PRECISION FLOATING POINT MATRIX TRACE",10,0
        fmt1    db      10,"This is the matrix:",10,0
        fmt2    db      10,"This is the trace (sequential version): %f",10,0
        fmt5    db      "This is the trace (AVX blend version): %f",10,0
        fmt6    db      10,"This is the tranpose: ",10,0
        fmt30   db      "Sequential version elapsed cycles: %u",10,0
        fmt31   db      "AVX blend  version elapsed cycles: %d",10,10,0
        fmt4    db      10,"Number of loops: %d",10,0

        align  32
        matrix dd 1.,      2.,      3.,      4.,      5.,      6.,      7.,      8.
               dd 9.,      10.,     11.,     12.,     13.,     14.,     15.,     16.
               dd 17.,     18.,     19.,     20.,     21.,     22.,     23.,     24.
               dd 25.,     26.,     27.,     28.,     29.,     30.,     31.,     32.
               dd 33.,     34.,     35.,     36.,     37.,     38.,     39.,     40.
               dd 41.,     42.,     43.,     44.,     45.,     46.,     47.,     48.
               dd 49.,     50.,     51.,     52.,     53.,     54.,     55.,     56.
               dd 57.,     58.,     59.,     60.,     61.,     62.,     63.,     64.

        loops  dq      1000
        permps dd      0,1,4,5,2,3,6,7   ;mask for permutation sp values in ymm
section .bss
        alignb       32
        transpose    resq   16

        trace        resq   1

        bbhi_cy      resq   1
        bblo_cy      resq   1
        ebhi_cy      resq   1
        eblo_cy      resq   1
```

```
        bshi_cy        resq    1
        bslo_cy        resq    1
        eshi_cy        resq    1
        eslo_cy        resq    1

section .text
        global main
main:
push    rbp
mov     rbp,rsp
; print title
        mov     rdi, fmt0
        call    printf
; print matrix
        mov     rdi,fmt1
        call    printf
        mov     rsi,matrix
        call    printm8x8

; SEQUENTIAL VERSION
; compute trace
        mov     rdi, matrix
        mov     rsi, [loops]

;start measuring the cycles
        cpuid
        rdtsc
        mov     [bshi_cy],edx
        mov     [bslo_cy],eax

        call    seq_trace

;stop measuring the cycles
        rdtscp
        mov     [eshi_cy],edx
        mov     [eslo_cy],eax
        cpuid
```

```
;print the result
      mov     rdi, fmt2
      mov     rax,1
      call    printf

; BLEND VERSION
; compute trace
      mov     rdi, matrix
      mov     rsi, [loops]

;start measuring the cycles
      cpuid
      rdtsc
      mov     [bbhi_cy],edx
      mov     [bblo_cy],eax

      call    blend_trace

;stop measuring the cycles
      rdtscp
      mov     [ebhi_cy],edx
      mov     [eblo_cy],eax
      cpuid

;print the result
      mov     rdi, fmt5
      mov     rax,1
      call    printf

;print the loops
      mov     rdi,fmt4
      mov     rsi,[loops]
      call    printf
```

```
;print the cycles
;cycles sequential version
        mov     rdx,[eslo_cy]
        mov     rsi,[eshi_cy]
        shl     rsi,32
        or      rsi,rdx

        mov     r8,[bslo_cy]
        mov     r9,[bshi_cy]
        shl     r9,32
        or      r9,r8

        sub     rsi,r9          ;rsi contains elapsed
    ;print
        mov     rdi,fmt30
        call printf

;cycles AVX blend version
        mov     rdx,[eblo_cy]
        mov     rsi,[ebhi_cy]
        shl     rsi,32
        or      rsi,rdx

        mov     r8,[bblo_cy]
        mov     r9,[bbhi_cy]
        shl     r9,32
        or      r9,r8

        sub     rsi,r9
    ;print
        mov     rdi,fmt31
        call    printf
leave
ret
;---------------------------------------------------------------
seq_trace:
push    rbp
mov     rbp,rsp
```

```
.loop0:
      pxor   xmm0,xmm0
      mov    rcx,8
      xor    rax,rax
      xor    rbx,rbx
      .loop:
      addss xmm0, [rdi+rax]
      add    rax,36    ;each row 32 bytes
      loop   .loop
      cvtss2sd      xmm0,xmm0
      dec           rsi
      jnz           .loop0
leave
ret
;-------------------------------------------------------------
blend_trace:
push   rbp
mov    rbp,rsp
.loop:
   ;build the matrix in memory
      vmovaps       ymm0, [rdi]
      vmovaps       ymm1, [rdi+32]
      vmovaps       ymm2, [rdi+64]
      vmovaps       ymm3, [rdi+96]
      vmovaps       ymm4, [rdi+128]
      vmovaps       ymm5, [rdi+160]
      vmovaps       ymm6, [rdi+192]
      vmovaps       ymm7, [rdi+224]

      vblendps      ymm0,ymm0,ymm1,00000010b
      vblendps      ymm0,ymm0,ymm2,00000100b
      vblendps      ymm0,ymm0,ymm3,00001000b
      vblendps      ymm0,ymm0,ymm4,00010000b
      vblendps      ymm0,ymm0,ymm5,00100000b
      vblendps      ymm0,ymm0,ymm6,01000000b
      vblendps      ymm0,ymm0,ymm7,10000000b
```

```asm
        vhaddps         ymm0,ymm0,ymm0
        vmovdqu         ymm1,[permps]
        vpermps         ymm0,ymm1,ymm0
        haddps          xmm0,xmm0
        vextractps      r8d,xmm0,0
        vextractps      r9d,xmm0,1
        vmovd           xmm0,r8d
        vmovd           xmm1,r9d
        vaddss          xmm0,xmm0,xmm1
        dec             rsi
        jnz             .loop
cvtss2sd xmm0,xmm0
leave
ret

printm8x8:
section .data
.fmt db        "%.f,",9,"%.f,",9,"%.f,",9,"%.f,",9,"%.f,",9,"%.f,",9,"%.f,",
9,"%.f",10,0
section .text
push    rbp
mov     rbp,rsp
        push    rbx             ;callee saved
        mov     rdi,.fmt
        mov     rcx,8
        xor     rbx,rbx     ;row counter
        vzeroall
.loop:
        movss           xmm0, dword[rsi+rbx]
          cvtss2sd      xmm0,xmm0
        movss           xmm1, [rsi+rbx+4]
          cvtss2sd      xmm1,xmm1
        movss           xmm2, [rsi+rbx+8]
          cvtss2sd      xmm2,xmm2
        movss           xmm3, [rsi+rbx+12]
          cvtss2sd      xmm3,xmm3
```

```
movss          xmm4, [rsi+rbx+16]
  cvtss2sd     xmm4,xmm4
movss          xmm5, [rsi+rbx+20]
  cvtss2sd     xmm5,xmm5
movss          xmm6, [rsi+rbx+24]
  cvtss2sd     xmm6,xmm6
movss          xmm7, [rsi+rbx+28]
  cvtss2sd     xmm7,xmm7
mov      rax,8 ; 8 floats
push     rcx          ;caller saved
push     rsi          ;caller saved
push     rdi          ;caller saved
  ;align stack if needed
xor      r15,r15
test     rsp,0fh               ;last byte is 8 (not aligned)?
setnz    r15b                  ;set if not aligned
shl      r15,3          ;multiply by 8
sub      rsp,r15        ;substract 0 or 8
call     printf
add      rsp,r15        ;add 0 or 8
pop      rdi
pop      rsi
pop      rcx
add      rbx,32     ;next row
loop     .loop
pop rbx      ;callee saved
leave
ret
```

The function blend_trace is an extension from 4×4 to 8×8 of the trace function we used in Chapter 36, in our matrix inversion code, with AVX instructions. The function seq_trace walks sequentially through the matrix, finds the trace elements, and adds them. When running this code, you will see that seq_trace is much faster than blend_trace.

Figure 38-2 shows the output.

```
jo@ubuntu18:~/Desktop/Book/47 performance2$ ./trace
8x8 SINGLE PRECISION FLOATING POINT MATRIX TRACE

This is the matrix:
1,      2,      3,      4,      5,      6,      7,      8
9,      10,     11,     12,     13,     14,     15,     16
17,     18,     19,     20,     21,     22,     23,     24
25,     26,     27,     28,     29,     30,     31,     32
33,     34,     35,     36,     37,     38,     39,     40
41,     42,     43,     44,     45,     46,     47,     48
49,     50,     51,     52,     53,     54,     55,     56
57,     58,     59,     60,     61,     62,     63,     64

This is the trace (sequential version): 260.000000
This is the trace (AVX blend version): 260.000000

Number of loops: 1000
Sequential version elapsed cycles: 48668
AVX blend  version elapsed cycles: 175509

jo@ubuntu18:~/Desktop/Book/47 performance2$ █
```

Figure 38-2. *trace.asm output*

If you want to know more about optimization, use the previously mentioned Intel manual. Here is another excellent source: https://www.agner.org.

Summary

In this chapter, you learned about the following:

- Measuring and computing elapsed cycles
- That AVX can speed up processing drastically
- That AVX is not suited for every situation

CHAPTER 39

Hello, Windows World

In this and the following chapter, we will start assembly coding in Windows. As with Linux, it is best to install a Windows virtual machine. You can download a license for a 90-day Windows 10 trial here: `https://www.microsoft.com/en-us/evalcenter/evaluate-windows-10-enterprise`. Install the trial version of Windows 10, and do the updates, which can take a while.

Getting Started

Microsoft has developed its own assembler, called MASM, and it is included in Visual Studio. Being able to use Visual Studio is certainly an advantage, because it is a comprehensive development tool. The assembler instructions used in MASM are the same as those in NASM, but the assembler directives are very different. Configuring and learning to work with Visual Studio has a learning curve, depending on your previous experience as a Windows developer.

To soften the culture shock, in this book we will use NASM on Windows and use the CLI. We already know NASM on Linux from the previous chapters, which gives us a head start. However, making the switch to MASM should not be too difficult to do on your own.

If you want to develop for Windows, learning to use Visual Studio is worth the effort. On the Internet you can even find how to use NASM with Visual Studio.

Find NASM for Windows on the Internet and install it (currently: `https://www.nasm.us/pub/nasm/releasebuilds/2.14.03rc2/win64/`). Make sure your Windows environment path variable has an entry that points to the folder where you installed NASM. See Figure 39-1. You can verify the NASM installation with `nasm -v` at the CLI.

© Jo Van Hoey 2019
J. Van Hoey, *Beginning x64 Assembly Programming*, https://doi.org/10.1007/978-1-4842-5076-1_39

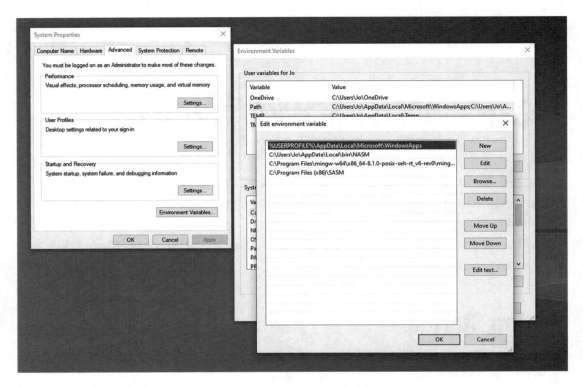

Figure 39-1. *Windows 10 environment path variable*

We will also use a version of MinGW (Minimalist GNU for Windows), which is a set of Linux development tools ported to Windows. MinGW will allow us to use the tools make and GCC, which we have used often in the previous chapters of the book. The version you have to install is MinGW-w64. Before you start downloading and installing, if you plan to use SASM on Windows, be aware that SASM installs NASM and some MinGW-w64 tools in its own subdirectories (except make). If you manually install SASM and MingGW-w64, you will end up with double installations. In the SASM settings, you can configure SASM to use your installed versions of NASM and GCC instead of the older versions that come with SASM.

Currently you will find the download files for MinGW-w64 here: http://mingw-w64. org/doku.php/download. Choose MingW-W64-builds, download and install it, and choose x86_64 in the installation window.

Go to the Windows environment variables, and add the path to the MinGW-W64 `bin` folder to the environment variable `path`, shown in Figure 39-1. The `bin` folder contains GCC. After updating the path variable, go to the PowerShell CLI and type `gcc -v` to verify the installation.

Download the win64 version of SASM (`https://dman95.github.io/SASM/english.html`), and if you want SASM to use the new versions of NASM and GCC, modify the build settings to your freshly installed NASM and GCC. Do not forget to update the Windows environment path variable with an entry for SASM.

If you do not have a preferred text editor on Windows, install Notepad++. It is simple and provides syntax highlighting for a large number of programming languages, including assembly. And you can easily set the encoding to UTF-8, UTF-16, and so on. You can find the assembly language setting on the menu bar under Language.

It is annoying that MinGW-w64 does not have a `make` command but provides only `ming32-make.exe`, which is a long command to use. To solve this, create a `make.bat` file with Notepad++ (run as Administrator) containing this line:

```
mingw32-make.exe
```

Save the file in UTF-8 format in the MinGW-W64 `bin` folder.

Here are some hints if you struggle with Windows:

- To open an application as administrator, right-click the application icon, and choose the option *Run as administrator.*

- It is always handy to have easy access to PowerShell, the Windows CLI. To open it, type **PowerShell** in the search field on the taskbar at the bottom and then click *Open.* A PowerShell icon will appear on the taskbar; right-click this icon and choose *Pin to taskbar.*

- In a window that shows icons for files or directories, press Shift and right-click at the same time, and on the menu that pops up, you can select *Open PowerShell window here.*

- To show hidden files and directories, click the File Explorer icon on the taskbar. Open the *View* menu item and select *Hidden items.*

- To find the environment variables, type **environment variables** in the search field on the taskbar.

Writing Some Code

Now you are ready to start coding. Listing 39-1 and Listing 39-2 show our first program.

Listing 39-1. hello.asm

```
; hello.asm
extern printf
section .data
      msg    db 'Hello, Windows World!',0
      fmt    db "Windows 10 says: %s",10,0
section .text
      global main
main:
push rbp
mov rbp,rsp
      mov    rcx, fmt
      mov    rdx, msg
      sub    rsp,32
      call   printf
      add    rsp,32
leave
ret
```

Listing 39-2. makefile

```
hello.exe: hello.obj
      gcc -o hello.exe hello.obj
hello.obj: hello.asm
      nasm -f win64  -g -F cv8 hello.asm -l hello.lst
```

There is nothing spectacular here, right? Or is there?

Well, first there is sub rsp,32, which in Linux we used to create stack variables. With this instruction, we create *shadow space* on the stack before calling a function. More on that later. After the printf function executes, we restore the stack with add rsp,32, which in this case is not strictly necessary because the stack will be restored by the leave instruction. The registers we use to pass arguments to printf are different from the ones used in Linux. That is because the calling conventions in Windows are different from the calling conventions in Linux. Windows requires you to use the Microsoft x64 calling convention, while Linux wants you to use System V Application Binary Interface, also called System V ABI.

You can find an overview of the Microsoft calling convention here: `https://docs.microsoft.com/en-us/cpp/build/x64-calling-convention?view=vs-2019`. This page tends to move from time to time; if you can't find it, search on the Microsoft site for the x64 calling convention. Here is the short version:

- Integer arguments are passed in `rcx`, `rdx`, `r8`, and `r9`, in that order.

- If you want to pass more arguments, you push them onto the stack.

- Floating-point arguments are passed in the `xmm0`-`xmm3` registers; further arguments are passed using the stack.

- Registers `rcx`, `rdx`, `r8`, `r9`, and, additionally, `rax`, `r10`, `r11`, `xmm4`, and `xmm5` are volatile, meaning that the caller has to save them if needed. The other registers are callee saved.

- The caller needs to provide a 32-byte space on the stack (*shadow space*) for four function arguments to be passed to the callee, even if the callee does not take that many arguments.

- As in Linux, the stack must be 16-byte aligned.

Figure 39-2 shows the output of our first program.

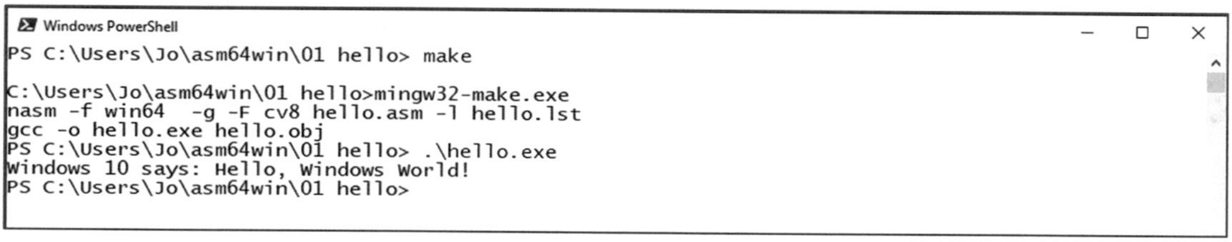

Figure 39-2. *hello.asm output*

Debugging

If you launch GDB to debug our first program, you are in for a surprise. You can execute a number of commands, but stepping through your code will not work. You will see the following message:

```
Single stepping until exit from function main,
which has no line number information.
0x0000000000402a60 in printf ()
```

This means that GDB is of limited use here! However, SASM comes to the rescue. SASM does not seem to have this problem. In our makefile we still include the debug flags; maybe in a future version of GDB this will be solved. In the makefile we specify cv8 (Microsoft CodeView 8) as the debugging format.

Syscalls

In our example code, we used printf instead of a syscall as we did with our first Linux assembly program. There is a reason for that: you do not use syscalls in Windows. Windows has syscalls, but they are for "internal" use only. You need to use the Windows API when you want to access system resources. Of course, you can dig around in the Windows code or on the Internet to find out what the Windows syscalls are, but know that newer versions of Windows can change the use of syscalls, and that can break your code if you use them.

Summary

In this chapter, you learned about the following:

- How to install and use NASM, SASM, and Linux development tools in Windows

- That calling conventions in Windows are different from those in Linux

- That it's better not use syscalls

CHAPTER 40

Using the Windows API

The Windows application programming interface (API) is a set of functions that can be used by a developer to interact with the operating system. As mentioned in the previous chapter, syscalls are not a reliable way to communicate with the operating system, but Microsoft provides a large set of APIs to accomplish just about everything you could think of. The Windows API is written with the C programming language in mind, but if we comply with the calling conventions, we can easily use the Windows API in our assembler programs. The description of the Windows API can be found here (at the time of this writing): `https://docs.microsoft.com/en-us/windows/win32/api/`.

Console Output

Listing 40-1 shows a version of a "Hello, World" program that makes use of the Windows API to display a message on the screen.

Listing 40-1. helloc.asm

```
; helloc.asm
%include "win32n.inc"
     extern WriteFile
     extern WriteConsoleA
     extern GetStdHandle

section .data
     msg              db        'Hello, World!!',10,0
     msglen   EQU     $-msg-1            ; leave off the NULL

section .bss
     hFile                        resq      1      ; handle to file
     lpNumberOfBytesWritten  resq      1
```

© Jo Van Hoey 2019
J. Van Hoey, *Beginning x64 Assembly Programming*, https://doi.org/10.1007/978-1-4842-5076-1_40

```nasm
section .text
      global main
main:
push  rbp
mov   rbp,rsp

; get a handle to stdout
;HANDLE WINAPI GetStdHandle(
;   _In_ DWORD nStdHandle
;);
      mov   rcx, STD_OUTPUT_HANDLE
      sub   rsp,32                  ;shadowspace
      call  GetStdHandle           ;returns INVALID_HANDLE_VALUE if no success
      add   rsp,32
      mov   qword[hFile],rax        ;save received handle to memory

;BOOL WINAPI WriteConsole(
;   _In_                   HANDLE       hConsoleOutput,
;   _In_      const VOID     *lpBuffer,
;   _In_              DWORD    nNumberOfCharsToWrite,
;   _Out_             LPDWORD      lpNumberOfCharsWritten,
;   _Reserved_        LPVOID       lpReserved
;);
      sub   rsp, 8                  ;align the stack
      mov   rcx, qword[hFile]
      lea   rdx, [msg]             ;lpBuffer
      mov   r8, msglen            ;nNumberOfBytesToWrite
      lea   r9, [lpNumberOfBytesWritten]
      push  NULL                   ;lpReserved
      sub   rsp, 32
      call  WriteConsoleA          ;returns nonzero if success
      add   rsp,32+8

; BOOL WriteFile(
;            HANDLE       hFile,
;            LPCVOID      lpBuffer,
;            DWORD        nNumberOfBytesToWrite,
```

```
;       LPDWORD        lpNumberOfBytesWritten,
;       LPOVERLAPPED     lpOverlapped
;);
        mov   rcx, qword[hFile]    ; file handle
        lea   rdx, [msg]           ;lpBuffer
        mov   r8, msglen           ;nNumberOfBytesToWrite
        lea   r9, [lpNumberOfBytesWritten]
        push  NULL                 ;lpOverlapped
        sub   rsp,32
        call  WriteFile            ;returns nonzero of success
leave
ret
```

The Windows API documentation uses thousands and thousands of symbolic constants. This makes the code more readable and makes it easier to use the Windows API, so we include the file win32n.inc at the beginning of our program. This is a list of all symbolic constants and their values. The win32n.inc file can be found here: http://rs1.szif.hu/~tomcat/win32/. However, be aware that including this file in your source will make the executable much larger than it needs to be. If space is important, just include only the constants you need in your program. If you use SASM, find the folder where SASM is installed and manually copy the file into the SASM include directory on your system.

In the code we copy the structure of the Windows function calls in comments so that it is easy to follow what is happening. We put the arguments in registers according to the calling convention, provide shadow space on the stack, call the function, and then restore the stack pointer.

The function GetStdHandle returns a handle if everything goes well; otherwise, it returns INVALID_HANDLE_VALUE. To keep it simple, we do no error checking, but in real production programs, you are advised to implement comprehensive error checking in your programs. Failure to do so can crash your program or, worse, can be the cause of security breaches.

When we have a handle, we continue to WriteConsoleA, passing the handle, the string to write, the length of the string, a placeholder for the number of bytes written, and NULL for a reserved argument. The first four arguments are passed in the registers, and the fifth argument is pushed onto the stack. This push will cause the stack to be unaligned; we have to anticipate this before we push the argument to the stack. If we aligned after the push, the function called would not find the argument on the stack. Just before we do the call, we create the shadow space on the stack.

Our program uses two methods to write to the console; one uses `WriteConsoleA`, and the other uses `WriteFile`. The `WriteFile` uses the same handle and considers the console as just another file to write to. After `WriteConsoleA`, we restore the stack for the shadow space and the alignment. After `WriteFile`, we do not restore the stack, because that will be done by the `leave` instruction.

If you do not find `WriteConsoleA` in the Windows API documentation, look for `WriteConsole`. The documentation explains that there are two versions, `WriteConsoleA` for writing ANSI and `WriteConsoleW` for writing Unicode.

When you run this code in SASM, you will see that the first method with `WriteConsoleA` does not work. The function returns 0 in `rax`, hinting that something went wrong. That is because we are interfering with the SASM console itself. The method using `WriteFile` works fine.

Figure 40-1 shows the output.

```
Windows PowerShell                                      —   □   ✕
PS C:\Users\Jo\asm64win\02 helloc> make

C:\Users\Jo\asm64win\02 helloc>mingw32-make.exe
nasm -f win64  -g -F cv8 helloc.asm -l helloc.lst
gcc -o helloc.exe helloc.obj
PS C:\Users\Jo\asm64win\02 helloc> .\helloc.exe
Hello, World!!
Hello, World!!
PS C:\Users\Jo\asm64win\02 helloc> _
```

Figure 40-1. *helloc.asm output*

Building Windows

Instead of using the console, we will now use the Windows GUI. We will not provide a full-fledged Windows program; we want to show you how to display a window. If you want to do more, you will have to dive into the Windows API documentation. Once you have seen how it works, it is just a matter of finding the right function in the Windows API documentation and passing the arguments in the registers and stack.

Listing 40-2 shows the example code.

Listing 40-2. hellow.asm

```
; hellow.asm
%include "win32n.inc"
extern ExitProcess
extern MessageBoxA

section .data
     msg    db 'Welcome to Windows World!',0
     cap    db "Windows 10 says:",0

section .text
     global main
main:
push    rbp
mov     rbp,rsp

;int MessageBoxA(
;       HWND hWnd,              owner window
;       LPCSTR lpText,         text to display
;       LPCSTR lpCaption,      window caption
;       UINT    uType          window behaviour
;     )

     mov    rcx,0           ; no window owner
     lea    rdx,[msg]       ; lpText
     lea    r8,[cap]        ; lpCaption
     mov    r9d,MB_OK       ; window with OK button
     sub    rsp,32          ; shadowspace
     call   MessageBoxA     ; returns IDOK=1 if OK button selected
     add    rsp,32
leave
ret
```

Figure 40-2 shows the output.

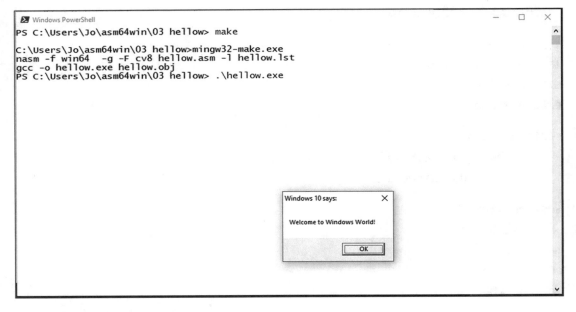

Figure 40-2. *hellow.asm output*

Of course, you can question if assembly is the right programming language to build a GUI for your Windows program. It is much easier to use C or C++ for that purpose and call in assembly for the computation-intensive parts.

Anyway, you can take any good book on Windows programming in C or C++, where the Windows API is explained, and translate all the function calls into assembly by providing the correct registers and then calling the function as demonstrated. Of course, complicated functionality such as error checking is needed, and that is just so much easier to develop in a higher-level language.

Summary

In this chapter, you learned about the following:

- How to use the Windows API

- How to write a message to the Windows CLI (PowerShell)

- How to use the instructions `GetStdHandle`, `WriteConsole`, and `WriteFile`

- How to create a window with a button

CHAPTER 41

Functions in Windows

Passing argument to functions is simple when you have four or fewer non-floating-point arguments. You use `rcx`, `rdx`, `r8`, and `r9` and provide shadow space on the stack before calling the function. After the call, you re-adjust the stack for the shadow space, and everything is fine. If you have more than four arguments, things are more complicated.

Using More Than Four Arguments

Let's first see why things get complicated with more than four non-floating-point arguments, as shown in Listing 41-1.

Listing 41-1. arguments1.asm

```
; arguments1.asm
extern printf
section .data
    first       db      "A",0
    second      db      "B",0
    third       db      "C",0
    fourth      db      "D",0
    fifth       db      "E",0
    sixth       db      "F",0
    seventh     db      "G",0
    eighth      db      "H",0
    ninth       db      "I",0
    tenth       db      "J",0
    fmt     db      "The string is: %s%s%s%s%s%s%s%s%s%s",10,0
section .bss
section .text
```

© Jo Van Hoey 2019
J. Van Hoey, *Beginning x64 Assembly Programming*, https://doi.org/10.1007/978-1-4842-5076-1_41

```
        global main
main:
push   rbp
mov    rbp,rsp
        sub    rsp,8
        mov    rcx, fmt
        mov    rdx, first
        mov    r8, second
        mov    r9, third
        push   tenth          ; now start pushing in
        push   ninth          ; reverse order
        push   eighth
        push   seventh
        push   sixth
        push   fifth
        push   fourth
        sub    rsp,32         ; shadow space
        call   printf
        add    rsp,32+8       ; restore stack
leave
ret
```

Look at the instruction sub rsp,8; it is there because when we call printf, the stack needs to be 16-byte aligned. Why not just use one instruction, such as sub rsp,40 just before the call? Well, the stack would be 16-byte aligned, but printf is likely to fail. If we decrease the stack by 40 instead of 32 just before the call, the arguments on the stack are not where printf expects them to be, just above the shadow space. So, we need to align the stack before we start pushing the arguments. Note that we need to push the arguments in reverse order. After the call, we restore the stack for the alignment and for the shadow space.

Figure 41-1 shows the output.

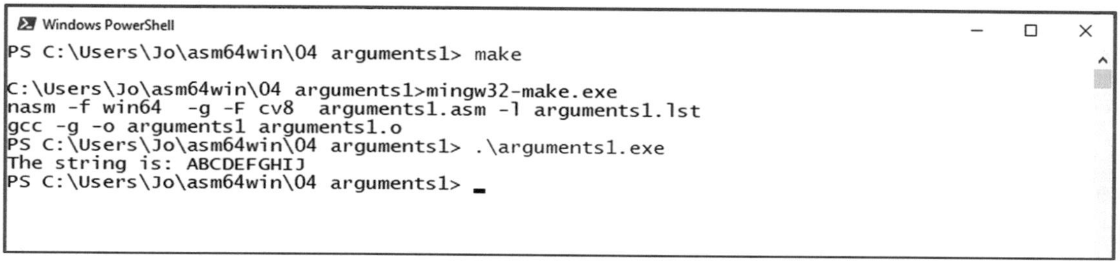

Figure 41-1. *arguments1.asm output*

You can also build the stack in another way. Listing 41-2 shows how it works.

Listing 41-2. arguments2.asm

```
;arguments2.asm
extern printf
section .data
        first         db      "A",0
        second        db      "B",0
        third         db      "C",0
        fourth        db      "D",0
        fifth         db      "E",0
        sixth         db      "F",0
        seventh       db      "G",0
        eighth        db      "H",0
        ninth         db      "I",0
        tenth         db      "J",0
        fmt      db       "The string is: %s%s%s%s%s%s%s%s%s%s",10,0
section .bss
section .text
        global main
main:
push   rbp
mov    rbp,rsp
        sub     rsp,32+56+8     ;shadow space + 7 arguments on stack + alignment
        mov     rcx, fmt
        mov     rdx, first
```

```
        mov     r8, second
        mov     r9, third
        mov     qword[rsp+32],fourth
        mov     qword[rsp+40],fifth
        mov     qword[rsp+48],sixth
        mov     qword[rsp+56],seventh
        mov     qword[rsp+64],eighth
        mov     qword[rsp+72],ninth
        mov     qword[rsp+80],tenth
        call    printf
        add     rsp, 32+56+8              ;not needed before leave
leave
ret
```

First use sub rsp,32+56+8 to adjust the stack.

- 32 bytes for shadow space

- 7 arguments to be pushed times 8 bytes, for a total of 56 bytes

Then you start building the stack, and when you see that you have to align the stack, another 8 bytes have to be subtracted from the stack pointer.

Now at the bottom of the stack, you have 32 bytes for the shadow space, and just above that you have the fourth argument, above the fifth, and so on. The stack that you build here looks the same as the one in the previous program. It is up to you to decide what you prefer.

Figure 41-2 shows the output.

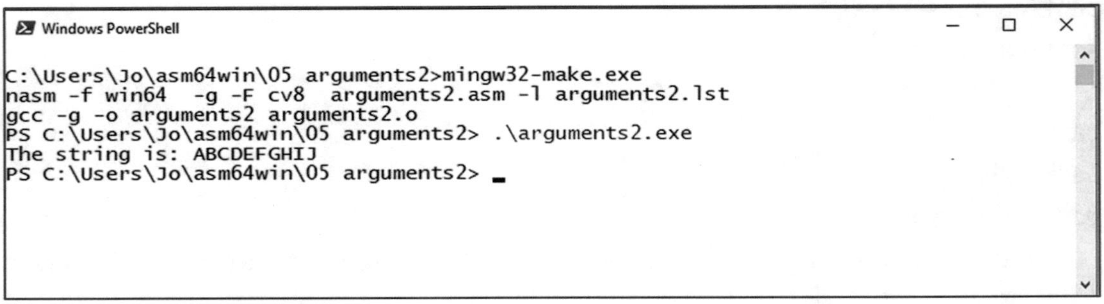

Figure 41-2. arguments2.asm output

How does this work in the called function? Listing 41-3 shows some example code that uses the function lfunc to build a string buffer to be printed by printf.

Listing 41-3. stack.asm

```
; stack.asm
extern printf
section .data
        first       db      "A"
        second      db      "B"
        third       db      "C"
        fourth      db      "D"
        fifth       db      "E"
        sixth       db      "F"
        seventh     db      "G"
        eighth      db      "H"
        ninth       db      "I"
        tenth       db      "J"
        fmt         db      "The string is: %s",10,0
section .bss
        flist   resb   14          ;length of string plus end 0
section .text
        global main
main:
push rbp
mov rbp,rsp
        sub rsp, 8
        mov rcx, flist
        mov rdx, first
        mov r8, second
        mov r9, third
        push tenth              ; now start pushing in
        push ninth              ; reverse order
        push eighth
        push seventh
```

```
        push sixth
        push fifth
        push fourth
        sub rsp,32        ; shadow
        call lfunc
        add rsp,32+8
; print the result
        mov rcx, fmt
        mov rdx, flist
        sub rsp,32+8
        call printf
        add rsp,32+8
leave
ret
;----------------------------------------------------------------------
lfunc:
push   rbp
mov    rbp,rsp
        xor rax,rax                ;clear rax (especially higher bits)
        ;arguments in registers
        mov al,byte[rdx]           ; move content argument to al
        mov [rcx], al              ; store al to memory
        mov al, byte[r8]
        mov [rcx+1], al
        mov al, byte[r9]
        mov [rcx+2], al
        ;arguments on stack
        xor rbx,rbx
        mov rax, qword [rbp+8+8+32] ; rsp + rbp + return address + shadow
        mov bl,[rax]
        mov [rcx+3], bl
        mov rax, qword [rbp+48+8]
        mov bl,[rax]
        mov [rcx+4], bl
```

```
        mov rax, qword [rbp+48+16]
        mov bl,[rax]
        mov [rcx+5], bl
        mov rax, qword [rbp+48+24]
        mov bl,[rax]
        mov [rcx+6], bl
        mov rax, qword [rbp+48+32]
        mov bl,[rax]
        mov [rcx+7], bl
        mov rax, qword [rbp+48+40]
        mov bl,[rax]
        mov [rcx+8], bl
        mov rax, qword [rbp+48+48]
        mov bl,[rax]
        mov [rcx+9], bl
        mov bl,0                ; terminating zero
        mov [rcx+10], bl
leave
ret
```

The main function is the same as in arguments1.asm; however, the function called is
lfunc instead of printf, which is called later in the code.

In lfunc, look at the instruction mov rax, qword [rbp+8+8+32], which loads the
fourth argument from the stack into rax. The register rbp contains a copy of the stack
pointer. The first 8-byte value on the stack is the rbp we pushed in the prologue of lfunc.
The 8-byte value higher up is the return address to main, which was automatically
pushed on the stack when lfunc was called. Then we have shadow space with 32 bytes.
Finally, we arrive at the pushed arguments. Hence, the fourth and other arguments can
be found at rbp+48 and higher.

When we return to main, the stack is aligned again, and printf is called.

Figure 41-3 shows the output, which is of course the same as before.

```
Windows PowerShell                                            —   □   ×
PS C:\Users\Jo\asm64win\06 stack> make

C:\Users\Jo\asm64win\06 stack>mingw32-make.exe
nasm -f win64 -g -F cv8 stack.asm -l stack.lst
gcc -g -o stack stack.obj
PS C:\Users\Jo\asm64win\06 stack> .\stack.exe
The string is: ABCDEFGHIJ
PS C:\Users\Jo\asm64win\06 stack>
```

Figure 41-3. *stack.asm output*

Working with Floating Points

Floating points are another story. Listing 41-4 shows some example code.

Listing 41-4. stack_float.asm

```
; stack_float.asm
extern printf
section .data
        zero    dq      0.0         ;0x0000000000000000
        one     dq      1.0         ;0x3FF0000000000000
        two     dq      2.0         ;0x4000000000000000
        three   dq      3.0         ;0x4008000000000000
        four    dq      4.0         ;0x4010000000000000
        five    dq      5.0         ;0x4014000000000000
        six     dq      6.0         ;0x4018000000000000
        seven   dq      7.0         ;0x401C000000000000
        eight   dq      8.0         ;0x4020000000000000
        nine    dq      9.0         ;0x4022000000000000
section .bss
section .text
        global main
main:
push rbp
mov rbp,rsp
        movq    xmm0, [zero]
        movq    xmm1, [one]
```

```
        movq   xmm2, [two]
        movq   xmm3, [three]

        movq   xmm4, [nine]
        sub    rsp, 8
        movq   [rsp], xmm4

        movq   xmm4, [eight]
        sub    rsp, 8
        movq   [rsp], xmm4

        movq   xmm4, [seven]
        sub    rsp, 8
        movq   [rsp], xmm4

        movq   xmm4, [six]
        sub    rsp, 8
        movq   [rsp], xmm4

        movq   xmm4, [five]
        sub    rsp, 8
        movq   [rsp], xmm4

        movq   xmm4, [four]
        sub    rsp, 8
        movq   [rsp], xmm4

        sub    rsp,32      ; shadow
        call   lfunc
        add    rsp,32
leave
ret
;------------------------------------------------
lfunc:
push   rbp
mov    rbp,rsp
```

```
        movsd  xmm4,[rbp+8+8+32]
        movsd  xmm5,[rbp+8+8+32+8]
        movsd  xmm6,[rbp+8+8+32+16]
        movsd  xmm7,[rbp+8+8+32+24]
        movsd  xmm8,[rbp+8+8+32+32]
        movsd  xmm9,[rbp+8+8+32+40]
leave
ret
```

There is no output for this little program because there is an oddity that we will explain in the next chapter. You will have to use a debugger to look at the xmm registers. For your convenience, we have provided the floating-point values in hexadecimal in the comments. The first four values are passed to the function in the xmm0 to xmm3 registers. The remaining arguments will be stored on the stack. Remember that the xmm registers can contain one scalar double-precision value, two packed double-precision values, or four packed single-precision values. In this case, we use one scalar double-precision value, and for the sake of the demonstration we stored the values on the stack without using a push instruction. This would be the way to store packed values on the stack, adjusting rsp every time with the appropriate amount. A more efficient way would be to push the scalar value directly from memory to the stack, as shown here:

```
    push   qword[nine]
```

In the function, we have to copy the values from the stack into the xmm registers, where we can process them further.

Summary

In this chapter, you learned about the following:

- How to pass arguments to functions in registers and the stack

- How to use shadow space on the stack

- How to access arguments on the stack

- How to store floating-point values on the stack

CHAPTER 42

Variadic Functions

A *variadic* function is a function that takes a variable number of arguments. A good example is `printf`. Remember, in Linux assembly, when we use `printf` with xmm registers, the convention is that `rax` contains the number of xmm registers that `printf` has to use. This number can also be retrieved from the `printf` format instruction, so often you can get away without using `rax`. For example, the following format indicates that we want to print four floating-point values, each with nine decimals:

```
fmt      db      "%.f",9,"%.f",9, "%.f",9,"%.f",10,0
```

Even if we do not comply with the convention to specify the number of floating-point values in `rax`, `printf` would print the four values anyway.

Variadic Functions in Windows

In Windows, the process is different. If you have xmm registers in the first four arguments, you have to copy them in the respective argument register. Listing 42-1 shows an example.

Listing 42-1. variadic1.asm

```
; variadic1.asm
extern printf
section .data
        one     dq      1.0
        two     dq      2.0
        three   dq      3.0

        fmt     dq      "The values are: %.1f %.1f %.1f",10,0
```

© Jo Van Hoey 2019
J. Van Hoey, *Beginning x64 Assembly Programming*, https://doi.org/10.1007/978-1-4842-5076-1_42

```
section .bss
section .text
      global main
main:
push  rbp
mov   rbp,rsp
      sub   rsp,32                    ;shadow space
      mov   rcx, fmt
      movq  xmm0, [one]
      movq  rdx,xmm0
      movq  xmm1, [two]
      movq  r8,xmm1
      movq  xmm2, [three]
      movq  r9,xmm2
      call  printf
      add   rsp, 32                   ;not needed before leave
leave
ret
```

When you create shadow space before calling a function, it is a good habit to delete the shadow space after you execute the function. In our example, add rsp,32 is not necessary because it immediately precedes the leave instruction, which will restore the stack pointer anyway. In this case, we called just one function (printf), but if you call several functions in your program, be sure to create the needed shadow space and do not forget to delete the shadows space every time you continue after a function.

Here you can see that we copy the floating-point values to xmm registers and to an argument general-purpose register. This a Windows requirement. The explanation is beyond the scope of this book, but it is a requirement when using unprototyped or variadic C functions. If you commented out the copy of the general-purpose registers, printf would not print the correct values.

Figure 42-1 shows the output.

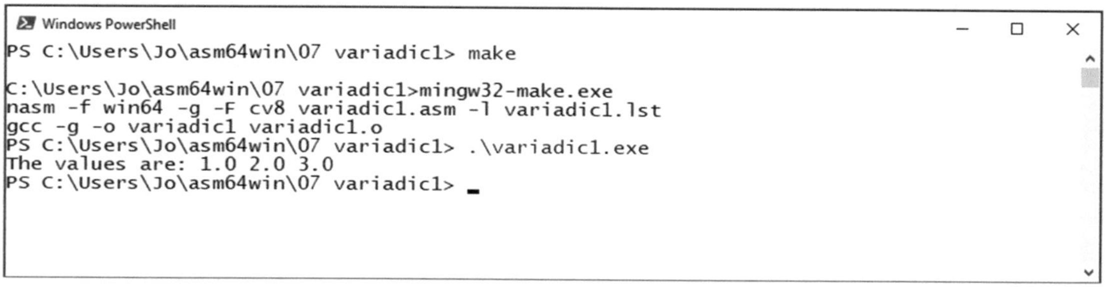

Figure 42-1. *variadic1.asm output*

Figure 42-2 shows the output without using the general-purpose registers.

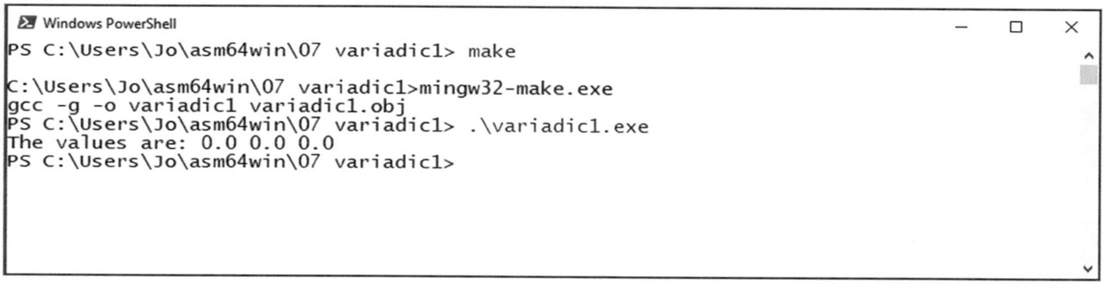

Figure 42-2. *variadiac1.asm erroneous output*

Mixing Values

Listing 42-2 shows an example with a mix of floating-point and other values.

Listing 42-2. variadic1.asm

```
; variadic2.asm
extern printf
section .data
        fmt     db      "%.1f %s %.1f %s %.1f %s %.1f %s %.1f %s",10,0
        one     dq      1.0
        two     dq      2.0
        three   dq      3.0
        four    dq      4.0
        five    dq      5.0
```

```
        A       db      "A",0
        B       db      "B",0
        C       db      "C",0
        D       db      "D",0
        E       db      "E",0

section .bss
section .text
    global main
main:
push rbp
mov rbp,rsp
        sub     rsp,8                   ;align the stack first
        mov     rcx,fmt                 ;first argument
        movq    xmm0,[one]              ;second argument
        movq    rdx,xmm0
        mov     r8,A                    ;third argument
        movq    xmm1,[two]              ;fourth argument
        movq    r9,xmm1
; now push to the stack in reverse
        push    E                       ;11th argument

        push    qword[five]             ;10th argument

        push    D                       ;9th argument

        push    qword[four]             ;8th argument

        push    C                       ;7th argument

        push    qword[three]            ;6th argument

        push    B                       ;5th argument
```

```
; print
        sub rsp,32
        call printf
        add rsp,32
leave
ret
```

As you can see, it is just a matter of respecting the order of the arguments, copying the xmm registers to general-purpose registers when needed, and pushing the remaining arguments in reverse order to the stack.

Figure 42-3 shows the output.

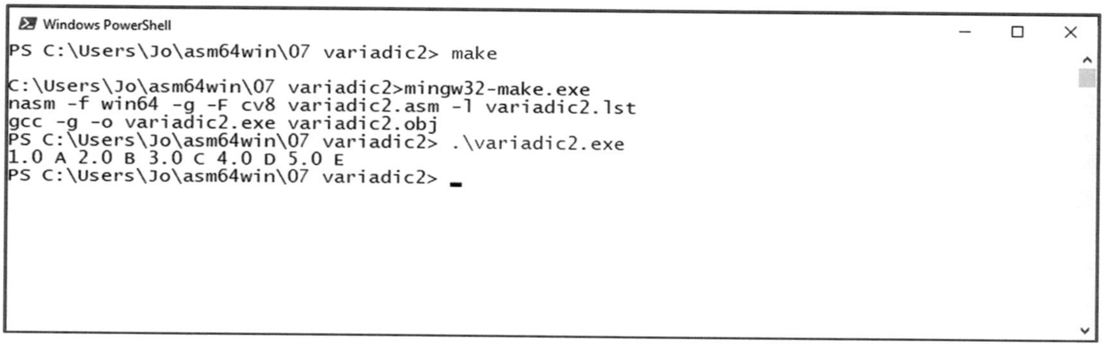

Figure 42-3. *variadiac2.asm output*

Summary

In this chapter, you learned the following:

- Floating-point values in xmm registers in the first four arguments need to be copied to the corresponding general-purpose registers.

- If there are more than four floating-point or other arguments, they have to be stored on the stack in reverse order.

CHAPTER 43

Windows Files

In Linux, we used syscalls to manipulate files. In Windows, we have to follow other rules. As mentioned in previous chapters, we use the Windows API.

Listing 43-1 shows the example code.

Listing 43-1. files.asm

```
%include "win32n.inc"
extern printf
extern CreateFileA
extern WriteFile
extern SetFilePointer
extern ReadFile
extern CloseHandle

section .data
    msg        db 'Hello, Windows World!',0
    nNumberOfBytesToWrite equ $-msg
    filename db   'mytext.txt',0
    nNumberOfBytesToRead   equ 30
    fmt        db "The result of reading the file: %s",10,0
section .bss
    fHandle                resq 1
    lpNumberOfBytesWritten resq 1
    lpNumberOfBytesRead    resq 1
    readbuffer             resb 64
section .text
        global main
```

© Jo Van Hoey 2019
J. Van Hoey, *Beginning x64 Assembly Programming*, https://doi.org/10.1007/978-1-4842-5076-1_43

```
main:
push    rbp
mov     rbp,rsp

;HANDLE CreateFileA(
;   LPCSTR                  lpFileName,
;   DWORD                   dwDesiredAccess,
;   DWORD                   dwShareMode,
;   LPSECURITY_ATTRIBUTES   lpSecurityAttributes,
;   DWORD                   dwCreationDisposition,
;   DWORD                   dwFlagsAndAttributes,
;   HANDLE                  hTemplateFile
;);
        sub         rsp,8
        lea     rcx,[filename]                      ;filename
        mov     rdx, GENERIC_READ|GENERIC_WRITE   ;desired access
        mov     r8,0                                ;no sharing
        mov     r9,0                                ;default security
; push in reverse order
        push    NULL                      ;no template
        push    FILE_ATTRIBUTE_NORMAL     ;flags and attributes
        push    CREATE_ALWAYS             ;disposition

        sub     rsp,32                   ;shadow
        call    CreateFileA
        add     rsp,32+8
        mov     [fHandle],rax

;BOOL WriteFile(
;   HANDLE          hFile,
;   LPCVOID         lpBuffer,
;   DWORD           nNumberOfBytesToWrite,
;   LPDWORD         lpNumberOfBytesWritten,
;   LPOVERLAPPED    lpOverlapped
;);
```

```
        mov     rcx,[fHandle]                       ;handle
        lea     rdx,[msg]                           ;msg to write
        mov     r8,nNumberOfBytesToWrite            ;# bytes to write
        mov     r9,[lpNumberOfBytesWritten]         ;returns # bytes written
        push    NULL
        sub     rsp,32                              ;shadow
        call    WriteFile
        add     rsp,32

;DWORD SetFilePointer(
;  HANDLE hFile,
;  LONG   lDistanceToMove,
;  PLONG  lpDistanceToMoveHigh,
;  DWORD  dwMoveMethod
;);

        mov     rcx,[fHandle]                       ;handle
        mov     rdx, 7                              ;low bits of position
        mov     r8,0                                ;no high order bits in position
        mov     r9,FILE_BEGIN                       ;start from beginning
        call    SetFilePointer

;BOOL ReadFile(
;  HANDLE          hFile,
;  LPCVOID         lpBuffer,
;  DWORD           nNumberOfBytesToRead,
;  LPDWORD         lpNumberOfBytesRead,
;  LPOVERLAPPED
;);
        sub     rsp,8                               ;align
        mov     rcx,[fHandle]                       ;handle
        lea     rdx,[readbuffer]                    ;buffer to read into
        mov     r8,nNumberOfBytesToRead             ;# bytes to read
        mov     r9,[lpNumberOfBytesRead]            ;# bytes read
        push    NULL
        sub     rsp,32                              ;shadow
        call    ReadFile
        add     rsp,32+8
```

```
;print result of ReadFile
        mov     rcx, fmt
        mov     rdx, readbuffer
        sub     rsp,32+8
        call    printf
        add     rsp,32+8

;BOOL WINAPI CloseHandle(
;    _In_ HANDLE hObject
;);
        mov     rcx,[fHandle]
        sub     rsp,32+8
        call    CloseHandle
        add     rsp,32+8
leave
ret
```

As before, we just use the C template of the Windows API function to build our assembly calls. To create the file, we just used the basic settings for access and security. When the creation succeeds, CreateFileA returns a handle to the created file. Note the parameters. You can read the Microsoft documentation to learn about the different parameters; there are quite a few possibilities that can help you in fine-tuning your file management.

The file handle will be used in WriteFile to write some text to the file. We already used WriteFile before to display a message on the console in Chapter 40.

After we have written the text to the file, we want to read the text back into memory, starting at location 7, where the first byte has index 0. With SetFilePointer, we move a pointer to the location where we want to start reading. If lpDistanceToMoveHigh is NULL, then lDistancetomove is a 32-bit value specifying the number of bytes to move. Otherwise, lpDistanceToMoveHigh and lDistancetomove together form a 64-value for the number of bytes to move. In r9, we indicate from where the move should start; the possibilities are FILE_BEGIN, FILE_CURRENT, and FILE_END.

When the pointer is set to a valid location, ReadFile will be used to start reading at that location. The bytes read are stored in a buffer and then printed. Finally, we close the file. Check your working directory, and you will see that the text file has been created.

Figure 43-1 shows the output.

```
Windows PowerShell                                        —  □  ×
PS C:\Users\Jo\asm64win\08 files> make

C:\Users\Jo\asm64win\08 files>mingw32-make.exe
nasm -f win64 -g -F cv8 files.asm -l files.lst
gcc -o files.exe files.obj
PS C:\Users\Jo\asm64win\08 files> .\files.exe
The result of reading the file: Windows World!
PS C:\Users\Jo\asm64win\08 files> _
```

Figure 43-1. *files.asm output*

Summary

In this chapter, you learned about the following:

- Windows file manipulation

- That there are plenty of parameters to help fine-tune the file handling

AFTERWORD

Where to Go from Here?

After you have worked your way through this book, you have mastered the basics of modern assembly programming. The next step depends on your needs. This afterword contains some ideas.

Security analysts can use the acquired knowledge to study malware, viruses, and other ways to break into computers or networks. Malware, in binary format, tries to get into computers and networks. You can take this binary code, reverse engineer it, and try to figure out what the code is doing. You would, of course, do that in an isolated lab system. Study how to reverse engineer and acquire the necessary tooling. You should consider learning ARM assembly for analyzing code on smartphones.

As a higher-level language programmer, you may consider building your own library of high-speed functions to be linked with your code. Study how you can optimize code; the code in this book was not written for high performance but for illustration purposes. In the book, we referred to a couple of texts that can help you write optimized code.

If you want a thorough understanding of the Intel processors, download the Intel manuals and study them. There is a lot of interesting information to digest, and knowing how the hardware and software works together will give you an edge in developing system software or diagnosing system crashes.

As a higher-level language programmer with a grasp of assembly language, you are now better equipped to debug your code. Analyze your `.obj` and `.lst` files and reverse engineer your code to see what happens. See how your compiler converts your code into machine language. Maybe using other instructions are more efficient?

405

© Jo Van Hoey 2019
J. Van Hoey, *Beginning x64 Assembly Programming*, https://doi.org/10.1007/978-1-4842-5076-1

Index

© Jo Van Hoey 2019
J. Van Hoey, *Beginning x64 Assembly Programming*, https://doi.org/10.1007/978-1-4842-5076-1

X

Y

Z

Printed in the United States
By Bookmasters